Crusader for Democracy

Crusader for Democracy

The Political Life of William Allen White

CHARLES DELGADILLO

 UNIVERSITY PRESS OF KANSAS

Published by the University Press of Kansas (Lawrence, Kansas 66045), which was organized by the Kansas Board of Regents and is operated and funded by Emporia State University, Fort Hays State University, Kansas State University, Pittsburg State University, the University of Kansas, and Wichita State University

Library of Congress Cataloging-in-Publication Data

Names: Delgadillo, Charles, author.
Title: Crusader for democracy : the political life of William Allen White /Charles Delgadillo.
Description: Lawrence, Kansas : University Press of Kansas, [2018] | Includes bibliographical references and index.
Identifiers: LCCN 2018004095 | ISBN 9780700626380 (cloth : alk. paper) | ISBN 9780700626397 (ebook)
Subjects: LCSH: White, William Allen, 1868–1944—Political and social views. Journalists—United States—Biography. | Emporia gazette (Emporia, Kan. : 1899) | Reformers—United States—Biography. | Political activists—United States—Biography. | Republican Party (U.S. : 1854–)—Biography. | Progressivism (United States politics)—History—20th century. | United States—Politics and government—1901–1953. | Middle class—Middle West. | Emporia (Kan.)—Biography.
Classification: LCC PN4874.W52 D45 2018 | DDC 070.92 [B]—dc23.
LC record available at https://lccn.loc.gov/2018004095.

British Library Cataloguing-in-Publication Data is available.

Printed in the United States of America

10 9 8 7 6 5 4 3 2 1

The paper used in this publication is recycled and contains 30 percent postconsumer waste. It is acid free and meets the minimum requirements of the American National Standard for Permanence of Paper for Printed Library Materials Z39.48-1992.

CONTENTS

ACKNOWLEDGMENTS

Any book is a collective effort, and I would like to acknowledge the following groups and individuals in seeing this project to completion. First and foremost, University of California at Santa Barbara professors Nelson Lichtenstein, Laura Kalman, and Salim Yaqub provided invaluable support, encouragement, and feedback through this project's many iterations. It would have been impossible to complete the research for this work without the help of a myriad of archivists at the Library of Congress, the Kansas State Historical Society, Emporia State University, the University of Kansas, the University of Indiana, and the Herbert Hoover and Franklin D. Roosevelt Presidential Libraries. Editors and advisors Kim Hogeland, Fred Woodward, and Jon Lauck gave me encouragement, constructive criticism, and many helpful pointers. Every penny counts on an adjunct's salary, and I am thankful for the financial support I received from Indiana University, the Hoover and FDR Presidential Library Associations, the George C. Marshall Foundation, the Dirksen Congressional Center, and the UCSB Labor and Employment Research Fund.

Crusader for Democracy

INTRODUCTION
THE MAN AND HIS METHODS

William Allen White, the editor of the *Emporia Gazette*, was a phenomenon. He established a national reputation as the voice of the midwestern middle class through his nationally syndicated journalism, his short stories, and the novels he penned. A man with White's talents could have joined a national newspaper at a hefty salary and made his career in Chicago, New York City, or Washington, DC. White had his share of such opportunities. For instance, the *Chicago Tribune* offered to hire him as a daily political columnist in 1903 at an annual salary of $12,000, which translates to more than $330,000 when adjusted for inflation in 2017.[1] White was sometimes tempted, but he ultimately refused any offer of employment away from his hometown of Emporia and his cleverly cultivated brand as a small-town newspaper editor sharing his view from "Main Street." The small-town image White projected was a real part of his personality, but he was also a sophisticated, well-traveled, and well-connected member of America's elite. White rubbed elbows with local, state, and national politicians, world-renowned journalists and authors, political activists of all kinds, and every president from William McKinley to Franklin Delano Roosevelt. His articles and editorials were nationally syndicated, and his magazine articles were in such demand that they earned him $1,000 apiece at the height of the muckraker era. Paradoxically, White was also an insurgent who fought a fifty-year crusade for liberal reform, usually through and sometimes against the Republican Party.[2] William Allen White was a phenomenon because he was able to fuse his "Main Street" persona with his mastery of insider politics to become a seemingly ubiquitous part of American political life during the first half of the twentieth century.

White's life work was the fight for democracy, which he reduced to the idea of equality of opportunity. To White, a democracy ought to guarantee every child a quality education and wholesome conditions, every worker the ability to provide a decent living for his or her family, every business owner or consumer the right to participate freely in the economy, and every citizen the right to good government. Although White would have preferred that people choose social justice through voluntary actions, he was a pragmatist who knew that it was necessary to use government to advance the general welfare. A wide variety of social, economic, and political reforms were included under White's definition of "general welfare," but one of his flaws was his almost singular focus on his own demographic of native-born, white, Anglo-Saxon Protestant men. White was troubled by the fact that women, nonwhites, and urban immigrants were left out of the American community, and he was particularly courageous in fighting discrimination in his local community. However, broader systemic solutions eluded him because he could not conceive of government as a tool for achieving major social changes. Woman suffrage and the prohibition of alcohol were the only two exceptions to this rule, and his support for government action was hardly innovative since both issues had been hotly debated in Kansas since the Civil War.

Midwestern ideals of community and neighborliness lay at the heart of White's liberal ideology, and they drove him during his half-century campaign to advance his vision for America. Such concepts inspired White to heroics at many points in his career. Midwestern ideals drove White during the Republican Party's factional warfare of the early 1900s, and they kept him engaged in public policy despite the conservative tide that inundated the nation during the 1920s. At the same time, White's midwestern values sometimes led him into functional alliances with conservatism when he felt culturally threatened. For instance, he served with distinction in both the conservative and liberal armies during the 1920s culture war as he fought against whichever side he felt was more threatening. White challenged the Ku Klux Klan, defended evolution, strained to understand Albert Einstein's theories, and urged his teenage daughter not to be afraid to come to him if she became pregnant. At the same time, he bristled against the Catholic Church; he asserted that America was a white, Anglo-Saxon Protestant nation; and he penned articles extolling the supremacy of rural America against the corrupt cities. One reason White was never able to fully embrace President Franklin D. Roosevelt even though he endorsed a laundry list of New Deal reforms was that he could not overcome his suspicions about Roosevelt's "slick" personality. White's midwestern values drew him toward liberalism, but they also represented a vulnerability that could be exploited to serve conservative ends.

The Republican Party was as central to White's political identity as his liberalism. The fact that White had been raised by his strong-willed Republican mother greatly inclined him toward the GOP, but there were practical reasons why he largely remained a lifelong Republican. First, Kansas was and remains a solidly Republican state, and anyone who wanted to have any say in state politics had to be a Republican. Second, like many Republicans, White saw the GOP as the party of middle-class, entrepreneurial, "Yankee" America, and he trusted his own demographic group with the reins of reform. In comparison, the Democratic Party had been a study in contrasts since its founding by archrivals Alexander Hamilton and Thomas Jefferson. By the late nineteenth century, the Democrats were an amalgam of western farmers, urban immigrants, and the racist South. The Democrats could never be a home to White because he knew that conservative southerners could "always ask the hill-billies, 'do you want your daughter to marry a nigger?' and stop any argument that means progress."[3] Throughout his life, White felt that the greatest threat to American democracy came from the uneducated, backward, shortsighted masses who were easily duped by smooth-talking demagogues.

Kansas was another essential part of White's identity, beginning with his hometown of Emporia. To White, midwestern towns like Emporia exemplified America's democratic ideals of social equality, civic-mindedness, and economic opportunity—the same notions that underpinned his concept of liberalism. In contrast, the social, economic, and political chasm between the wealthy, the middle class, and the impoverished masses in cities like New York was so vast as to raise the danger of class stagnation. From White's point of view, it was easier for a person to become a civic leader, an activist, or an entrepreneur in a small town than it was in the big city. Similarly, White idealized Kansas as the heir to New England's imagined cultural purity, terming the state "the child of Plymouth Rock" because it had been settled by the Yankee pioneers who fought against slavery during the mid-nineteenth century. The state's strong support for the Union during the Civil War had made it thoroughly Republican, and Union Army veterans dominated its political leadership until the early twentieth century. The state's reform tradition was so engrained that Theodore Roosevelt exaggeratedly proclaimed that "Kansas was in fact founded by the Progressive Movement in the 'fifties." To White, Kansas was both typically American and exceptionally democratic and mystical. Kansas was "a state of mind, a neurotic condition, a psychological phase, a symptom, indeed something undreamt of in your philosophy, an inferiority complex against the tricks and the manners of plutocracy, social, political, and economic."[4]

White's rhetoric of the Midwest's importance was not an idle boast, and his ideas were widespread during the era. The Midwest's cultural significance had its expression in early twentieth-century politics. The Progressive movement had flourished in the Midwest from 1900 through 1916, led by governors such as Wisconsin's Robert La Follette, Sr., Iowa's Albert Cummins, Kansas's Edward Hoch, and Missouri's Joseph Folk. Two midwesterners led the progressive Republican insurgency against the party's conservative wing in Congress during William H. Taft's presidency: Kansas representative Victor Murdock and Nebraska representative George W. Norris. The Bull Moose Progressive Party relied on the Midwest as one of its primary pillars of support after the excitement of 1912 faded. Reformers survived in the Midwest during the conservative 1920s through Senator Norris; Idaho senator William E. Borah, formerly of Kansas and Illinois; and Senator Arthur Capper of Kansas. Every Republican presidential nominee from 1928 to 1944 was from the Midwest:

Iowa-born Herbert Hoover in 1928 and 1932, Kansas governor Alf Landon in 1936, and Indiana's Wendell Willkie in 1940. Four of the six Republican National Committee chairmen from 1928 to 1944 were midwesterners, and eleven of the party's thirteen national conventions were held in the Midwest from 1900 to 1944. White's career coincided with a period in which the Midwest was arguably at its political and cultural apex.[5]

Politics has always been an interpersonal profession, and White's ability to befriend leading figures and weave them into a universe of friends, allies, and collaborators was key to his success. White was a charismatic, cheerful, energetic, and sometimes impish soul who loved interacting with others. His small-town midwestern manner helped him charm many hard-bitten politicians, who came to value his ability to provide sincere advice generously leavened with empathy. One reason White was able to make and maintain enduring friendships with political figures was his ability to see politicians as honorable individuals as long as they respected his code of political ethics. A man could be a bare-knuckles political brawler and still be honorable as long as he avoided personal enrichment and kept the bargains he made. Politics was, to White, a story "dramatized around heroes and villains just as sport is dramatized around gladiators," and he gauged his political friends by "how [a man] wears his clothes, how he walks, what his attitude is toward brave men and fair women, lovely gardens, wise dogs, colonial antiques, and all the notable things of the world." Political disagreements with friends were inevitable for a man as steeped in politics as White, but he had the rare ability to be able to separate individuals and issues. Even when he disagreed vehemently with his political friends, he tried to bear in mind that "politics is always the choice between evils."[6]

Journalism was another essential component of White's success. Mechanization allowed the newspaper industry to mature into a true instrument of mass communication just as White entered the field during the late nineteenth century. White's trajectory from newspapers to politics was common during the period, and it is easy to rattle off a list of leading politicians who were connected with the newspaper industry. In Kansas alone, White saw fellow newspaper publishers Clyde Reed, Arthur Capper, Joseph Bristow, Edward Hoch, George Hodges, and Henry J. Allen rise to become governors and US senators. Still, he refused to follow the same course and enter politics himself, choosing to maintain strict "monastic vows against office holding." One cannot understand White's political significance without understanding that he sought "influence in politics rather than place or prestige." He wanted a seat at the table or opportunities to whisper into decision makers' ears, and it was no idle boast when White stated that his refusal to seek office had made him "one of the fellows that had to be considered in Kansas and the Middle West." The fact that White was a journalist, an activist, or a friend rather than a rival office seeker gave him the opportunity to "stand aloof where I [can] from the more bitter conflicts and offer practicable compromise in deadlocks." His status as a journalist allowed him to try to make his "private sentiments to a degree controlling public opinion" without being accused of being a politician with an ax to grind.[7]

As an activist, White was a tireless reformer who fought for change on multiple fronts. As White put it, a broad-based approach to change ensured that his "political eggs are never in one basket and I can write a book or edit the paper or play horse-around New York and be just as happy whether I win any particular election or not." In the end, White had faith that "the curious thing about reform is that the fellow who has one idea or two or three ideas doesn't get forward with any of them but the fellow who dumps a basket full into the hopper gets a few of them out." Changing the world required patience, and White was willing to work by small increments and suffer the slings and arrows of outrageous fortune to advance the cause. There were times when White found himself "irked with the slow moving van of progress," but he was careful to stay "with the procession" rather than risk getting too far ahead of what was possible. Ultimately, he believed that change was inevitable, and it came "step by step from the ground up and not from the top down."[8]

The editorials White wrote for his *Gazette* were cited far and wide as a barometer of midwestern liberal thought, but the newspaper was also a business that allowed Publisher White to practice the ideas that Editor White preached. Managing editor Laura French and other women were employed in positions of responsibility at the *Gazette*, and White humorously silenced shop rumors about a coworker's suspected homosexuality by remarking, "Hell, I never did care a damn what a man's religion was." White consistently editorialized that all workers had a democratic right to a living wage and a voice in the workplace, and he implemented policies making good on these ideas at the *Gazette*. The newspaper's workers were unionized by the National Printers' Union at White's request, although he freely admitted that he "did this for selfish reasons. I was paying the highest wages in town and the union label was an asset." A sketch of the *Gazette*'s wages and benefits circa 1929 proves that White's statement was no idle boast. The *Gazette* employed approximately fifty workers at wages ranging from $30 to $100 per week, with a firm policy against layoffs during slack times. Every employee received two weeks of paid vacation per year, paid holidays, up to three months of paid sick leave annually, a share of an annual bonus pool that totaled $4,000, and a partially subsidized life insurance benefit. White was proud of the fact that "a man has a job-right on the *Gazette*," and it is not surprising that the average employee stayed with the newspaper for thirteen years. Many of the young men White mentored, known affectionately as his "boys," went on to become important figures in their own right: David Hinshaw, journalist and Herbert Hoover White House staffer; William S. Culbertson, lawyer, diplomat, and administrator; and Brock Pemberton, Broadway producer and founder of the Tony Award.[9]

In his personal life, William Allen White was happily married to Sallie Lindsay for nearly fifty years. The couple were a good match: he was enthusiastic and ebullient, and she was serious and level-headed. Indeed, it was the strongly prohibitionist Sallie who was responsible for ending White's brief experimentation with beer as a young reporter in Kansas City, Missouri. Sallie helped White suppress his occasional emotional outbursts in politics, and she provided crucial feedback as he wrote his novels. The Whites had two children, Mary and Bill, Jr. Mary was a bright, vivacious girl who shared her father's upbeat and dynamic personality. Sadly, she died in a tragic riding accident at the age of sixteen in 1921. Bill inherited his mother's sobriety and his father's writing talent, making his own journalistic name as a reporter and novelist during World War II. The White home was a happy one despite the family's occasional tragedies, and the house itself played a supporting role in White's career. Many a leading politician, famous artist, or reform activist made the pilgrimage to Emporia to spend an evening as White's honored guest, including Theodore Roosevelt, Herbert Hoover, and a host of lesser lights. White described the recipe for a successful evening at his home as "cabbage, turnips, carrots, onions, beets, and boiled beef with a nippy horse radish sauce which is one of Mrs. White's culinary achievements. Stoke in from eight to twenty ounces each into four competent fiddlers and then turn them loose on old man Beethoven's 'c Sharp Minor Quartette,' and you've got something for your money."[10]

White had always wanted to "be somebody," and both he and Sallie thoroughly enjoyed their status as part of America's journalistic and political elite. Still, this national prominence was not without cost to the couple's health. White's strategy of having many irons in the fire meant that he was often juggling the tasks of writing editorial copy for the *Gazette,* producing magazine articles and novels, corresponding with national politicians, dabbling in state and local politics, and traveling between Kansas and Chicago, Washington, DC, New York City, Europe, the Middle East, and East Asia. The strain White placed on himself led to frequent "nervous breakdowns," an ambiguous condition of dubious medical validity that was probably the social expression of stress in a rapidly modernizing world. Americans of White's era were obsessed with nervous breakdowns, and White frequently suffered crippling breakdowns until he learned to counterbalance his personal and professional burdens with frequent vacations. Physically, White's ample appetite led to obesity and diabetes that eventually forced his doctors to place him on a strict low-carbohydrate diet of meat, vegetables, and fruit.[11] Mrs. White suffered from her own maladies, including lifelong cardiovascular problems, crippling gastrointestinal disturbances, and chronic bouts of emotional depression.

The Rocky Mountains were the Whites' lifelong refuge from their medical and emotional difficulties, and they spent part of nearly every summer at their cabin in Moraine Park, Colorado. The nearby town of Estes Park was a popular destination for Kansans fleeing brutal summertime heat, and White guessed that at least a thousand such refugees owned cabins in the Rockies. The Whites' cabin was luxurious, featuring a bedroom, a living room, and a screened-in porch with kitchen facilities and a breathtaking mountain view. White had his office in a smaller building up the hill from the main cabin, and there were two detached sleeping cabins for guests. The fare often included mountain delicacies such as wild huckleberries and raspberries, forest mushrooms, and freshly caught trout, and White's children took full advantage of the area's potential for summer adventures. A number of prominent guests were entertained at the White cabin over the decades, including social reformer Jane Addams, defense attorney Clarence Darrow, and Edith Willkie, wife of 1940 Republican presidential candidate Wendell Willkie. Through one of the most tumultuous epochs in American history, White always had the serenity of the Rocky Mountains to soothe his soul.[12]

Naturally, White's prominence in American politics has attracted the attention of historians and biographers who have interpreted him through the lenses of their time. The first full biography of White was written by noted University of Chicago historian Walter Johnson beginning in the 1930s. Johnson had the benefit of White's full cooperation, along with access to his voluminous correspondence and the *Gazette*'s archives. The work was finally published in 1947, and *William Allen White's America* strongly reflected the Second World War's spirit of national unity at a time of global crisis. Johnson's White was a middle-class, midwestern everyman who embodied America's inevitable drift toward liberalism. A generation passed, and White was rediscovered during the turbulent 1970s as a grassroots protest

White's cabin at Moraine Park, Colorado, as it appears today. The structure was considerably more rustic when he purchased it in 1912. Courtesy of the Library of Congress, HABS COLO, 35-ESPK.V, 2A-1.

leader in John DeWitt McKee's *William Allen White: Maverick on Main Street* (1975). McKee's White was a deceptively amiable Progressive Era insurgent who waged a fierce campaign against the Republican establishment and faded away after World War I brought progressivism to an end. Scholars began to focus on White's cultural philosophy by the 1990s as Americans faced globalization and yet another divisive culture war. Sally Foreman Griffith's *Home Town News: William Allen White and the* Emporia Gazette (1989) examined White as a journalist at the height of the Progressive Era, concluding that his progressivism was a defense of his local community during the rise of corporate capitalism. Similarly, Edward Argan analyzed White's popular literature in *Too Good a Town* (1998) and placed him as the popularizer of an idealized vision of an American civilization built on small-town, midwestern community values.

The aforementioned studies are all worthy pieces of scholarship, but the fact is that White has not been fully reevaluated as a political figure in more than four decades. Furthermore, many of the studies that have been completed since Johnson published *William Allen White's America* in 1947 have focused on White's career during the Progressive Era. As a result, he has been somewhat pigeonholed as the voice of a fading small-town civilization, an exemplar of progressivism's interesting but ultimately naive reformers, or as a quote-generating machine for other studies of the period. Ironically, White's name is most widely circulated today in connection with Thomas Frank's 2004 book *What's the Matter with Kansas?* Frank argued that cultural politics drove formerly left-leaning midwestern states like Kansas into the conservative column. He chose the same title as White's famously conservative 1896 anti-Populist editorial to highlight this shift, which is both apt and tragic considering that White spent more than forty years as a liberal living down his moment of conservatism.[13]

Every generation asks its own questions of the past, and the highly charged political landscape of recent years has sparked a new wave of political biography. Historians such as Doris Kearns Goodwin and Brad Snyder have recently penned biographies that emphasize the way that prominent leaders crafted and interacted with networks of reformers. William Allen White fits this pattern as a leader, a crafter, and a member of several reform networks as he fought a lifelong campaign for democracy in an era of vicious political warfare between liberals and conservatives. White was one of the "hell-raisers" who waged an insurgency against his own party, he managed to help reshape a democracy whose basic mechanisms were initially dominated by powerful interests, and he bravely challenged ugly ideologies based on hatred and supernationalism. How did White and his cohort of Progressive Republican activists manage to organize a rebellion that threw the national Republican machine into turmoil? How did a liberal such as White manage to not only persevere during the 1920s but also have a voice in a decade that was so conservative that it crushed many other reformers? Why was White so suspicious of a New Deal liberalism that achieved reforms he had spent decades fighting to enact? How did a small-town Kansas newspaper editor help the United States become one of the world's leading internationalist powers? What does White's trajectory as a midwestern liberal tell us about the fate of liberalism in the twentieth century? The battles White waged, the victories he won, the defeats he suffered, and the ideas that inspired him when his cause seemed futile are as relevant to Americans today as they were a century ago.

CHAPTER ONE
"HE WANTS NO OFFICE!"

Mid-nineteenth-century Kansas was a microcosm of the dramatic social, political, and economic changes that were reshaping the United States. Battles were fought in territorial Kansas between abolitionists and proslavery militants during the 1850s, a period that came to be known as Bleeding Kansas. The fledgling Republican Party successfully deployed Bleeding Kansas as a recruiting tool in the North during the antebellum period, and Union Army veterans flooded Kansas after the Civil War because they received preferential treatment in settling federal land. As a result, Republican Union veterans dominated Kansas's politics for a generation after the war, and the GOP became a fundamental part of the state's cultural identity.[1] Meanwhile, the arrival of railroads such as the Atchison, Topeka and Santa Fe or the Missouri, Kansas and Texas tied Kansas's producers into the national economy. At the same time, railroads and other corporations increasingly dominated state affairs. Kansas became a hotbed of reform movements that included woman suffrage, temperance, and railroad regulation during the late nineteenth century, partly as an echo of the abolitionist tradition and partly as a reaction to the harsh realities of frontier life. The men and women who made their homes in Kansas at this time were in a peculiar position: they were at once on the frontiers of civilization and at the center of a modernizing, industrial America.

William Allen White's parents were part of the pioneer wave that settled Kansas. The White family traced its American roots to Nicholas White, who landed in Massachusetts as part of the first generation of English Puritans in 1639. Like many Americans, the White family joined the inexorable westward movement over the years until Allen White was born on an Ohio farm in 1819. Allen White received rudimentary training as a country doctor and got married before moving to frontier Kansas in 1854. Bleeding Kansas spurred Dr. White to push on to Texas, but he returned in 1859 and settled near Emporia. A young woman of Irish rootstock named Mary Ann Hatten made the same decision to move to Emporia several years later. The Hattens had settled in Canada in 1829, had a daughter named Mary Ann in 1830, and relocated to upstate New York later that year. Mary Ann was orphaned in 1846 and moved to Illinois to live with a foster family, where she attended the strongly abolitionist, coeducational Knox College. Miss Hatten was inspired to join the newborn Republican Party after watching Republican candidate Abraham Lincoln debate Democrat Stephen Douglas on campus during the race for Illinois's US Senate seat in 1858. She settled in Council Grove, Kansas, to work as a teacher in 1865, only to be fired when she challenged segregation in her school. Miss Hatten found another teaching job in Emporia that year and met Allen White, then separated from his first wife, at a community dance. Dr. White secured a divorce and married Mary Ann on April 15, 1867. William Allen White later remarked that his parents were "a curious mixture" of old Yankee blood and Irish immigrant stock that embodied the two major demographic currents in nineteenth-century America. To White, the combination made for "a thrifty, hard-working, resourceful, cheerful family."[2]

The Whites set up housekeeping in a modest Emporia home and soon welcomed a son into the world on February 10, 1868. Allen, a staunch Democrat, named the boy William Allen after a Democratic politician he had admired in Ohio. Ironically, William's namesake later defected to the Republicans, foreshadowing young White's eventual shift to the GOP. Newspapers were part of William's life from the beginning, and he passed the hours at his mother's knee learning the alphabet from the pages of the *Emporia News* that papered the kitchen walls. The frontier's twilight days left an indelible impression on young White. As an adult, he vividly recalled "primeval groves, beside clear, rock bordered streams, . . . the lisping of the long, lush grass, . . . the antelope, the prairie chicken, the quail." Dr. and Mrs. White moved to nearby El Dorado to establish a drugstore in 1869. Years later, their son recalled memories of his hardworking neighbors reduced to the shame of asking for credit during hard times.

Dr. White sold his drugstore and bought a farm in 1874, but this short-lived experiment ended because he was an incompetent farmer and his wife missed town life. The couple sold their farm and built a new house in town that they operated as a hotel. The "White House" was a source of tremendous satisfaction for White's father, whose affinity for good food and entertaining made him perfectly suited for inn keeping. Allen set the finest table in town and thoroughly enjoyed his role as hotelier, but the business never turned a profit. The hotel did benefit young William by exposing him to vigorous table conversation from a parade of guests that included notables such as suffrage activist Susan B. Anthony. The Whites ultimately shuttered the hotel because Mrs. White hated it as passionately as her husband loved it, and she rebelled in 1881.[3]

Allen and Mary Ann White were both strongly political individuals who supported suffrage and prohibition, and each contributed to their son's early political education. William described his father as "an old fashioned Jacksonian Democrat" who established the Democratic Party's organization in Butler County. He was also a bare-knuckled political warrior who was burned in effigy by the residents of a nearby town on accusations that he had stuffed the ballot box during a hotly contested county seat election. Young William learned a great deal about the interpersonal art of politics by accompanying his father on Democratic Party canvassing trips, and he seemed destined for the Democrats until Allen's sudden death on October 4, 1882. A fourteen-year-old William inherited his father's charisma, his affinity for good company, his taste for a hearty meal, and his correspondingly ample waistline. Both were enterprising men who were constantly striving for something more, whether in business, in politics, or in society. White spent the rest of his life compensating for his loss by seeking fatherly figures, beginning with Allen's Kansas cronies and ranging through a succession of governors, senators, and presidents.[4]

In the near term, the death of White's father left his mother as the dominant influence in his life. Mrs. White was a woman with a forceful personality, a profound sense of moral duty, a love of good books, and a strong commitment to the GOP, all of which she impressed on her son. Nineteenth-century sons generally followed the partisan example set by their fathers, and Allen White's Democratic colleagues were naturally brokenhearted when William gravitated toward the Republicans. The move would have been logical regardless of his mother's influence, since anyone who wanted to have any say in Kansas politics had to be a Republican. Mrs. White also cultivated her son's literary interests by reading him poetry and Victorian novels by English authors such as Charles Dickens, George Eliot, and Anthony Trollope. Where Allen White had made his mark by cultivating his son's political skills and by infusing him with an enterprising spirit, Mary Ann developed her son's creative mind, his appreciation for good writing, and his zeal for reform. Mrs. White remained a constant daily presence in White's life, living with or next door to him until her death at the age of ninety-four.[5]

Kansas was basking in the aura of an economic boom created by high grain prices and eastern credit when young Will graduated from El Dorado High School in 1884. Emporia College beckoned, but Will found the college's academic program uninspiring and struggled to find a social niche during his freshman year. More appealing social opportunities were available in town, and he established a particularly strong friendship with future Stanford biologist Vernon L. Kellogg. Will returned home for the summer of 1885 to work as a printer's devil on the *El Dorado Democrat,* followed by a stint as a typesetter and cub reporter for the *Emporia News* after his mother forced him to resume his studies at Emporia College in January 1886. He spent the following summer working on Thomas "Bent" Murdock's *El Dorado Republican.* This gave White a crucial opportunity to learn the technical and business sides of running a newspaper, and he established a lifelong friendship with a young Republican named Henry J. Allen. The academic menu at Emporia College proved as unappetizing the second time around, and White took Kellogg's advice that he join him at Kansas University in Lawrence that fall.[6]

KU offered White the kind of vibrant student life that had eluded him at Emporia College, and he quickly developed a slew of enduring friendships. Iconoclastic professor James H. Canfield befriended White and encouraged him to challenge such orthodoxies as the Republican Party's devotion to economic protectionism. Kellogg sponsored White for membership in KU's Phi Delta Theta fraternity, but White's preference for loud clothing and his youthful exuberance made a poor impression. Kellogg spent the next five months lobbying the group before White was allowed to join. "Phi Delt" introduced White to an array of future leaders that included Charles F. Scott, who became a Republican congressman and journalist; Charles Gleed, a director of the Santa Fe railroad; future US Army general Frederick Funston; and William E. Borah, who served as a Republican senator from Idaho for forty years. White's childhood political education paid off in student government when he discovered that he had his father's gift for "backstairs politics." The newspaper experience White had acquired yielded dividends when he joined the campus newspaper, worked on the school's literary review, and edited the KU yearbook. White also contributed campus news pieces to the town's newspapers, and his copy was sometimes reprinted around the state. "Bent" Murdock continued to mentor his young protégé into the newspaper business by giving him summer work on the *Republican*.[7]

Phi Delt also introduced White to his lifelong emotional refuge from the pressures of life, career, and politics: the Rocky Mountains. White, Kellogg, and Funston were part of a company of a dozen young KU men, mostly Phi Delts, who embarked on an epic, three-month vacation in the Rockies near Estes Park, Colorado, in June 1889. The group established "Camp Jay Hawk" at a rented cabin in Moraine Park, which lies at the heart of what later became Rocky Mountain National Park. The impoverished students lived off the land primarily, foraging for wild berries, hunting mountain sheep and other game, and fishing for trout from the nearby Big Thompson River. There was plenty of time for White to lounge with his books and enjoy the company of his friends once he had fulfilled his share of camp chores. Despite his lack of athleticism, White was able to keep

White and friends, hiking to Longs Peak, Colorado, during the summer of 1889. Left to right: White, Helen Sutliffe, Schuyler Brewster, Herbert Hadley, and Janice Sutliffe. Courtesy of Emporia State University, Special Collections and Archives.

up with the group on strenuous excursions that included a multiday, forty-mile trek to the recently deserted silver-mining town of Lula, or the harrowing climb to the 14,259-foot summit of Longs Peak. The summer climaxed with a 145-mile meandering hike across the Great Divide to Golden, Colorado, where the Jayhawkers entrained for Kansas. A newlywed White and his bride honeymooned in Estes Park four years later, and they rarely missed a summer in the Rockies over the decades that followed.[8]

Everything about college life strongly agreed with young White except for the academics, and his failure to pass a required geometry course after almost four years made his graduation unlikely. White dropped out of KU in December 1889 to accept Murdock's job offer managing the *El Dorado Republican*, which freed the latter to focus on politics as the Republican boss of Butler County. Self-dealing, influence peddling, and bribery were an accepted part of Gilded Age politics, and Murdock used his position as a Kansas state senator to drum up campaign donations, free travel passes from the Santa Fe railroad, and advertising contracts from banks, insurance companies, and packing houses. Manager White's duties included selling advertising, supervising the staff, ordering supplies, and doing anything else required for the daily operation of the newspaper. Any empty space was his to fill with his own poetry and prose, which was occasionally reprinted in regional newspapers such as the *Kansas City Star*. Murdock still wrote most of the editorial copy, but he helped White tremendously by mentoring him away from his penchant for florid writing.[9] The decision to drop out of KU worked out well for White, who had profited from his time at the university and was ready to make his own way.

White once described Gilded Age Kansas as a state that "might well have been named for Jefferson" because it was possible for a man to make his way with minimal capital compared to later decades. At the same time, as White correctly acknowledged, lack of access to capital was the driving force behind the periodic protest movements that flourished in the region. Farming was transforming into a more capital-intensive industrialized operation during the late nineteenth century. At the same time, the political system ignored the farmers' calls for legislative action while responding to those of other interests. Populism was the last and most intense of the many protest movements that emerged from this dynamic, and the rise of populism coincided with White's tenure at the *Republican*. Populism was an outgrowth of the Farmers' Alliance, an agricultural cooperative that began in Texas in the mid-1870s. The alliance quickly evolved into a mass movement across the Great Plains after millions of farmers were crushed by a crippling drought that began in 1887. The Kansas alliance boasted 470 suballiances with twenty-five thousand members by the time it began dabbling in politics in November 1889. The group became politically potent when it developed a platform and asked its members to vote for candidates who pledged their support. The Kansas alliance soon swelled to a hundred thousand members, and it held a statewide convention at Topeka to establish a formal political organization in March 1890. The alliance's convention endorsed proposals for a mortgage payment grace period for farmers, the regulation of railroad rates, the direct election of US senators, and other measures broadly designed to relieve the farmers' suffering.[10]

The unrefined and impoverished profile of those who joined the alliance particularly grated on White, who was temperamentally inclined to distrust what he regarded as a mob of motley malcontents, professional goldbricks, and uncouth half-wits preaching such blasphemies as an inflationary monetary policy. Actually, the movement's leadership in Kansas was solidly middle class and highly educated, and most made their livelihood in professional occupations other than farming. The alliance's membership offended him more than its leadership. Kansas's newspaper establishment was largely opposed to the alliance, and White gleefully joined the general assault on the movement in his editorials for the *Republican*. The viciously clever sallies White launched against the alliance won him recognition from his colleagues and from Emporia's middle and upper classes, and it helped sustain the newspaper's circulation. Once again, White found his pieces being picked up by the Associated Press, the *Kansas City Star*, and major newspapers in Saint Louis, Chicago, and New York. The pieces also earned White a place as an effigy in the alliance's protest marches through town, further embellishing his reputation with the Republican establishment. Murdock shared White's disdain for the alliance, but he was a savvy politician who quickly recognized that the farm revolt had real momentum. Murdock joined a group of Republicans who sought to co-opt the farmers' momentum by adopting elements of their program, and he gently instructed White to temper his rhetoric.[11]

Murdock was right about the energy behind the Kansas Farmers' Alliance, and the group blossomed into the Populist Party in June 1890. The new party held its convention in August, where it endorsed a platform of banking and tax reform, restrictions on financial speculators, government ownership of the railroads and other communications infrastructure, and an inflationary monetary policy. Farmers flocked to the Populist Party, which tore through the political scene like a Kansas tornado. Crowds packed its rallies to listen to orators such as firebrands Mary Lease and "Sockless" Jerry Simpson, the latter so nicknamed by the anti-Populist press after he mocked a wealthy campaign opponent's expensive silk socks. The intended slur was a major blunder because many farmers were themselves "sockless," and Simpson wore the moniker as a badge of honor in his victorious campaign for Congress. In contrast, the Republican and Democratic Parties both struggled to attract votes by co-opting the Populist agenda. The best attacks White and the Republican press deployed failed to hamper the Populist campaign. The Populists won 96 of the 125 seats in the state legislature and four congressional seats, and their 120,000 votes effectively tied the Republicans' overall result.[12]

The 1890 campaign was a disaster for the Republican Party in Kansas and around the nation, but it opened doors of opportunity for White as a journalist and as a political operative. Dozens of Kansas editors had read and reprinted his pieces in Murdock's *Republican*, helping build his reputation as a promising young newspaperman with the state's journalistic community. White cut his political teeth and established a lasting friendship by campaigning against the Populists alongside future vice president Charles Curtis during the summer of 1891. The state party widely circulated White's short story titled "The Regeneration of Colonel Hucks," which revolved around a lifelong Republican turned Populist who returned to the GOP for sentimental reasons. White later summed up the piece, which had been written as filler for the *Republican*, as "all emotion, all sentiment, and probably all nonsense," but it bore fruit in the form of two job offers. Wealthy real estate developer William R. Nelson offered him a position on the politically independent *Kansas City Star*, while Charles Gleed, a prominent railroad attorney and White's KU Phi Delt brother, offered him a job at the *Kansas City Journal*. The *Journal* was solidly Republican while the *Star* had supported Democrats in the past, and White chose the *Journal* because he felt he would be happier at a "loyal" Republican newspaper.[13]

Kansas City offered White a myriad of new experiences when he arrived in October 1891, including cultural activities, culinary adventures, and social opportunities. Unfortunately, White soon learned that the *Journal* was a hack newspaper devoted to the Republicans right or wrong. Worse, the newspaper's midlevel staff saw him as a young upstart to be cut down to size. White also missed his mother terribly, writing her that "I want you. I want a home; I am sick of boarding [houses]." The young reporter was thrilled when Gleed sent him to Topeka as the *Journal*'s political correspondent for Kansas in March 1892. The job was ideal for White, who crisscrossed the state attending Democratic, Republican, and Populist political events, cultivating relationships with politicians of all kinds, and helping establish a social organization of young Republican leaders called the Kansas Day Club that remains an important institution. Kansas's archetypal political boss, Cyrus Leland, was by far the most important acquaintance White made at this time. Leland was a pragmatic former Union cavalry officer who ran the state's Republican machine using a web of personal relationships, political favors, and railroad money. Leland religiously adhered to the Gilded Age's political code of honor, which allowed a man to take bribes, barter political offices, backstab rivals, and engage in all manner of "honorable" corruption as long as he kept the bargains he made. White never missed an opportunity to mention Leland favorably in his articles, and Leland gradually took White under his wing as a machine acolyte. The two men developed a genuine friendship, and White came to admire Leland as another fatherly figure in his life.[14]

Ironically, the Populist Party that White so disdained gave him the spur he needed to emancipate himself from the mediocre *Journal*. Kansas's Populists faced a key decision in 1892: would they fuse with the Democratic Party to defeat the Republicans, or remain independent and pure, with little chance of expanding their vote beyond the farm? The *Journal* dispatched White and a colleague to report on the Kansas Populist Convention as it settled the question that August. White had built a friendship with Populist leader "Sockless" Jerry Simpson while covering Kansas politics, and he privately tipped White that the convention would vote for fusion. White and his colleague immediately telegraphed their scoop to the *Journal* before boarding a train for Kansas City. The pair were expecting to celebrate a triumph on their arrival, but they were horrified to discover en route that the *Journal*'s telegraph editor had vindictively buried the story. White resigned on the spot after the guilty man refused his demand for a fistfight. The *Kansas City Star* was looking for an editorial writer, and White was hired the next day to write editorials, cover Kansas issues, and contribute literary filler.[15]

The *Kansas City Star* was a first-rate newspaper owned by "Colonel" William R. Nelson, a tireless crusader for municipal reform who became another journalistic father figure for young White. Unlike the lackluster *Journal*, the *Star* had principles. The incorruptible Colonel Nelson assigned him to investigate price gouging in the city's gas industry and horrid conditions in its slums even though his friends reaped handsome profits under the status quo. Another point of difference between the *Star* and the *Journal* was that Colonel Nelson treated his staff as respected professionals, and he allowed them their journalistic freedom. White generally wrote what he pleased, the editors explained any revisions they made, and a journalist always had the opportunity to defend himself if he disagreed with the editors. The *Star* was a shining model for White of how a newspaper ought to be run. First, a newspaper ought to report the news honestly and professionally, and second, it ought to be an advocate for the best interests of the community it served.[16]

The *Star* generously allowed a twenty-five-year-old White to remain on the payroll when he departed on an extended western honeymoon following his marriage to Sallie Lindsay, then a twenty-four-year-old schoolteacher from Kansas City, Kansas, on April 27, 1893. The newlyweds traveled for free on a Santa Fe railroad pass and received a steep discount at the railroad's luxury Montezuma Hotel in New Mexico. Both were standard practices railroads used to

Sallie Lindsay White, circa 1900. Courtesy of Emporia State University, Special Collections and Archives.

purchase goodwill from influential men. Mr. and Mrs. White spent a month in New Mexico before continuing to a log cabin in Moraine Park, Colorado, but the *Star* wanted its reporter back and recalled him by telegram. The *Star* fired him when he refused to abandon his honeymoon, and the newlyweds' situation further darkened the next day when the Colorado bank where White had deposited his savings failed in the Panic of 1893. Broke and unemployed was an inauspicious way to begin a marriage, but fortune smiled on White when one of his former colleagues at the *Star* suffered a mild stroke. The newspaper offered to reinstate White if he agreed to return immediately, and the chastened reporter wasted no time in finding his way back to Kansas City. The couple's finances were so dire that Sallie had to wait in Colorado until her husband had saved enough to pay for her return train fare.[17]

White had recovered his position sufficiently to consider new options in 1895. The professional journalists at the *Star* had given him the best possible education, and he was able to provide a comfortable living for his family. Colonel Nelson liked White and gave him plum reporting assignments, including the task of accompanying future presidential candidate Governor William McKinley (R-OH) aboard his special train touring the Midwest. Boss Leland had taken the young reporter into his circle, and Colonel Nelson allowed White the latitude to cover Leland's activities in a manner that would please the boss. It would have been perfectly reasonable for White to remain in Kansas City and build his career at the *Star,* laying the foundation for a move to a national newspaper in Chicago or New York City. No one would have blamed him for choosing such a course, but White wanted more than just a byline and a comfortable life. He wanted his independence, he wanted to deal with influential men as an equal rather than as a hireling, and he longed to return to the small-town Kansas life he loved. The only way to accomplish these goals was for White to become an editor in his own right. He began searching for a newspaper he could afford to purchase, in a college town, with an educated, middle- to upper-class readership. A struggling newspaper

Cyrus Leland, Jr., Kansas's archetypal political boss of the 1890s, seated at right. Courtesy of the Kansas State Historical Society.

that had been founded by the Populists in 1890, the *Emporia Gazette,* seemed to meet these criteria, and White purchased it for $3,000 in the spring of 1895. The deal was financed primarily by White's political contacts: Boss Leland convinced Republican governor Edmund Morrill, a banker, to lend White $1,000, the family of US senator Preston Plumb (R-KS) lent him $1,250, and "Major" Calvin Hood, an Emporia banker and the town's political boss, helped arrange financing for the remainder.[18]

The new owner of the *Gazette* was confronted with a dilemma when he arrived in Emporia to finalize the sale on May 25. The cost of acquiring the *Gazette* and relocating from Kansas City had exhausted his savings, leaving just $1.25 in his pocket. An announcement had been made that White was purchasing the *Gazette,* and the fact that he had spent many years as a reporter in Emporia meant that he would be easily recognized. A hired hack cost twenty-five cents, and it would have been perfectly reasonable for White to save money by walking to the boardinghouse. Yet to be seen lugging his own bags into town was not without cost, since some would be reluctant to do business with an editor who seemed financially distressed. White took the hack on the shrewd calculation that riding into town would give him an air of prosperity that would pay dividends. The next morning he surveyed his new domain: a sixty-by-twenty-five-foot print shop with a rotary press. The *Gazette*'s books showed that the newspaper's paid circulation was significantly below the promised seven hundred, and its accounts were already in the red because the prior owner had not paid his bills. Still, White was pleased with his purchase and determined to make the business a success.[19]

The *Gazette* was officially transferred to White on June 1, and the twenty-seven-year-old editor published a statement of principles two days later explaining his commitment to the town. White promised his readers three things. First, the *Gazette* would be a vehicle for the "best people" to improve their town, and he asked for his readers' cooperation and assistance in their common effort. Second, White promised that the *Gazette* would report the news as it happened and confine his staunchly Republican politics to the editorial page. Third, White declared that the *Gazette* was a business venture and would be operated as such, rather than as a partisan rag or as its editor's hobbyhorse. All in all, White intended the *Gazette* to be the voice of people like himself: young, middle-class, educated, ambitious Kansans who were determined to show the world that their town was cosmopolitan and modern. To begin this campaign, White relied on a staff consisting of a foreman, two reporters, a printing and typesetting crew, and occasional help from Sallie. The newspaper's declining revenue meant that White's first problem was making his forty-five-dollar-per-week payroll. Emporia's Republican politicians helped keep White afloat by purchasing fifty dollars' worth of advertising space for their declarations of candidacy, but he still had to borrow $120 to meet his first two months of expenses.[20]

The *Gazette* steadily increased its circulation by focusing on local news presented in a lighthearted manner and by covering local events, the antics of the town's youth, church news, and national news through wire services. The *Gazette* ran circles around its crosstown rival, the *Republican,* which was owned by a man forty years White's senior named C. V. Eskridge. A rivalry was inevitable because Eskridge represented a faction of town bosses led by Charles S. Cross's First National Bank of Emporia, while White was allied with the faction led by Major Hood of the Emporia National Bank. Eskridge personalized the rivalry by ridiculing White at every opportunity in the *Republican,* but White quickly realized that the best way to get revenge was to ignore the attacks, improve the *Gazette,* and capture Eskridge's political patronage. The *Gazette* soon eclipsed the *Republican,* and the First National Bank failed spectacularly when federal examiners discovered that it was insolvent in 1898. The failure wiped out many depositors, and both Eskridge and Cross committed suicide within a year. The dual tragedies exemplified the ruthless cruelty of nineteenth-century capitalism, which later became an important theme in White's Progressive Era fiction.[21]

Emporia was also politically divided into Populist and anti-Populist factions, and White's *Gazette* was firmly in the latter camp. Like many Americans, White regarded a deflationary "gold standard" monetary policy as one of the foundations of civilization, and he fiercely denounced Republicans who tacked toward the Populists' demands for inflation. The *Gazette* supported McKinley for the presidency in 1896 solely because he was for the gold standard, and White remained as vicious as ever in his anti-Populist editorial denunciations. Emporia's Populists returned the vitriol in kind, regularly haranguing White as he walked through town. The morning of August 13, 1896, was a typical Kansas summer scorcher, and White once again found himself surrounded by Populists who insisted on debating the money question. White was not the kind of man who enjoyed wrangling face to face, and he was in a hurry to catch the next train to Colorado to join Sallie on vacation. He squirmed his way past his Populist persecutors and returned to the *Gazette*'s office angry and flustered, only to be informed that he had not provided enough editorial copy to be printed in his absence. Impulsively, White dashed off an editorial about the Populist movement in Kansas before rushing to catch the Santa Fe's next train to Colorado. As usual, he was traveling on a free pass provided by the corporation.[22]

The editorial, titled "What's the Matter with Kansas?" was published on Monday, August 15, 1896. Kansas was an economically stagnant national joke, White argued, and the Populists were to blame. The Populists were fools "who hate prosperity," who wanted to "Give the prosperous man the dickens!" and "Legislate the thriftless man into ease." The party's candidates were mercilessly mocked. One individual was ridiculed as a "shabby, wild-eyed, rattle-brained fanatic," and another as "an old human hoop skirt who has failed as a businessman, who has failed as an editor, who has failed as a preacher." The editorial concluded with:

What's the matter with Kansas?

Nothing under the shining sun. She is losing her wealth, population and standing. She has got her statesmen, and the money power is afraid of her. Kansas is all right. She has started in to raise hell, as Mrs. Lease advised, and she seems to have an overproduction. But that doesn't matter. Kansas never did believe in diversified crops. Kansas is all right. There is absolutely nothing wrong with Kansas.[23]

The piece was almost never published because both the *Gazette*'s typesetter and his assistant were Democrats and they refused to print it, but the assistant eventually relented. A Santa Fe vice president noticed the editorial and forwarded it to the *Chicago Times-Herald*. Other newspapers soon reprinted it, and Republican boss Mark Hanna distributed a million copies through McKinley's presidential campaign. Populism had challenged the American myth that hard work alone leads to material success, and White's piece resonated because it succinctly summarized anti-Populist sentiment.[24]

The world had come knocking on William Allen White's door, but ironically, he was not at home to answer. Anxiety invaded his Rocky Mountain retreat when Monday's *Gazette* arrived in the mail, and

Sallie feared that the controversial editorial would harm the news-paper. White shivered when he returned to Emporia one week later to find a large stack of mail on his desk, but he soon discovered that most correspondents praised him for his anti-Populist screed. The Populists made gains in the 1896 election despite McKinley's presidential victory. White's contribution earned him an invitation to address the Ohio Republican League's Lincoln Day dinner at Zanesville on February 12, 1897. He was introduced to Boss Hanna, who was shocked and impressed when the young man declined an offer of a patronage job as a reward for his service. Hanna sent White to meet President-Elect McKinley with a note exclaiming, "He wants no office!" The speech White delivered at the banquet vigorously denounced both the Populists and the Republicans who sought to win by adopting their ideas. "What's the Matter with Kansas?" did pay White material dividends by winning him a contract to publish several of his short stories about Kansas life as an anthology titled *The Real Issue*. The work's critical success spurred *McClure's* magazine to order six additional short stories for $3,000, which more than cleared White's debts.[25]

"What's the Matter with Kansas?" had launched White's career overnight, but its most significant consequence was that it brought him into contact with the man who became his great friend and political inspiration, Theodore Roosevelt. The two men were introduced after local Republicans secured White's nomination to Emporia's postmastership without his knowledge. The nomination advanced to President McKinley's desk before White learned of it, and Mr. and Mrs. White immediately embarked for Washington, DC, to halt the process in June 1897. Washington insiders were more used to office seekers than office shirkers, and McKinley was amused when he granted White's request that he return the commission unsigned. The Whites were free to tour the capital and socialize with prominent national figures such as future secretary of war and state Elihu Root and Senator Henry Cabot Lodge (R-MA). Representative Charles Curtis, now Emporia's congressman, relayed a request from Assistant Secretary of the Navy Theodore Roosevelt to meet the author

*White at his desk in the original Gazette office, 1896. The wall above his desk
was soon filled with portraits of famous Americans he had befriended. Courtesy of
Emporia State University, Special Collections and Archives.*

of "What's the Matter with Kansas?" and *The Real Issue*. White was immediately enthralled, and he gushed a half century later that Roosevelt had "sounded in my heart the first trumpet call of the new time that was to be." In particular, Roosevelt had discussed the need for balance among corporations, the powerful politicians who were in their pocket, the working class, and the public. More broadly, White found in Roosevelt the sense of civic duty and national vision that the older machine establishment lacked, and Roosevelt gave reform a more respectable veneer than the unwashed Populists. Roosevelt was an ember that slowly smoldered in White's soul.[26]

The vane had begun to tip away from machine politics and toward reform in White's heart, but he remained a machine creature in the near term. White wanted no patronage for himself, but he had no compunction about using the political capital he had earned with "What's the Matter with Kansas?" to further Boss Leland's interests while in Washington, DC. President McKinley had appointed Leland as pension commissioner for the Midwest, a powerful position that gave him political leverage by virtue of the hundreds of thousands of Union Army pensions he disbursed. Leland had paid White's expenses in Washington, and White had run several political errands on Leland's behalf. In return, the boss rewarded White's loyalty by giving him a Pension Commission printing contract worth $3,000 per year. White also took the opportunity to meet the staff of *McClure's* magazine in New York City, building friendships with publisher Samuel McClure and Ida Tarbell, a pioneering muckraker. A steady stream of magazine assignments flowed to White from *McClure's*, which led to contracts from the *Saturday Evening Post, Scribner's*, and other periodicals.[27] Overall, White's East Coast trip was a resounding success that helped lay the foundations for his future political, journalistic, and literary success.

The Klondike gold strike of 1896 dramatically increased the money supply, bringing an end to the hard times that had fueled the Populist Party. Ironically, although the Populists' argument that inflation would solve the 1890s depression had been validated, their party shriveled as the economy gained steam. Emporia rebounded as new businesses opened and existing firms expanded, which translated to a stream of advertising revenue for the growing *Gazette*. White's editorials cheered the return of prosperity and the consequent erosion of Populism, crowing that "the farmer has ceased complaining. He is out of politics. He is in business." The receding Populist threat freed White to consider the farmers' fundamental argument that the economy was rigged.[28] The changing times were reflected in three problems that particularly grated on White: the control that large corporations had over western businesses, the dominant role machines played in political affairs, and the implications of America's imperialistic foreign policy.

The *Gazette*, like the rest of Emporia's business community, relied on the railroads to obtain essential supplies and to reach eastern markets. The railroads' plan to capitalize on the economic recovery by raising freight rates outraged White and other town businessmen, particularly since railroad workers did not receive higher wages. It was difficult for White to understand why freight rates ought to increase when costs remained fixed, and he called on the railroads to explain the need for higher rates. If the increase could not be justified on business grounds, then he warned that the railroads risked unleashing a new "litter of [Kansas's Populist senator William A.] Peffers, Leases and Simpsons." White gave the railroads space in the *Gazette* to make their case while encouraging businesses to organize against higher rates.[29] For the moment, White remained a conservative, arguing against a government role in railroad regulation on the theory that business disputes were best settled through discussion. Subsequent events disproved White's thesis, and the issue of railroad regulation spurred him to embrace a broader economic role for government over the years to come.

American civic life also needed reform, and White denounced the "selfishness of men in all classes and conditions" that he saw impeding good government. White attacked those who used their wealth to further their own greed in ways that harmed society, but he again displayed his persistent conservatism by rejecting a government role in correcting this condition. Education was the best tool for bringing greed under control because educated individuals would be inspired to spend the money they earned in a manner consistent with the national interest. Similarly, White saw education rather than government as the solution to the problem of party conventions that nominated self-serving candidates. Reformers in Wisconsin demanded primary election laws designed to take the nominating process away from political machines and give it to the electorate, but White argued that it was folly to change the system as long as voters remained ignorant and apathetic.[30] Like many progressive reformers of the late nineteenth century, White was driven by the belief that American civic life needed to shift away from parochialism and toward nationalism. He was a machine politician who knew that the levers of democracy were dominated by powerful individuals and corporations, but he looked forward to a day when the people would govern themselves. For the moment, White was too suspicious of the electorate to trust it with real power. White gradually discovered that the powerful would not surrender the keys willingly, and he eventually became one of the nation's leading advocates of the democratizing reforms that were being pioneered in Wisconsin.

Finally, the erection of an American empire in the Spanish-American War troubled White, who opposed imperialism throughout his life. The idea that that the Spanish had anything to do with the explosion of the USS *Maine* in Havana harbor on February 15, 1898, struck White as preposterous. He asked, "Why should America play into the hands of a lot of adventurers, who are using the name of Cuba to juggle with?" Patriotism spurred White to support the United States once the war began in April, but he rejected the notion that America ought to retain the conquered Spanish territories in order to civilize them. White pointed out that America had established an ignoble record toward dark-skinned people. He cited as evidence the extermination of Native Americans, murderous assaults on Chinese immigrants in the West, and the periodic lynching of African Americans. White remained a product of his era even though his attitudes on race were more advanced than many of his contemporaries.

For instance, another of his arguments against imperialism was that it would be nearly impossible to civilize millions of "half-naked black people who can't read, and whose idea of human relations are little above the ideas of the beasts of the fields." The war's most important impact on White's career was that it made Theodore Roosevelt a national hero by virtue of his Rough Rider exploits. White loudly called for his friend to be "made governor of New York and President of the United States." Roosevelt eventually won both offices, catapulting White into the front ranks of the Progressive movement.[31]

William Allen White and the *Gazette* were institutions after four short years. The *Gazette*'s rapidly increasing circulation spurred White to build a new office building that was completed in the summer of 1899, and his improving financial situation allowed him to purchase a new home for his family that year. The newspaper had been noticed nationally, and White capitalized on his growing reputation by selling advertising space to national corporations. At the same time, he carefully cultivated his image as a simple, small-town newspaper editor with facile protests that his was "simply a little country daily and weekly, devoted entirely to chronicling the important fact that Bill Jones brought in a load of hay today." The man who had arrived in Emporia four years earlier with $1.25 in his pocket was now one of the town's leading citizens, a fact demonstrated by White's chairmanship of the committee organizing the first annual Emporia street fair.[32] The event was to be held in late September 1899, and White had to find ways to entertain a family crowd without the advantage of ticket revenue, since it was free. A successful street fair would also increase White's prestige, helping attract advertising and subscribers to the *Gazette*.

The network of leading business and political figures White had established proved to be an invaluable advantage. He raised $4,000 for the fair from Emporia's business community and from corporate sponsors such as the Kansas City office of the Armour Company. Excursion trains were required to transport the legions of attendees and entertainers, which included bands, log-rolling teams, and acrobat and vaudeville acts. Funds had been raised for this purpose, and White wrote his friend W. J. Black, passenger manager of the Santa Fe Railroad, to request his assistance in making the arrangements. White assured Black that this personal favor would be repaid at some future date, and Black obliged him by donating the cost of transportation for several exhibits. Boss Leland helped White by using his political contacts at the Department of the Interior to arrange "corn dance" performances by groups of Kickapoo and Pottawatomie Indians from Nebraska's Nemaha Reservation.[33]

The Emporia street fair was a rousing success, drawing approximately twenty thousand attendees from the region. Popular exhibits included a French automobile owned by prominent Chicago attorney Edward Brown, a display of color photography, and Santa Fe's "King Corn" statue, which was a thirty-five-foot-tall corn king figure crafted entirely of corn. Local farmers and ranchers displayed their finest produce, and prizes were awarded in categories such as "best sweet corn." White and his fellow Emporians thought nothing of humiliating the local African American community for their own amusement. One of the fair's events was a "colored baby show," which consisted of twelve African American mothers and their infants dressed in their finest outfits. The contest had just begun when one of White's confederates told the band to play a popular tune called "All Coons Look Alike to Me," amusing the crowd while the outraged mothers stormed off. A similar incident occurred during the flower parade. The fair committee paid two dozen African American boys a dime apiece to dress in corn husk loincloths and be marched in the parade as mock Filipinos captured in the ongoing Philippine-American War. Once again, the town's African American mothers intervened before the exploitative procession began, hauling their children back to Emporia's "Stringtown" African American quarter.[34] Overall, the street fair helped White prove that he had the clout and the organizational skills to stage a major event, and it showed that he was moving toward progressivism. As White put it, the fair proved that "Emporia has changed . . . from the country village, to the energetic, enterprising town" of his dreams. The same could be said of the young man who faced a mighty struggle just to make the *Gazette*'s weekly payroll four years before.[35]

William Allen White was part of a younger generation that was determined to make its place in the world, and he was well on his way to success by the end of the nineteenth century. His fiction was well received, and he was churning out short stories that highlighted the corrupting influence of powerful corporations. He was a nationally known journalist, the *Gazette* was established as Emporia's newspaper, and Emporia itself was maturing into a thriving midwestern town. The doors to the inner sanctum of politics were opening to him as a rising Republican operative in the service of Boss Leland's political machine. Sallie bore him a son in June 1900, William Lindsay White, who would follow in his father's footsteps as a journalist and novelist. White was approaching a fork in the road, and the course he chose determined that of his career. In one direction lay the path of his mentors "Bent" Murdock, Calvin Hood, and Cy Leland: he could become a Republican boss in his own right and keep the *Gazette* as a vehicle for his political aspirations. Or he could choose the crusader's route, following the course laid out by his mother, by Colonel Nelson's fearless *Kansas City Star,* and by Theodore Roosevelt's pursuit of a greater destiny. Like many who became Progressives, White eventually chose the latter, but for the moment he remained loyal to the old political system he knew best.[36]

CHAPTER TWO

HELL-RAISER

William Allen White burned with the desire to join his fellow countrymen as they marched to war against Spain in 1898, his patriotic fervor having trumped his concerns about the implications of an American empire. The thirty-year-old's martial fantasies were dashed when his wife, Sallie, became ill, and he watched from afar as the United States seized Cuba, the Philippines, and other Spanish possessions in the New World. Colonel Theodore Roosevelt's exploits with his Rough Riders in Cuba particularly impressed White, who was overjoyed when Roosevelt was elected to the New York governorship in November. Roosevelt obliged White's gushing request for an autographed portrait in his Rough Rider uniform, which White displayed above his desk for nearly five decades as a reminder to stand up for his beliefs. White felt that America needed the Rough Rider in the White House, and he resolved to help elect Roosevelt to the presidency as an act of national service.[1] At the same time, Roosevelt had attracted White by his forceful personality more than his political ideas, and White remained a loyal cog in Cyrus Leland's political machine. The contrast between Roosevelt's high ideals and the daily reality of White's participation in machine politics forced him to choose a path. Young men and women around America were having to face the same decision, and White was one of many who cast their lots with the budding progressive movement.

The near certainty that Republican president William McKinley would seek a second term in 1900 meant that Governor Roosevelt's first real chance to head the ticket would be in 1904. White immediately began laying the groundwork for the anticipated campaign. His first move was to persuade Roosevelt to stop in Emporia to meet midwestern journalists in June 1899, explaining that it would help to have a good relationship with the region's newspapermen in 1904. Roosevelt's path to the White House deviated from that White had envisioned when word leaked out that the governor would be nominated as McKinley's vice presidential running mate in 1900. Roosevelt had clashed with Thomas Platt's New York state Republican machine, and the boss aimed to bury Roosevelt in the vice presidency. Governor Roosevelt initially agreed with White that he should refuse the nomination, but he changed his mind after concluding that the Platt machine would stymie his reform agenda in New York. The vice presidency also seemed to offer Roosevelt more avenues to significant positions in the future. For instance, Roosevelt thought that the vice presidency might lead to an appointment as governor-general of the Philippines, where he could help build a new democracy in Asia. White accepted Roosevelt's decision, surmising that God had a different plan for Roosevelt than the one he had envisioned.[2]

President McKinley won reelection in 1900 with Roosevelt as his vice president, but White's organizing for Roosevelt's expected 1904 campaign hardly missed a beat. Vice President Roosevelt made White his midwestern campaign manager for his 1904 run, assigning him responsibility over Kansas, Nebraska, Missouri, Oklahoma, Colorado, and Utah. His first task was to attend a political dinner given by several Colorado Republican Party leaders in Roosevelt's honor in August 1901. Roosevelt insisted that White act as a "witness" as the attendees pledged support for his nomination, which he hoped would spark a western boom that would blunt Platt's efforts against his candidacy. White was the ideal man for the role: he was one of Roosevelt's close friends, he was in contact with an impressive array of influential people as a journalist, and he was a highly placed member of Cyrus Leland's political machine. Roosevelt and White continued to confer on the train back to Emporia, and Roosevelt asked him to survey the Kansas and Missouri Republican establishments to assess their support for his nomination.[3]

As a machine man, White's first step was to establish an alliance between Roosevelt and Boss Leland's machine in Topeka. White assured Leland that Roosevelt "wants the friendship of our fellows," and that he would "show his appreciation of that friendship in a substantial and manly way" if he won the nomination. The transaction was an accepted part of politics under the old system that White would later challenge, but at the moment, he remained one of its acolytes. Leland reciprocated the overture, and White found so much support on his visits to Topeka and Kansas City that he wrote Roosevelt that his candidacy was "kind of a popular uprising like the crusades." Roosevelt welcomed the news, and he signaled his willingness to take Leland "into my inmost councils and have him one of the men who shape the whole course of events." Even as he bargained for the support of political machines, Roosevelt insisted to White that his campaign had to rest primarily on the support of "men like you . . . like the farmers, small business men and upper class mechanics who are my natural allies." The public narrative for his campaign, Roosevelt continued, had to be that the professional politicians had bowed to a tidal wave of grassroots support when they endorsed his nomination. The Roosevelt campaign was well under way by the end of the summer, and in September 1901 White turned his attention to pressing magazine assignments that brought him to Chicago, Buffalo, New York City, and Washington, DC.[4]

Anarchist Leon Czolgosz seemed to validate White's casual remark that fate had a different plan for Roosevelt when he shot President McKinley at the Pan-American Exposition in Buffalo on September 6. The president initially appeared likely to recover, and Roosevelt wrote White the next day expressing confidence that "when you receive this the president I am sure will be out of danger." The two men made arrangements to confer on political matters when White arrived in Washington, DC, but McKinley died after his condition suddenly worsened early on the morning of September 14. Roosevelt took the oath of office in Buffalo that afternoon, and White dashed an emotional note to the new president lamenting the terrible burden that fate had placed on his shoulders. White assured Roosevelt that God had equipped him to handle the challenges to come, that the American people trusted him, and that he should be bold in addressing "the duties [God] has raised you up to perform." President Roosevelt invited White to dine in Washington, DC, on September 20, 1901, the day after McKinley's funeral, and the editor was enthralled as Roosevelt outlined his vision of reform motivated by a powerful sense of national purpose.[5]

One of the first decisions President Roosevelt had to make concerned White's position in Kansas politics, in the form of Boss Leland's reappointment as pension commissioner. The Kansas Republican Party was locked in a savage internecine war between Boss Leland's faction and an anti-Leland group that called itself the Boss Busters. Many Boss Busters were sincere reformers, but the group's membership consisted primarily of Leland's political enemies. The Boss Busters were led by Joseph R. Burton, an ambitious Republican who had built his political career as a skilled anti-Populist orator and state legislator in Kansas during the 1890s. Burton had supported reform-minded measures in the legislature, such as the regulation of railroad rates, but he also displayed a disturbing willingness to leverage his position for personal profit. Leland and Burton were intense rivals who shared a deep personal enmity, and Leland had used his influence to suppress Burton's political career on several occasions. Burton began to gain the upper hand when he was elected to the US Senate in 1900. Leland's Pension Commission appointment was due to expire in 1902, which placed Senator Burton in position to administer a strong blow against his enemy by challenging his renomination.[6]

White well knew that both Leland and Burton were political bosses who exercised power by corrupting the democratic process, but he felt that there were substantial differences between the two men that justified supporting Leland. First, White owed a great deal to Boss Leland, and he felt honor-bound to stand by his friend. Leland and his machine had helped finance White's purchase of the *Gazette* in 1895, and Leland kept the newspaper afloat by giving White a highly profitable pension printing contract during the *Gazette*'s early days. Second, White excused Leland as an older man who had entered public life during a period when politics and machines were inseparable. Simply put, Leland knew no other political way of life. Third, White respected Leland as an honorable man who kept his bargains even when he could gain an advantage by reneging. In contrast, White despised Senator Burton as a corrupt, untrustworthy, backstabbing politician with no principles whose word counted for nothing when there was a profit to be had.[7] By supporting Leland, White was helping a longtime friend, repaying old debts, and fighting against a man he considered a crook.

Leland's position seemed secure. President McKinley had promised to reappoint him, and incoming president Roosevelt had announced that he intended to honor his predecessor's patronage commitments. Nevertheless, Leland was concerned enough to ask his trusted lieutenant, Fourth Assistant Postmaster General Joseph L. Bristow, to work with White in shepherding his reappointment through Washington. Although White was inexperienced, Leland noted that he could be tremendously useful because he had "the confidence of the new President." Senator Burton alleged that Leland had abused his office for personal gain, and White defended him to Roosevelt as a machine politician who was nonetheless an honest and honorable man. He argued that Leland deserved reappointment unless Burton could prove his allegations beyond a reasonable doubt, and the president replied that additional endorsements would facilitate the matter. Leland's chances seemed to brighten when White corralled an impressive array of recommendations from the state's political establishment. White even took the liberty of asking the president for the privilege of allowing him to "break the news to the old man first" in the event of a favorable decision.[8]

The first sign that Leland's appointment was in real trouble came when Roosevelt informed White that he had received a confidential accusation that Leland had engaged in misconduct. The disclosure spurred White to write Roosevelt frankly admitting that Leland was "a blunt man with primitive passions" who had made many enemies over the decades. By the same token, White stated that he had been Leland's friend for six years and that he had never abused his position for personal profit. The president dashed any remaining hope that Leland might win an easy reappointment when he lamented that the patronage nominees before him were "not bad enough for me to get anything tangible against them, and yet not good enough for me to feel satisfied if I appoint them."[9]

Roosevelt's letter hurt White deeply because he interpreted it as a personal rebuke for his support for Leland. In reply, White wrote that his friendship with Roosevelt had "lifted me and strengthened me and given me a wider moral intelligence than I could ever have without it." It appeared to White that Roosevelt thought he was either being "deceived by a bad man [Leland], or ignoring his vices. Either proposition is painful to contemplate because I want . . . your respect." The fight was really all about Burton, whom White described as an "arrogant coward" and "a mercenary" who would "run from you and your administration like a hungry cat" when it served his ends. The same day, the president wrote White that Professor James Canfield, his KU mentor, had stated that there was no material difference between Leland and Burton. Roosevelt had no desire to take sides unless the issue was greater than mere factionalism, and White again conceded that Leland was "not and never was and never will be a man of ideals." Nevertheless, he asserted that Kansas had changed since Leland's day. Describing himself as well as his state, White explained that "men have grown, have revealed themselves, have developed" through the progressive movement. The progressive reforms being enacted in the states would prevent anyone from being able to control Kansas in the way that Leland had in his heyday.[10] White requested Leland's reappointment on the grounds that he had spent decades in honorable service and no one would be harmed by allowing the old man to remain at his post.

Leland's fortunes had reversed so suddenly and drastically that he launched a frantic, last-ditch effort to save his appointment. The boss dispatched White to Washington, DC, to ask President Roosevelt to hold his decision until influential Rock Island Railroad attorney Marcus Low arrived. The Rock Island wanted peace in the Kansas Republican Party, and Low was irritated that Burton had broken his promise not to prosecute his war against Leland. Bristow felt that White and Low's combined influence would reinvigorate Leland's chances, and their conference with the president on December 5 seemed successful. In fact, the intervention went so smoothly that White left Washington for Emporia the next day, convinced that Leland had won the battle. Although Leland regarded White as young and inexperienced, the boss wrote Bristow that he liked White because he was a "fighter [who] will stay." Bristow agreed, praising White for having "acted with fine discretion" in the matter.[11]

The bottom fell out of Leland's nomination the day after White's departure. Senator Burton confronted Roosevelt with endorsements from half of Kansas's congressional delegation supporting Wilder Metcalf, a Spanish-American War veteran who had been named as a neutral candidate. Furthermore, the senator complained that Roosevelt had treated him unfairly by rejecting his patronage nominees on unproven allegations while Leland remained under consideration despite similarly unproven allegations. Roosevelt was still considering the matter when Burton tried to force the issue by falsely informing the press that Leland would be prosecuted on December 13. White immediately protested to President Roosevelt that the nomination of anyone other than Leland would be a triumph for Burton's brand of underhanded politics. He begged Roosevelt "not for [Leland] . . . but for the welfare of a state" to allow Low the time he needed to unite the state's congressional delegation for Leland.[12]

Roosevelt acquiesced to White's request for more time, but he finally appointed Metcalf on December 19. Burton was ecstatic, believing he had scored a mortal blow that would destroy Leland and establish himself as the power in Kansas Republican politics. Boss Leland accepted his defeat with dignity because he wisely recognized that Burton had alienated many Republican leaders by breaking his promise not to stir up party quarrels. White respected Roosevelt's decision and he acknowledged that Metcalf was a sound choice, but the defeat stung. Boss Buster–allied newspapers celebrated Metcalf's appointment as the triumph of good government over a wicked political boss, and a few also mocked White as a paper tiger. The factionally neutral *Kansas City Journal* noted that the state's voters were completely ignored in the personal fight between Leland and Burton.

Presciently, the *Journal* predicted that the voters would soon take control of the party from both factions.[13]

White was too glum to see matters clearly, but the *Kansas City Journal* had gauged the situation correctly. Metcalf's appointment was painful for both White and Leland, but it was hardly the twilight of democratic government in Kansas that White had bewailed. Both Leland and Burton were machine politicians who corrupted the democratic process. The heart of the matter from White's perspective was his personal loyalty to the fatherly Boss Leland, his obligations as a member of Leland's machine, and his visceral hatred for the opportunistic Burton. White's support for Leland was understandable, but his emotional investment caused him to assign outsized importance to the appointment. Although White saw the truth only vaguely, his future lay with the younger generation of reformers who would fight to democratize America. Leland's defeat was a necessary step in that evolution.

The emotional blow of Leland's defeat coincided with a fierce controversy over one of White's articles profiling America's leading political figures for *McClure's* magazine. The December 1901 installment featured Senator Thomas C. Platt, the longtime boss of the New York state Republican machine who had clashed with Roosevelt during the latter's tenure as governor. Platt had been a vigorous political warrior in his youth, but the senator was now nearly seventy and had clearly entered his declining years. Roosevelt helped White by arranging interviews with both Platt and several of the senator's disillusioned former confederates, and the piece reflected Roosevelt's antipathy toward the old boss. White was merciless in his depiction of Platt as a "quarrelsome, petulant, and suspicious" man who was driven by "an itch for power" and a "love for money." Platt was a machine, White explained, who could be "taken apart without finding a soul." Gleefully, he recounted how Governor Roosevelt had forced old Boss Platt and his machine to heel in a nomination fight, remarking that Platt had later tried to "punish [Roosevelt] for his integrity" by sidelining him in the vice presidency. "Fate itself" had intervened and elevated Roosevelt to the White House when McKinley was assassinated. White concluded that Platt's career was all but over, and the once powerful boss was now a doddering old fool marked by "the dry, purple-pink parchment skin of senility."[14]

The offensive article naturally incensed Senator Platt, who correctly deduced that President Roosevelt had provided White's information. An enraged Senator Platt stormed to the president to demand that White be declared persona non grata at the White House, and he publicly threatened both White and *McClure's* with a libel suit. White was aghast. He apologized to Roosevelt for having involved him in a controversy, and he asked for help in explaining to Platt that he was solely responsible for the article. The affair amused Roosevelt, who assured White that there was no need for an apology. Indeed, Roosevelt capitalized on the episode to play a practical joke on Platt, who had publicly boasted that White would never again be admitted to the White House. White was in the Oval Office visiting Roosevelt several months later when Platt arrived to request a favor. Platt knew White only by name, and Roosevelt asked him to remain while Platt made his statement. The senator delivered his message without ever realizing that he had just shared the Oval Office with the man he swore would never again be admitted to the White House. Platt's promised libel suit never materialized, but the controversy added to White's burdens of overwork, of scrimping to pay off his home mortgage, and of a severe cold in December 1901.[15]

The strain proved to be too much, and the dam burst around Christmas. White arrived at his office "feeling rather like a wobbly legged calf," and he began to dictate a routine letter ordering a carload of newsprint for the *Gazette*. Suddenly, he began trembling, sweating profusely, and struggling to get his words out. His face and shirt collar were soaked with perspiration before he had dictated three lines. White asked his staff to finish the letter and turned his attention to writing an editorial, only to find himself "weak as a cat" before he had completed half a column. He abandoned the office for his sickbed, but the next morning he found that he could not read the newspapers or his mail without suffering another attack. The diagnosis was nervous exhaustion, and his doctors prescribed a vacation. Mr. and Mrs. White arrived at California's Catalina Island in February 1902, while their toddler son, William, remained in Kansas with White's mother. The couple spent weeks lounging on the beach and enjoying rustic island cuisine in their rented cabin. The mail was a particular problem because White's letters often involved political matters at home, and he confessed to Roosevelt that his nerves were so shattered that "every time I see a letter from Emporia in the mail I go to bed." Sallie initially kept all mail away from her husband, but gradually she was able to read his letters to him aloud, tease out his thoughts, and compose replies in his name.[16] By the spring of 1902, White had regained enough strength to begin a leisurely return to Kansas that took him through Los Angeles, Yosemite, Salt Lake City, and Colorado Springs.

The Whites arrived in Emporia to find the war between Leland's machine and the Boss Busters still raging in the form of a battle over the town's postmastership. Post offices were at the center of small-town civic life, making postmasterships highly desirable patronage positions that paid tremendous financial and political dividends. Potential vacancies frequently triggered town squabbles as competing candidates and factions vied for their congressman's endorsement, which weighed heavily in the president's final selection. Emporia's incumbent postmaster was associated with Leland, while the town was represented in Congress by a Burton ally named James M. Miller. White and other leading Emporians were outraged when Miller nominated John Wiggam, a man with a reputation for treachery within the Republican Party. The matter should have been settled when the postmaster general declared Wiggam unsuitable for the office, but Miller insisted that he would nominate no other man. Roosevelt was in a bind. White, Emporia's leading citizens, and the postmaster general were against Wiggam. However, Representative Miller was Senator Burton's ally, and Roosevelt needed Burton's vote for a bill establishing free trade with Cuba on a reciprocal basis. The reciprocity issue was thorny for Roosevelt because it neatly divided the GOP between the industrial northeast, which wanted access to

William and Sallie traveling, circa 1900. White was a true Rooseveltian who enjoyed America's natural splendor, including visits to the Grand Canyon, Catalina Island, Yosemite, and the Rocky Mountains. Courtesy of Emporia State University, Special Collections and Archives.

Cuban markets, and midwestern sugar beet producers who feared cane sugar competition. Burton was likely to vote against reciprocity if Roosevelt denied Miller his patronage appointee.[17]

The postmaster fight had begun just as White's nervous breakdown was erupting, and he played little role in the controversy until his condition improved in April 1902. White shied away from expressing his frank opinion about Wiggam despite the president's persistent requests for advice because he sensed that he had lobbied Roosevelt too vigorously in the pension commissioner battle. Indeed, White took pains to discount his opinions by stating that the matter was not of national importance and that he understood that Roosevelt needed to consider Burton's vote on Cuban reciprocity. Roosevelt saw that White was pulling his punches, and he insisted that White give him his thoughts "straight from the shoulder." White could hardly deny such a request, and he gave Roosevelt both barrels: Wiggam was an "incompetent disreputable fellow," he was backed by men who were under indictment in the failure of the First National Bank of Emporia in 1898, and his appointment would make bosses of his corrupt backers. All this notwithstanding, White told Roosevelt that he did not want his opposition to produce a nasty battle that might endanger the president's legislative agenda.[18]

The path to Wiggam's appointment seemed to clear on May 28, when Senator Burton publicly endorsed reciprocity as long as Kansas's beet sugar producers were protected against Cuban imports. Leland dropped his machine's opposition to Wiggam after he and Burton agreed to a temporary cease-fire in the spring of 1902, which was motivated by a desire to unite against the Democrats. Roosevelt signaled that he was leaning toward appointing Wiggam after Bristow, a Leland lieutenant, stated that the issue was a matter of factions rather than principle. Bristow scolded White that his continued opposition was "embarrassing [Roosevelt] in matters of national policy in dealing with Congressman Miller and Senator Burton," and White wrote Roosevelt that he would stand down if his opposition was harming the administration. However, he also arranged for Wiggam's pastor to send Roosevelt a letter describing the nominee as

Panorama of downtown Emporia in the spring of 1909. Courtesy of the Library of Congress, LC-USZ62-58682.

"unfit, incompetent, and unreliable." Still, Wiggam's appointment seemed imminent by mid-June.[19]

White was all but licked when Senator Burton swooped in to snatch defeat from the jaws of victory. Burton validated White's warnings that the senator was a dishonorable man who would not keep his bargains when he joined a caucus of staunchly antireciprocity senators in Washington, DC. Still, President Roosevelt pursued Burton's support by sending a special message to Congress asking the Senate to ratify the reciprocity bill while requesting legislative measures to protect the beet sugar industry. Even Burton's supporters were shocked when he rose as one of only two senators to speak against the administration in a Republican caucus meeting. Roosevelt was enraged, and Burton's fate was sealed as other examples of the senator's duplicitous behavior emerged. The president immediately informed White that Wiggam would not be appointed, he chose the man White named to fill the position, and he arranged a conference with White and Leland in Kansas.[20] The White House was now at war with Burton, and White began to comprehend his folly in giving his loyalty to a political machine. White hated Burton with a visceral passion, he saw Wiggam as a man exquisitely unfit for the office he

sought, and he had served the Leland machine to the point of physical and mental exhaustion. He could not have ignored the fact that neither his loyalty nor his ideological values had counted for anything when the machine decided to back an unfit candidate.

The contrast between White's budding ideals and the corrupt reality of machine politics was on full display when he helped Leland broker the election for Kansas's US Senate seat in 1903. The voters elected a Republican state legislature in November 1902, and the fact that senators were chosen by state legislatures meant that a Republican was sure to win the seat when the legislative session opened in January. Senatorial elections usually turned Topeka into a buzzing hive of ambitious politicians, political bosses, and powerful corporate figures, all seeking to use the election to advance their interests. Friends prevailed on friends, political offices were traded, and bribes were paid, often in the form of free travel passes that railroad company attorneys doled out to legislators and journalists. White was as guilty as anyone else in this regard. He carried passes granting him free travel on the Santa Fe, Missouri-Pacific, Rock Island, and Union Pacific railroads, and other passes that granted him free telegraph services, express freight services, and free meals while traveling. Lining up railroad support was a key task for any senatorial campaign manager, because whoever obtained the backing of these powerful corporations was likely to win the election. White's job was to help Leland line up votes for his faction's candidate at Topeka, and the experience showed him that he had to choose between his democratic ideals and his machine ways.[21]

The Republican caucus was divided between Leland's and Burton's factions in the senatorial election, and Leland's faction was itself divided between supporters of the popular congressman Chester I. Long and outgoing governor William Stanley. Senator Burton was officially neutral in the race because he was a sitting senator, but his Boss Buster faction favored Representative Charles Curtis. Leland was ostensibly neutral in the contest between Long and Stanley, but the boss knew that Long was very close to winning enough railroad support to take the seat. Stanley never had enough votes to be a serious competitor, but Leland ordered White to lock up his votes by keeping him in the race until Long sealed his bargain with the railroads. Meanwhile, Bristow collaborated with Wall Street financier and future Progressive Party chairman George Perkins to negotiate with the railroads on Long's behalf in New York City. Long emerged victorious after Kansas's five leading railroads agreed to give him the Senate seat in January 1903, and White played one final role in Long's corrupt bargain the day after the election. Major Hood was White's patron and one of Leland's allies, and he visited the *Gazette*'s office to ask for a favor. Hood explained that he had lent Stanley and Long $1,500 each for their expenses in Topeka, and he wanted White to tell Long to repay Stanley's note. White obeyed, knowing perfectly well that the "loan" was a bribe to keep Stanley from raising a ruckus about his defeat.[22]

Decades later, White cited his participation in the senatorial election as the moment when he realized that machine democracy was a fraud because the people played no real role in politics. Representatives and senators were elected and platforms set by a handful of political elites, powerful railroad attorneys, and financial moguls in New York or Chicago, who traded Kansas's elected offices in the same way they traded coal or wheat or any other commodity. In 1903, White's outrage was subordinated to his singular focus on wiping "the smut-spot of Burton from the Senate." White hoped that electing Long would help end the kind of factional "wrangling and rag-chewing and back biting" that had aided Burton, while giving Roosevelt a reliable supporter on the Kansas Republican delegation. The president soon informed Senator Long that he would be consulted exclusively on Kansas patronage matters, and Long had eclipsed Leland as the boss of the state's Republican machine by 1904.[23]

Long's star was rising while Senator Burton's was falling, and White helped deliver the final blow against the man he hated with a visceral passion. In July 1903, White reported to Roosevelt that Senator Burton had attempted to intercede with the US Postal Service as general counsel for the Rialto Grain and Securities Company of Saint Louis. The company was under investigation by the Postal Service for securities fraud, and Burton had escorted one of the company's officers to the postmaster general's office to inquire about the case. A Civil War–era statute made it a federal crime for a member of Congress to represent a private company in cases in which the US government had an interest. A raid on the Rialto Company's offices substantiated the allegations, an indictment was brought, and Burton was convicted by a federal court on March 28, 1904. The senator maintained his innocence and refused to resign his seat, remaining in the Senate for two more years as his appeals wound through the court system. The US Supreme Court rejected Burton's final appeal in 1906, which left him with no choice but to resign his seat and begin serving his six-month prison sentence. Former senator Burton spent the rest of his life in a futile attempt to exonerate his name in the court of public opinion.[24]

The year 1904 proved consequential for White. In his personal life, Sallie gave birth to Mary, their second child, on June 18. In public affairs, Burton's conviction eliminated him as a force in Kansas, and the ties that bound White to machine politics were finally severed. The first tie was White's sincere esteem for the fatherly Leland. The affection between White and Leland remained, but affection alone was not enough to keep White permanently bound to Leland's political initiatives. Second, White had cleared his ledger with Leland by 1904, and the old Leland machine was now led by Senator Long, to whom White owed nothing. Third, White had felt that he needed the Leland machine's help in his battle against Burton, but the senator's own misdeeds severed this tie. Republican and Democratic reformers in state parties across America were waging war against their parties' respective machines, and Senator Burton's downfall freed White to join the Republican reformers.[25] Finally, Theodore Roosevelt had inspired him with a new vision of politics as an act of national service. White was ready to join the hell-raisers.

The Progressive movement was blossoming in Kansas just as White was becoming emancipated from machine politics in early 1904. Ironically, the shift was driven partly as a reaction against White's friend Governor Willis J. Bailey. The governor had been heavily criticized in 1903 for his perceived failure to address petty graft in state government, spurring his detractors to organize the Kansas Republican League to agitate for reform. The group resembled the defunct Boss Busters in that it was primarily a vehicle for railroad attorneys and Burton factionalists, but it included a few sincere reformers. The Republican League's railroad element was frightened out of the group by two such reformers, Walter R. Stubbs and Edward W. Hoch. Stubbs was a wealthy, charismatic railroad contractor who entered politics as a state legislator in 1902, rising to the state Republican Party chairmanship in just two years. Hoch was the publisher of the *Marion County Record* and an established politician who shocked the state machine by securing enough support to win the Republican gubernatorial nomination well in advance of the party convention in 1904. Stubbs and Hoch were younger men of White's post–Civil War generation, and the editor admired both as "big broad-gauged Americans" who could bring Kansas into the current of national reform led by President Roosevelt.[26]

White had repented his machine-operative ways, and he demanded that both Stubbs and Hoch prove themselves faithful to the

Progressives' higher standards in the 1904 election. Stubbs and Hoch had built a slate of nominees partly by agreeing to support a machine man for treasurer, but the candidate faced unresolved allegations of fiscal irregularities in several previously held elected offices. White knew that politicians sometimes had to craft unpalatable deals, and he had helped arrange some of those deals as part of Leland's machine. As a newly minted Progressive, White wrote Hoch that it was "farce" to "talk good government" with a possibly corrupt man on the ticket. Citing Roosevelt's call for politicians to employ more than "mere passive honesty," he asked Hoch and Stubbs to endorse an investigation that would either refute or validate the allegations. The state attorney general undermined White's call for action a few days later when he revealed that his investigation had failed to sustain the charges, but the incident highlighted White's rapid conversion from machine acolyte to Progressive zealot.[27]

Hoch, Stubbs, and other state reformers triumphed in Kansas and elsewhere in the November 1904 election, and President Roosevelt won reelection. White celebrated the outcome in an article for the *Saturday Evening Post* arguing that the election proved that Roosevelt was inspiring the people to democratize their nation. He explained that the government's sole concern during the late nineteenth century had been to protect those who had acquired wealth, with little regard for the social cost. President Roosevelt's "Square Deal" had aimed to force organized wealth to earn a fair profit in a more responsible manner, and he had won important national reforms despite stubborn resistance from the GOP's conservative establishment. Roosevelt's legislative accomplishments were significant, but White saved his greatest praise for the way the president had spurred the post–Civil War generation toward "Civic Righteousness." The president had inspired White and millions of younger Americans to abandon the Gilded Age's crass materialism and embrace social justice; this new wave of reformers would continue the fight to tame capital long after the president's term had expired. The article pleased Roosevelt, who remarked that the two men "both stand for the same thing." In particular, Roosevelt appreciated White's point that national leaders were important as symbols who inspired individuals to organize and change their own communities.[28]

Kansas was at the forefront of the Progressive movement after Hoch won the governorship and Stubbs became the Speaker of the Kansas House of Representatives in the 1904 election. The Progressive agenda they advocated was based partly on Wisconsin governor Robert La Follette's pioneering reforms, which aimed to democratize state government. Hoch and Stubbs won measures converting the plum patronage office of state printer into an elected position, beefing up enforcement of Kansas's prohibition statute, enacting limited woman suffrage, creating a juvenile justice system, and regulating railroad rates. Railroad reform was the issue that truly energized midwesterners because the region was heavily reliant on the railroads to access the national market. Roosevelt used his annual message to Congress in December 1904 to call for the federal Interstate Commerce Commission (ICC) to be given the power to set railroad rates, but the measure stalled due to conservative opposition in the Senate. Kansas's reformers focused on railroad rate discrimination, which made shipping rates a function of cargo type and destination rather than weight and distance. The policy made it more cost-effective to ship Kansas's raw materials to eastern factories than to manufacture goods locally, and the state's boosters argued that it discouraged industrialization. Hoch and the legislature passed a bill that required the railroads to file their rate books with the state Board of Railroad Commissioners and broadened the board's regulatory powers. The direct primary was the most important Progressive reform Hoch and Stubbs pursued because the machines' and corporations' control over Kansas politics was based on their ability to buy support under the caucus system. Unfortunately, the measure failed in the face of the establishment's fierce opposition.[29]

Illness left White sidelined during the fight to enact Hoch's agenda in the Kansas legislature, but the editor's condition paid a greater dividend by inadvertently deepening his Progressive faith. White departed for five weeks' rest in Colorado on doctor's orders in late

January 1905, which gave him an opportunity to consult Idaho's William E. Borah regarding a land investment. Borah and White became acquainted as fraternity brothers at the University of Kansas, and Borah had risen to become a prominent land attorney and politician. The "investment" was actually a scheme to establish a cantaloupe farm in partnership with Idaho governor Frank W. Hunt and a number of speculators. The speculators would use the Desert Lands Act to acquire public land at practically no cost, White would purchase or lease the land for the farm under assignment from them, others would operate the farm, and White would market and distribute the fruit in the Midwest. The scheme was a commonly used method of obtaining land for next to nothing, but Borah advised White that the arrangement constituted fraud even if the crime was unlikely to be detected. White panicked because the Roosevelt administration had begun prosecuting fraudulent land claims of exactly this type all over the West. Borah helped White deed the land back to the original owner and quietly withdraw from the deal, but the editor retained the private shame of having publicly demanded honest government while secretly, if perhaps unwittingly, participating in a corrupt enterprise.[30] The incident gave White a visceral reminder of the kind of pervasive corruption that had been commonplace during the Gilded Age, of the need for Rooseveltian conservation, and of the way that a good man could become a criminal after a momentary lapse in judgment.

White returned from Colorado in March more determined than ever to work for Progressive reform, and he had his opportunity when Governor Hoch appointed him to serve as a University of Kansas regent. White firmly believed that editors should maintain their journalistic independence by religiously avoiding public office, but he leapt at the opportunity to remold KU along midwestern lines. The university was focused on constructing buildings, increasing enrollment, and training young people to be technicians, and White felt that its course was too materialistic. Instead, he believed that KU's true mission was to cultivate a strong sense of citizenship based on midwestern values among its students. The school needed to churn out young men and women who would "help to make Kansas a cleaner decenter, more livable state—more livable in that its citizens see the folly of piling up unnecessary riches, and see the wisdom of neighborly kindness and gentility towards one another." White believed that improving faculty pay would be a good first step because it would create a faculty that was so zealously devoted to the university "that it will become a religion to them." Chancellor Frank Strong shared White's vision of KU as a counterpart to the University of Wisconsin at Madison, and the two men collaborated to advance KU as a leading midwestern higher education institution working for the public good.[31]

Railroad regulation was another avenue of reform, but there were limits to what Progressives could accomplish at the state level. Muckrakers such as White had kept the pressure on Congress to act on Roosevelt's proposal to allow the ICC to set railroad rates through 1905, and Kansas's reformers were thrilled when President Roosevelt used his annual message to Congress in December 1905 to call for renewed action. The Hepburn bill was the House's version of Roosevelt's proposal, but opposition solidified in the Senate. In Kansas, Stubbs worked with the Wichita Chamber of Commerce to create the Kansas Civic Voters' League in January 1906, which enlisted a thousand of the state's leading citizens to lobby for the Hepburn bill. The group received White's strong support, but it placed Senator Long in a difficult position. The Hepburn bill was too popular for Long to resist if he hoped to retain his seat in 1908, but he could not afford to alienate the railroad companies that had made him a senator. Long played the issue masterfully. He was able to claim that he supported reform because he helped ensure the Hepburn Act's passage by advancing a conservative amendment paring back the ICC's new powers. At the same time, he cultivated internal dissent in the Voters' League in a bid to destroy the group.[32] Senator Burton's resignation in mid-1906 gave Long his opportunity. The Voters' League was critically weakened when Stubbs, White's friend Henry J. Allen, and Senator Long's disaffected lieutenant Joseph Bristow all pursued the Senate seat instead of rallying around a single candidate. In contrast,

Senator Long, the state's railroad companies, and its political machines united behind conservative Republican representative Charles Curtis.

The machines' unity in the face of the reformers' disarray was a bad omen for the Progressives, but White felt that the railroads were making a fundamental mistake by behaving as if politics remained as usual. He sought to explain the people's anger to his friend Santa Fe Railroad vice president George T. Nicholson. White acknowledged that railroad executives were understandably frustrated to be "suddenly pounced upon and called thieves and liars and criminals" by reformers, when they were merely trying to operate their lines. However, he warned that the people "don't kick unless some one is prodding them. And here is the prod: the so-called railroad attorney[s]" who used company assets to establish themselves as kingmakers in state politics. White argued that railroad attorneys playing politics had advanced the careers of unfit men such as Burton and Curtis, which ultimately harmed the company because the public blamed the railroads for the outcome. Summing up the Progressive call to arms, White stated that the railroads could not "name senators, pack state conventions, run legislatures and boss politics generally with passes, and then successfully maintain that the railroads are private concerns doing a private business. So long as there are Harrimans and Goulds," men of wealth who interfered in politics, "there will be La Follettes and Tillmans," who were Progressives demanding that the public have a greater say in the companies' operations. Progressives in other states, such as Governor Albert B. Cummins (R-IA), expressed similar sentiments.[33]

The Kansas Republican Party held its convention in May 1906, and as White had feared, Curtis, the railroad attorneys, and the political machines entirely ran the board. The reformers had imitated the Wisconsin Plan by calling for platform planks demanding a complete assessment of railroad assets for tax purposes, banning the issuance of free railroad passes, and replacing the convention system with a direct primary. Unfortunately, Long and his supporters used every means at their disposal to stymie the Progressives even though Roosevelt's ideas had wide popular support in Kansas. Curtis won the

Republican nomination for former senator Burton's seat, and Governor Hoch was forced into an alliance with the machines to win renomination. Soon after, Governor Hoch outraged the Progressives by unilaterally committing Kansas to join the Missouri-Kansas-Texas railroad's land claims lawsuit against the federal government even though the state had no interest in the case.[34]

Hoch's bargain was an inexplicable act of betrayal to White, who warned the governor that the "great big revolt" against political machines and railroad attorneys was real. The only way Hoch could save his job, White argued, was to stand up, admit his mistake, and declare his independence from the interests. As much as White liked and respected Hoch personally, he confessed that his "high hopes of you as Governor" had been dashed. This feeling was so distressing to White that he conferred with three other pro-Hoch newspaper editors to determine whether he had judged the governor too harshly. All agreed that the governor had chosen the wrong course. The general consensus among Emporians was that Hoch was an honest man who was too weak to stand up to the machines that really ran Kansas. White punctuated his disappointment in Hoch by plaintively asking the governor, "How could you do it?"[35] The Kansas Civic League disbanded, and Kansas's Progressives seemed to be defeated.

The Progressives came roaring back over the summer. White's old mentor, Thomas "Bent" Murdock, rescued the movement by founding a new reform organization called the Square Deal Republican Club, which included White, Stubbs, Bristow, and most of the Voters' League's former members. The Square Dealers needed a prominent voice to rally their group and attack Senator Long, and White sent Senator La Follette, whom he knew only by reputation, a "Macedonian cry" to "Come and help us!" White explained that the people of Kansas were locked in a struggle with the railroads for control of the Republican Party, and he asked La Follette, Long's fierce opponent in the Senate, to speak at the Square Deal Club's August rally. La Follette accepted the invitation and gave a speech that electrified the state, but White was disappointed that the region's newspapers failed to cover the meeting. He helped address this by chiding his old contacts at the

Kansas City Star for missing out on "the biggest explosion fizzling in the fuse out here that the state has seen since 1890." White fully expected that the Progressive candidates would unite to defeat Curtis in 1907, and "when the union is made . . . there will be the devil to pay." One of Senator Long's lieutenants had reached the same conclusion, privately writing that La Follette's speech had "sowed eagle's claws" that could prove deadly in Long's 1908 reelection campaign.[36]

The Square Deal Club's activities generated a great deal of energy, but Long might have taken solace in the thought that his machine had limited the group's impact on the 1906 election. Such optimism would have been misplaced. White and his friend Congressman Victor Murdock ingeniously used the Square Deal Club to counter the machine's control of the platform and nominees. At their instigation, the group surveyed 185 Kansas Republican candidates about their support for a range of highly popular Progressive proposals such as the direct primary, the anti-pass law, and an assessment of railroad property for tax purposes. The move forced the candidates to choose between pledging to support popular reform measures and outraging the electorate by standing with the machines. More than two-thirds of the candidates completed the surveys, and White had the final product bound into a widely circulated booklet called "The Square Deal Hand Book." White rightly crowed to President Roosevelt that the machines had been outfoxed. The gambit was a clever way for the Progressives to place the machine's candidates on record in support of reform, and White was reasonably confident that the incoming state legislature would be friendly to the Progressive agenda.[37]

The prospects for a Progressive victory in the election to fill Kansas's vacant US Senate seat were significantly dimmer. Senators were chosen by state legislatures until the Seventeenth Amendment was ratified in 1913, which meant that the election would be held when the new legislature convened in January 1907. The Progressives were almost certain to lose because their forces were divided between Stubbs and Bristow, and White feared that a poor Progressive showing would hamper the group's ability to act on its legislative agenda in the statehouse. White supported Bristow, although he recognized that Stubbs had a right to campaign vigorously for the position. Electing a Progressive was what mattered in the end, and White wrote Stubbs proposing an understanding with Bristow that would unify the Progressives. Drawing on his experience as a dealmaker for Leland's machine, White suggested that each man promise to support the other if and when it became obvious that his own candidacy was not viable. The man who was elected senator could then lobby the legislature to adopt the direct primary, which would allow the defeated man to campaign directly to the people when Senator Long's seat came up for reelection in two years.[38]

The senatorial election finally began in January 1907, and White held out hope that the Progressives might eke out a victory as he held vigil in a Topeka hotel room. It was not to be. The railroads and the machines combined their forces as expected, overwhelming the Progressives and electing Representative Curtis to the seat. The news came in the middle of the night, and White released his frustration by walking out into the street and whistling his way through the midnight darkness. Curtis and White had been friends since the 1880s even though their politics had diverged, and White hoped that he would do well while suspecting that he had been "lifted up this way for no good." The defeat highlighted the fact that the machine politicians would always win "so long as politics is played under the present rules of the present game." He implored his friend Henry Allen, now a newspaper publisher, to "join the hell raisers" by committing his newspapers to support the move for a direct primary and a living wage. The failed senatorial election had convinced White that the two issues were inextricably linked. As he explained to President Roosevelt, any man willing to work had a right to a wage sufficient to live in reasonable comfort, to enjoy time off for self-improvement, and to be able to "educate his children so that Democracy may have an enlightened conscience at the ballot box." The lack of an enlightened electorate, White argued, was "at the bottom of all our trouble."[39]

The Progressives' defeat in the senatorial election was painful, but the outcome spurred White to become a leader in the fight to democratize the Kansas Republican Party overall, and the state's electoral process in particular. White's observation that the Progressives had a strong hand going into the 1907 Kansas legislative session proved accurate, and the Republican establishment was forced into a rearguard action against reform. Senator Long sought to blunt the Progressives' momentum by having his cronies in the legislature advance toothless versions of Progressive proposals. For instance, the legislature finally passed the law White had endorsed banning railroads from distributing free passes, but corporations had already developed more subtle and effective strategies for buying influence. The Long machine watered down a proposal to limit railroad passenger fares to two cents per mile by converting it from a universal flat fare to a limited travel voucher system. The direct primary was by far the biggest threat to both the railroads and Senator Long, since the measure would help shift the center of power away from party conventions that were easily controlled by the machines and corporations. The primary was too popular for Senator Long to attack directly, so he had his lieutenants in the state senate change the terms of the proposal in ways that favored his power base in western Kansas. Long's men also inserted a provision that threw the nomination back to a party convention if no candidate won a majority. The bill failed after Stubbs and the Progressives refused to accept the eviscerated primary measure, which suited Senator Long perfectly.[40]

Kansas's political establishment had scored a temporary victory by defeating the primary, but White recognized that the outcome only fueled popular support for the reform movement. He credited technological advances in the newspaper industry for having helped drive this process, explaining to President Roosevelt that Americans were now "getting daily papers on rural routes, and they are talking over their rural phones, and they watch the legislative proceedings of their various states carefully. They <u>know</u> who beats the primary law, and the anti-pass law and the corrupt practices law, and the people <u>know</u> that the local attorneys for the railroads are prostituting local government." White closed his letter with the comment that Kansans would be happy to treat the railroads fairly if they would "stop trying to name our Senators and Governors, and let us govern ourselves." Roosevelt was of the same mind when it came to the power of mass communications in politics, and he liked White's sentiments so much that he decided to incorporate his arguments into his next speech on the railroad question.[41]

Kansas's reformers had been temporarily foiled in their effort to reform the nominating process, but White helped put at least one additional Progressive into the US Senate. William E. Borah had obtained all but three of the votes he needed in the Idaho state legislature to win the state's US Senate seat in early 1907. Borah's rival for the seat refused to release the five votes he held even though he had no real chance of victory because he was convinced that the Republican boss, Senator Mark Hanna, supported his candidacy. White had not accepted a political office for himself as payment for "What's the Matter with Kansas?" but he again proved that he was willing to ask for favors on behalf of his friends. After explaining the situation and assuring Senator Hanna that Borah was no bomb-throwing radical, White asked Hanna to publicly declare that he had no candidate in the race. Hanna obliged with a letter to the influential Idaho *Statesman* declaring his neutrality, which helped Borah obtain the necessary votes.[42]

One obstacle still prevented Borah from claiming his Senate seat, and White was once again well positioned to be of assistance. Soon after Borah's election, the US attorney for the District of Idaho filed criminal charges alleging that he had conspired to defraud the government while working as corporate counsel for the Barber Lumber Company. Specifically, Borah was accused of helping his client acquire government land using straw purchasers, which was the same strategy used in White's cantaloupe farm scheme. Borah claimed that the charges were politically motivated, and he prevailed on White to intercede with President Roosevelt. White immediately wrote the president that he had come to know Borah as an honorable man, a reformer, a defender of the rule of law, and a good friend since their days as fraternity brothers at KU. The same day, White assured

Borah that Roosevelt "wants to be fair, and if he can get the right line on a matter, he is brave enough." Borah hoped that White would persuade Roosevelt to delay the corruption case against him until he had completed his prosecution of the Western Federation of Miners labor union for alleged complicity in the murder of Idaho governor Frank Steunenberg. White had his work cut out for him, since Roosevelt's initial response was that the judge, the district attorney, and the grand jury all seemed to feel that Borah was at least "morally guilty."[43]

An independent investigation by S. S. McClure, the muckraking publisher of McClure's magazine, seemed to validate White's instinctive decision to support Borah. McClure had traveled to Boise during the summer of 1907 expecting to find that the evidence substantiated the charges, but he returned convinced that Borah was the victim of malicious prosecution. At White's request, Mark Sullivan of Collier's magazine conducted a second investigation that reached the same conclusion. The McClure and Sullivan reports proved to White that the charges against Borah were retaliation for his fight for good government in Idaho, and he asked President Roosevelt to give Borah an opportunity to make his case in person. Roosevelt shied away from a personal encounter, explaining that he feared that such an event would attract the ire of those on the left who hated Borah for prosecuting a union, and those on the right who hated Borah for being a Progressive. Instead, Roosevelt proposed that Borah send a lawyer to confer with him, White, and US Attorney Charles Bonaparte at Oyster Bay.[44] Borah and White accepted the offer, and they agreed that White, Sullivan, and Borah's attorney would visit the president in early August to try to persuade him to drop the charges. Roosevelt was unwilling to go that far, but the parties agreed to measures designed to ensure that Borah received a fair trial. A subsequent investigation revealed that the local US attorney had packed the jury to obtain an indictment, and Roosevelt removed him from the case several weeks later. Borah's trial began on September 23, and the jury returned an acquittal after just fourteen minutes of deliberation. The outcome convinced Roosevelt that "Borah is all right," and the senator became one of White's reliable contacts at the highest levels of government for the next four decades.[45]

White had helped Idahoans get their Progressive senator, and he was determined to do the same for the people of Kansas in 1908. Senator Long had once been one of the state's most popular politicians, but by April 1907 his conservative "bourbon" tendencies signaled to White that "he can't make the riffle." Long was vulnerable, but White feared that the senator would be saved in 1908 by the same Stubbs-Bristow rivalry that had helped elect Senator Curtis in 1907. Stubbs's friends wanted to clear his path to the Senate by having Bristow run for governor, while Bristow's friends hoped for the reverse. White believed that practical politics ought to settle the issue. The gubernatorial election was a statewide race involving hundreds of thousands of votes, and Stubbs's superior campaign skills made him likely to win in November. The senatorial election was held in the state legislature the following January, and the untested Bristow would only have to win a few dozen votes to capture the seat. Furthermore, newly elected Governor Stubbs could use his prestige to help Bristow's senatorial campaign during the three-month period between the gubernatorial and senatorial elections. The decision was Stubbs's to make, but White assured him that he had his support regardless of his chosen course. Stubbs dithered for most of 1907 because he wanted to be a senator, and a frustrated White complained that "Stubbs is a mule, and a balky mule at that . . . a good worker, but essentially a mule, too blame stubborn."[46]

Meanwhile, persistent lobbying by White and other Progressives persuaded Governor Hoch to call a special session of the state legislature for early 1908 with the goal of enacting a direct primary. Senator Long's efforts to derail the measure failed the second time around, and the legislature passed a primary law that empowered the voters to choose party nominees for most state offices. The law also allowed legislative candidates to have their preference for the senatorial election printed on the primary ballot, which placed them under a moral obligation to vote for that candidate. Although complex, the new primary law was an accomplishment because it used sunshine to prevent the kind of wrangling that had defined senatorial elections. The primary law gave White the ammunition he needed to persuade Stubbs's and Bristow's representatives to cooperate, summoning them to a secret conclave that aimed to forestall a second round of costly infighting. Bristow's and Stubbs's proxies finally agreed that Stubbs should run for the governorship, where he could accomplish more reform and help serve as a party conciliator, while Bristow would run for the Senate. Bristow announced his candidacy for the senatorial nomination on the evening of February 15, and Stubbs did the same for the governorship after some prodding from White. The outcome pleased Senator Long, who felt that he could defeat Bristow more easily than Stubbs. However, Long's chief advisor, Mort Albaugh, warned the senator that Kansas had "taken up with the wildest form of radicalism," and the people resented his conservatism. Stubbs's campaign quickly gathered momentum, and White was pleased as he easily became the prohibitive front-runner by launching a vigorous drive against Senator Long and his machine.[47]

White managed Bristow's campaign, which was not an easy task because Bristow was an inexperienced politician with all the charisma and spice of a Puritan. Bristow should have had an easy time against the deeply unpopular Long, who faced defections, demoralized supporters, and a political climate that one aide described as "so impregnated with this rampant La Folletteism, that lots of men who act sensible and sane under ordinary circumstances, are inclined to side in with this foolishness without stopping to analyze it." In White's view, Bristow's difficulty stemmed from the perception that he was "'cold' and that is a worse sin than dishonesty" in a campaign. The prescription was to humanize Bristow, and White convinced his friends at the Kansas City Star to supply "a little newspaper ginger" by printing a series of candidate sketches that White had penned. Money also helped, and White solicited prominent friends in search of funds for a massive direct-mail campaign. The effort paid off when White's friend and fellow Kansan Ida Tarbell arranged a $5,000 donation from wealthy Chicago industrialist Charles Crane. The money paid for five thousand copies of White's Bristow sketch and a pamphlet outlining Long's voting record, and White circulated the printing plates to other Kansas newspapers so that they could print more copies. He also solicited endorsements on Bristow's behalf, obtained political intelligence, and arranged statements from respected elements of Kansas's political establishment attacking Long.[48]

White's active management was beginning to pay off by late spring, but Bristow's tendency to rely on facts and figures rather than fiery rhetoric dampened his campaign against Long. An endorsement from the influential *Kansas City Star* would prove invaluable, but the editorial board was reluctant to do so because they felt that Bristow lacked fighting spirit. Indeed, rumors had begun to circulate that Bristow had agreed to throw the campaign to Long in exchange for a postal appointment. White urged Bristow to prove his mettle by challenging Long to a debate. Bristow was shaken and disappointed, especially since White's letter had arrived just as he was wrapping up an exhausting, ten-day, fifteen-speech trek covering 125 miles by horse and buggy in poor weather. Bristow deeply appreciated White's efforts on his behalf, but he complained that none of his other political friends had worked to advance his campaign. The *Star*'s attitude stung the most because Bristow felt that the newspaper had egged him into the race and then ignored his pleas to cover his rallies. White telephoned the *Star*'s Colonel Nelson to request his personal intervention, and the newspaper immediately endorsed Bristow.[49]

The Bristow campaign was revived, and Senator Long soon received his own dose of brutally honest advice when his private secretary warned him that the opposition was gaining strength. Bristow had hardly improved as a campaigner, but "just the same he stirs up the hellraising spirit, and this is the thing that will beat you if anything does." Stubbs and Bristow were barnstorming the state and "sowing the seed wherever they go, and much of it is taking root." Long's campaign manager, Morton Albaugh, explained that even when poor weather depressed turnout at Bristow's meetings, he managed to attract "a few fellows of the rabid, rampant sort and gets them imbued with his feverish self-righteous notions and they immediately go to work on his line." A third operative wrote the senator that the people were for Bristow because they believed he would do what they wanted. The correspondent warned Senator Long that a "populistic wave" was looming that he could not see from "down there in Washington surrounded by your friends." All three sources advised Long to return from Washington to campaign in person as soon as possible.[50]

The campaign hit full stride when White wrote a bombshell article that was published in the *Kansas City Star*, the *Topeka Capital*, and the *Wichita Eagle* on May 18. The article was based on information from Senator La Follette outlining thirty-five instances in which Long had allegedly voted against Kansas's interests and with those of the corporations in the Senate. Long's campaign staff urgently telegrammed the senator that they were encountering the article's harmful effects wherever they went, and that it had "dazed a great many who were inclined to be for you." The staff proposed a rebuttal article, but Long suggested a more theatrical response. The senator wanted to challenge White's claims at a public meeting in Emporia, with White as an invited guest. Long planned to ignore Bristow entirely. Instead, he would focus on smearing White as a political boss and on refuting his article, which Long described as "based upon the imagination of a novelist rather than on a statement of facts." Long's campaign staff agreed that the scheme was "an opportunity to change the drift of this whole campaign," and they began making the necessary arrangements.[51]

The Emporia Opera House was booked for the June 10 event, and Senator Long was so keen on ensuring White's presence that he asked his lieutenants, Albaugh and W. Y. Morgan, to deliver the invitation personally. White, Albaugh, and Morgan had all worked together on the state party's central committee, and they remained friends despite their political disagreements. Albaugh and Morgan told White that Long had invited him to attend the rally as a gesture of esteem, and they assured him that Long's speech was entirely friendly. White had agreed to attend on the condition that he would maintain a low profile, but he arrived to find that he had been seated prominently on stage. Long began his speech, and White soon discovered that he had been invited "not as a friend, but as a target." The only way for White to avoid a scene was to sit there as a prop for Long's attack, but he still felt honor-bound to shake the senator's hand as a gesture of sportsmanship at the end of the event. White recognized that he was a legitimate political target as Bristow's campaign manager, but the senator's underhanded methods violated White's lifelong belief that men could disagree about politics without personal rancor. The fact that Long lacked the moral fiber to abide by this political code of honor proved that Long was "essentially a coward."[52]

The attack on White backfired spectacularly because it spurred Henry J. Allen, Bent Murdock, and other prominent Republicans off the sidelines and into Bristow's camp. White shrugged off the attack, reiterated his allegations, and continued to focus on coaching Bristow, whom he criticized for "hiding out in the small-towns" instead of campaigning in major population centers such as Wichita or Topeka. White complained that Bristow lacked "advertising sense" and energy, and that he was too inclined to give speeches that were "full of figures and data and not full of fire and brimstone. It is fire and brimstone that count." Bristow's lack of vigor against Long had created the impression "that you are afraid of him," and White suggested that Bristow challenge him to a debate. The scolding had its intended effect, and Bristow held a rally in Wichita on July 10 that Long's campaign manager reported was both well attended and highly effective. Bristow also acted on White's advice that he challenge Long to a debate, and White encouraged him to aggressively pepper the senator with questions designed to force him to explain why he had supported the railroads instead of the people.[53]

The Kansas progressive Republicans' Senate campaign reached its peak at Bristow's Emporia rally on August 1, which built on foundations White had established. Earlier in the campaign season, he had asked La Follette to deliver a Senate speech attacking Long's argument that railroad rate discrimination was a boon that allowed Kansas farmers to outcompete their eastern rivals. La Follette obliged after being assured that "what you say will count" in Bristow's fight against Long, and the speech was so well received that White asked La Follette to reprise it at the Emporia rally. The meeting was held in a rented circus tent, and La Follette spent three hours railing against Long in the sweltering summer heat. The increasingly desperate Long played his last card three weeks before the election: he asked President Roosevelt to make good on his promise of a letter of recommendation for distribution in Kansas.[54]

Not even a letter from Roosevelt could save Long. Kansas's Progressives scored a tremendous victory when Stubbs won the nomination by more than fifteen thousand votes and Bristow by more than ten thousand in the August 1908 Republican primary. White had played a key role in clinching the victory, and his typewriters bore the scars: both had to be repaired after he smashed them in fits of campaign-season frustration. Such conduct was highly unusual for the happy-go-lucky White, reflecting the campaign's ferocity. White was gracious in victory, asking his fellow journalists to be compassionate toward Long despite the fallen senator's treachery at the Emporia Opera House. The outcome boosted White's stature as one of Kansas's reform leaders, but he downplayed his own role as "insignificant. The people were radical and Long was conservative and that's all there was to it." Long's defeat sparked conservative chatter that Populism had resurged in Kansas, and a concerned Roosevelt wrote to White to ascertain what the situation was. White dispelled this notion, crowing that "in Kansas it was the bankers and the merchants and the large farmers, and the professional men who defeated Long." White had the right to help lead the Kansas Republican Party's late August strategy council as the victorious campaign manager, but he declined, partly to show that he had no aspiration of becoming a boss.[55]

The fact that Kansas was a thoroughly Republican state meant that the general election was a mere formality. Stubbs was swept into office by a huge majority in November 1908, Bristow was elected by the legislature the following January, and White placed himself at their disposal in working to make "Kansas the foremost state in the

White working at his typewriter in his Gazette *office, circa 1909. Courtesy of Emporia State University, Special Collections and Archives.*

United States, in the matter of liberal laws and wise policies." He proposed an agenda that included ballot, prison, and school reforms, auditing the state's railroads for tax valuation purposes, and regulating public utilities. Governor-Elect Stubbs embraced this program at a meeting of the state's legislative leaders, the attorney general, and other political allies held at his home shortly after the election. The group endorsed a broad agenda based on the reforms La Follette had advanced as governor of Wisconsin from 1900 to 1906, including a legislative reference library to help legislators make good laws, restrictions on lobbying, the commission plan for city government, and the nonpartisan primary, initiative, and referendum for incorporated cities. Kansas's legislature passed bills inspired by all of these proposals by the end of the legislative session in March 1909, and

White had good reason to feel satisfied with the outcome. Stubbs's Progressive accomplishments were the most direct gains of the 1908 election in Kansas.[56]

A second important outcome of the 1908 campaign was that it gave White a visceral understanding of the national scale of the fight for reform. He began reaching out to Progressives of both parties in order to advance the cause across the Midwest as soon as Bristow's primary victory was assured. White sent his campaign research files and other advice to Missouri's John W. Folk, a progressive Democrat whom White supported for governor, and to Iowa's Albert Cummins, a progressive Republican candidate for US Senate. In particular, White was a tireless evangelist for the direct primary in neighboring states, advising Indiana Progressives that "all your reforms will be temporary" without the power of the primary to make the politicians listen to the people. He urged Senator Borah to persuade reformers in Idaho to work for a direct primary, pointing to Bristow's recent victory as proof that "wherever the people have got a crack at the machine they have smashed it." White offered to help Colorado Progressives organize bipartisan citizens' groups to push for the primary, and he fielded a request from New York governor Charles E. Hughes for a brief on the measure.[57]

The election of 1908 had shown White that Progressives were part of a "distinct movement towards fundamental democracy all over the country," but he felt that too many were "fighting alone for state freedom from machine control." The Progressive movement would accomplish more if reformers united around a common agenda, and White worked to encourage collaboration toward that goal across state lines. He wrote a primer on the strategies Progressive Kansans had employed in 1908 for *La Follette's* magazine, and he penned a series of articles exploring progressivism for *American Magazine* under the general title "The Old Order Changeth." The series traced "the movement to divorce business from politics, and control business by politics, first in cities, second in states, and third in the federal government" over the preceding decade. The American people were enjoying their first opportunity to have a real say in government through direct democracy, and White hoped they would use this new power to tame both capital and the Congress it controlled. The series, with appended examples of progressive legislation enacted around the country, was ultimately republished as a guidebook for reformers called *The Old Order Changeth*. The guidebook played an important role in inspiring Progressives in other states, such as South Dakota state senator Peter Norbeck, who later rose to become his state's governor and US senator.[58]

William H. Taft's election as president was a third outcome of the 1908 campaign, but White was not significantly engaged in the national election. Taft had befriended White when he visited Kansas in 1906, but the latter harbored deep reservations about Taft's fitness to lead the Progressive movement. Taft seemed to lack the strength of will required to inspire the Progressives and fight the conservative establishment. Only loyalty to Roosevelt motivated White to help unite the Kansas delegation for Taft, and to write a laudatory article portraying him as another Roosevelt for the *American*. However, White had been disturbed by the way that conservatives had exulted over Roosevelt's looming departure from the presidency during the Republican National Convention in June 1908. White hinted at his concerns when he wrote Roosevelt to ask him to devote part of his final annual message to Congress to a discourse on his efforts "to make this government more democratic." An increasingly conservative Congress had resisted Roosevelt's agenda for two years, and White argued that the outgoing president had a duty to leave "a text for those of us who are to stay in the fight." A rousing statement of principles, White explained, would help Taft in his efforts to organize public opinion. White was thrilled when Roosevelt subsequently delivered a message to Congress that sounded a clarion call for government action to address a raft of national problems.[59]

Taft won the White House in November, and White remained only vaguely hopeful that the president-elect would stand up to the GOP's conservative establishment. White telegrammed President Taft shortly after the inauguration explaining that Kansas supported the congressional Republican insurgency that was building against conservative Speaker of the House Joseph Cannon in Washington, DC, but the president's reply was hardly inspiring. Boss Cannon had an iron grip on the House, and Taft explained that he had little choice but to work with the party establishment if he wanted to achieve his legislative agenda. Taft seemed to blame the insurgents for disrupting the Republican caucus, and he expressed the desire for a cease-fire until Congress finished the pending tariff revision bill. White assured Taft that he had the West's support and that nobody expected him to join the insurgency, but many hoped that the president would "work out a compromise, or sit by and hold the coats of the combatants" in Congress. Taft was under no illusions: he knew that many westerners suspected that he was a reactionary, but he asked White to withhold judgment until he had a chance to prove himself. As Taft lamented, Roosevelt was able to inspire men by his ability to "communicate his feelings. I find myself unable to do so."[60]

Roosevelt left Washington for an extended African safari immediately after Inauguration Day in March 1909, and Mr. and Mrs. White, their two children, and White's elderly mother did the same for a six-month European vacation. The trip was well earned. White had spent almost two years running the *Gazette*, writing magazine articles, and managing the Kansas Progressives' political campaigns. In just over a decade, he had rocketed from being a mere cog in Boss Leland's machine to being one of the generals leading the progressive Republican insurgency in Kansas. He had risen from a small-town newspaper publisher on the brink of insolvency to a financially secure, nationally recognized midwestern journalist. Finally, the forty-year-old White had finished his first major novel in 1908. The work, titled *A Certain Rich Man*, dramatized the way that unrestrained capitalism shaped ordinary people in small towns like Emporia. The book was the product of three years' labor, and White summarized the plot as the tale of a "prodigal son of predatory power and wealth" who discovered after a shameful scandal "that he can do more good by personal service . . . than he can by getting money greedily and trying to do good with that." Decades later, White described the novel as a proxy for his own arc from conservatism to progressivism: a conceited, materialistic young man who believed that he was better than the world, who slowly discovered his ignorance, and who finally found his way to the truth.[61]

The Whites embarked for Europe on the SS *Cretic* at New York City on April 3 and arrived in Naples two weeks later. The family then traveled northward, stopping at Rome so that White's mother, who had been raised as a Catholic, could see the pope at Saint Peter's Basilica before proceeding to Switzerland, Germany, the Netherlands, and England. Progressivism was an international phenomenon involving transnational conversations between reformers, and like many Progressives, White hoped to learn about the "progress [that] has been made in democracy in Europe, and what the democratic progress has brought to the average man in the way of comfortable living and opportunity for mental and spiritual growth." He was especially interested in German socialism, the English labor movement, and cooperative efforts in the Low Countries. White later described his six months in Europe as a transformative experience that exposed him to the broader world, and he was particularly pleased to find that the European working class was striving toward the same democratic ends as their American brethren.[62] The discovery thrilled him because it proved that the Progressive movement he had fought so hard to advance in Kansas was part of a much larger, international phenomenon. The movement toward democracy could not be reversed, but White soon discovered that it could be stalled.

CHAPTER THREE

A WAR OF CONQUEST

William Allen White was still in Europe when his first novel was published during the summer of 1909, and the forty-one-year-old was thrilled to see newspaper advertisements for *A Certain Rich Man* while homeward bound. The story traced the rise and fall of John Barclay, a promising young man from a small, midwestern town who had traded his happiness for power, who used treachery to become a robber baron, and who learned the error of his ways only after his actions caused manifold tragedies for himself and others. *A Certain Rich Man* had no hero, according to White. The book reflected his belief that "human nature runs some good and some bad. There seems to be a regression which brings us all to the same moral average." Politically, *A Certain Rich Man* was a parable about the dangers of the nineteenth century's unrestrained capitalism and rampant materialism. The work sold thirty thousand copies in its first four months on the market, aided by its saliency to the ongoing Progressive movement and by critical acclaim from the likes of Mark Twain. In praising the book, *La Follette's* magazine demanded to know how a democratic nation could allow a man like Barclay to wreak such havoc without running afoul of the law. White sent a copy to Theodore Roosevelt, still on safari in Africa, who praised it as "a real, and very effective, tract for the times" that would help advance "the cause of righteousness in our country." *A Certain Rich Man* was White's most successful novel, selling more than 250,000 copies over the next two decades and establishing his place in American literature.[1]

Similarly, the progressive Republican movement White helped lead had mushroomed beyond "insurgency—it is revolution." Conservative Republican Speaker of the House Joseph Cannon had used his iron grip on power to blockade national progressive reform, and White now recognized that the fight to transform America into a democratic community was in "the congress and not in the states, except incidentally." The conservative faction's control of the national Republican Party had to be broken in order for progressivism to succeed, and White threw himself into the cause. White and other progressive Republicans were forced to declare war against the party establishment, eventually spurring them to establish the Progressive Party in 1912. World War I erupted as the Progressive Party withered two years later, and the United States was increasingly drawn into the European conflict. Like many Progressives, White came to see the war as an opportunity to transform the entire world into a community of democratic nations.[2] Neither the domestic nor the international campaign White waged for democracy succeeded as thoroughly as he had hoped, but he lost none of his ardor for the fight. Instead, White reacted to these setbacks by steeling his resolve and looking toward the day when the seeds he had helped sow, at home and abroad, bore fruit.

President William H. Taft asked White to suspend his editorial judgment until he had a chance to demonstrate the character of his administration when he took office in March 1909. Since White was about to depart for six months in Europe, it was easy for him to abide by the request. In the meantime, Taft outraged many Progressives by replacing most of Roosevelt's cabinet, by signing the protectionist Payne-Aldrich Tariff Act, and by supporting Secretary of the Interior Richard Ballinger's efforts to overturn Roosevelt's conservation policies. White returned to Emporia on August 27 convinced that the president had embraced the GOP's conservative faction, and Taft's Winona Speech soon confirmed his belief. The president was on a national speaking tour to build support for his policies when he stopped in Winona, Minnesota, on September 17 to endorse Representative James Tawney, a conservative leader who had fought Roosevelt to a standstill in 1908. Taft was a habitual procrastinator, and his speech had been hastily prepared and ill considered. The president went out of his way to praise the bitterly divisive Payne-Aldrich Tariff as "the best tariff bill that the Republican Party ever passed," to attack the Progressive insurgents, and to thank the conservative establishment.

The speech proved to be a spectacular blunder that shocked Progressives around the country. White remarked that Taft's speech had left Kansas's Progressives feeling "persecuted by those in high authority," that it had failed to persuade them to stand down, and that it showed them that "the President has turned his back" on Roosevelt, progressivism, and the West. White summed up Taft's offenses for one correspondent as

> His endorsement of Aldrich,
>> His endorsement of Ballenger,
>> His endorsement of Tawney,
>> His endorsement of standpatism,
>> His rebuke of the insurgents,
>> all piled on top of one another make western Republicans feel
> that they are leaning on a broken reed.[3]

The president and White were now opponents in an epic battle, but they remained on good personal terms partly because White saw Taft's decision to side with Cannon as an act of weakness rather than one of ideological conviction. The Progressive movement was strongest in the West, and Taft appeared to have surrounded himself with an eastern "phalanx of selfish, reactionary leaders" who had "persuaded him that everything west of the Alleghanies [sic] is bad." The administration had declared war on the progressive Republicans, and White reacted by recruiting "the finest line-up of insurgent candidates in the whole country" who would challenge conservative Republican congressmen in every Kansas district. Although it seemed hopeless, White acceded to insurgent leader Representative Victor Murdock's (R-KS) request that he make a last-ditch effort to persuade Taft to adopt a neutral stance. He wrote the president that he had "wished for five months, ever since I returned from Europe to find some decent opportunity to tell you that if you will just let the insurgents alone they will come home like little Bo-peep's sheep." Meanwhile, the congressional insurgency against Cannon finally succeeded when the insurgent Republicans combined with the Democratic minority

*Emporia's homecoming reception for the White family after their European travels,
1909. Courtesy of Emporia State University, Special Collections and Archives.*

to strip Cannon of some of his powers on March 19, 1910. Taft was
pleased by the outcome because he disliked Cannon, but he did not
profit from the turn of events. The president responded to White's
letter by inviting him to lunch at the White House in May, and White
took the opportunity to discuss Taft's leadership with business leaders in several eastern cities. The result convinced him that "there is
a unanimous opinion in all classes in all parts of the United States"
that the president was failing. At lunch on May 21, White discovered
that the president was befuddled by his situation between the Progressive insurgents on his left and the conservative establishment
on his right.[4]

Progressive reform was blockaded as long as conservatives dominated the GOP, and White redoubled his efforts on behalf of the
insurgency. He managed the entire Kansas progressive Republican
campaign in 1910, consulting on strategy, planning events, and writing campaign literature. White wrote a piece endorsing a congressional bill to stop federal attempts to prosecute labor unions under

the 1890 Sherman Antitrust Act that was distributed nationally by the American Federation of Labor. Money was short, and White used innovative tactics to maximize grassroots support. For instance, he organized a postcard campaign asking five hundred rural farmers to use their party telephone lines to canvass for Congressman Murdock. Kansas's Progressives triumphed in the August Republican primary, winning a majority in the state legislature, control of the state Republican Central Committee, renomination for Governor Walter R. Stubbs, and six of the state's eight Republican congressional nominations.[5]

The Kansas insurgents' lopsided victory gave them the right to craft the state Republican platform, and White, Stubbs, and Senator Joseph Bristow (R-KS) used the opportunity to produce a model for reformers in other states. The platform advocated conservation, a federal income tax, a presidential primary, the direct election of senators, railroad reform, direct democracy, and an expert commission to set tariff rates. Kansas's conservative Republicans denounced the platform as a radical manifesto, but White pointed out that the document incorporated ideas that were percolating in states across the nation. The platform was actually conservative, White argued, because it aimed to forestall the kind of truly radical changes that would result without reform. He crowed that the Progressive movement was gaining momentum and would not rest until it had taken control of the entire Republican Party. White sent copies of the platform to Senator William E. Borah, the leading progressive Republican in Idaho; Senator Robert M. La Follette, the leading progressive Republican in Wisconsin; and to Walter Lippmann, an up-and-coming progressive journalist in Connecticut.[6]

Former president Roosevelt energized the increasingly successful Republican insurgency when he made his highly anticipated return to politics in the summer of 1910. White had kept Roosevelt apprised of Taft's failings and of the insurgents' activities while the former president made his way back to the United States, but Roosevelt seemed unlikely to challenge Taft for the nomination. Instead,

White expected the conservative Republican establishment to continue to abuse the insurgents, leading to an "ineffectual bolt of Republicans from the Republican convention in 1912." The failed bolt would then clear the way for the formation of a truly progressive third party that would unite the Republican and Democratic Parties' left wings against their respective conservative establishments. Only by nominating Roosevelt could the GOP avoid a bolt in 1912, but White believed that the former president would not accept the nomination. Although nothing was certain, White suspected that Roosevelt preferred to serve as the Progressive movement's elder statesman. Meanwhile, Taft further outraged the insurgents by strongly supporting a failed conservative effort to deny insurgent senators Albert Beveridge (R-IN), Albert Cummins (R-IA), and Jonathan Dolliver (R-IA) their respective nominations.[7]

Roosevelt planned to make his return to public affairs by delivering the keynote address at the John Brown Memorial Park dedication ceremony in Osawatomie, Kansas, on August 31. The former president aimed to help define the Republican Party's future agenda and harmonize its warring factions, partly by moderating what he saw as the insurgency's radicalism. However, the speech Roosevelt eventually delivered at Osawatomie was more radical than it might have been because it was written primarily by former chief forester Gifford Pinchot, whose firing in early 1910 had convinced many that Taft had turned his back on Roosevelt. White had sent Roosevelt and Pinchot copies of the Kansas Republican platform, and many of its ideas were incorporated into the speech. Roosevelt spent the night before his address visiting with White, and the next day he delivered an unabashedly progressive speech that reflected the Kansas platform. Compared to the policies Taft's conservative allies embraced, the Osawatomie speech was practically revolutionary in its call for a "New Nationalism" that used government as an agency of human welfare.[8]

The Osawatomie speech returned Roosevelt squarely to the national spotlight, but White was not convinced that he ought to run for president in 1912. As much as White admired Roosevelt and his

New Nationalism, he felt that centering the Progressive movement on Roosevelt "would make it seem like a one-man movement which distinctively it is not." Expressing a long-held concern, White worried that Roosevelt's reputation as "a man of rather supernatural powers" might make the people dependent on him to "do great wonders" instead of learning to walk on their own. White was certain that Taft would lose to a Democrat in 1912, and he was equally certain that a Democratic administration would prove that neither the Democrats nor the Republicans were capable of serving as America's reform party. In that event, Roosevelt would be able to accomplish more as "a preacher of righteousness" than as an officeholder. Roosevelt would be the elder statesman who could spur the Democratic and Republican Parties' reform wings to combine into a truly progressive third party in 1916. Perhaps Roosevelt was the man best suited to be the new party's candidate for president in 1916, but White felt that an immediate campaign would be less than ideal. Nevertheless, he believed that President Taft's implosion and the lack of a plausible Republican candidate would probably force Roosevelt to accept the presidential nomination in 1912.[9]

As White and other progressive Republicans had expected, Taft's unpopularity helped the Democrats romp to victory in the 1910 midterm election, gaining twelve Senate seats, fifty-seven seats in the House of Representatives, the House Speakership, and state and local offices across the country. Kansas's Republicans bucked the national trend, capturing the state's entire congressional delegation, the governorship, both houses of the state legislature, and all statewide elected offices, albeit by narrower margins than expected. White argued that the national party had been defeated because its conservative leadership had tried to impose its ideology on a thoroughly progressive electorate, while Kansas Republicans beat the Democrats "because we had a straight-forward, clean-cut, progressive platform." The national party might have fared better had it made "the Osawatomie speech into a political promissory note," White asserted, although Roosevelt felt that the conservatives had angered the electorate so deeply that the entire Republican brand had suffered. The

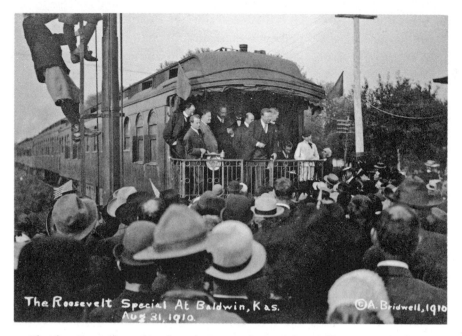

The Roosevelt Special At Baldwin, Kas.
Aug 31, 1910.
©A. Bridwell, 1910

Theodore Roosevelt speaking from the Roosevelt Special *at Baldwin, Kansas, after the Osawatomie Speech on August 31, 1910. Henry J. Allen stands behind him. White holds a white hat to Roosevelt's right, while Senator Joseph L. Bristow stands behind White. Courtesy of the Library of Congress, LC-USZ62-78373.*

party's prospects for 1912 seemed grim either way, and many leading progressive Republicans shared White's concern that Taft's name at the head of the ticket would drag down the entire slate.[10]

Unfortunately for White and other progressive Republicans, the ranks of potential Republican presidential candidates were perilously thin. Senator La Follette or recently defeated senator Albert Beveridge (R-IN) were possibilities, but White recognized that neither man had the eastern support required to win the White House. Roosevelt's chances of victory were good, but the former president's letters to White and his unwillingness to challenge the conservatives at the 1910 New York State Republican convention showed that he wanted to be a moderating force in the party. Roosevelt still seemed to regard the western Progressives as "ultra-radical," and White privately worked to persuade the New Yorker that the time for compromise had passed. Roosevelt applauded an article White wrote for *American Magazine* describing the Republican insurgents as the "scouts of the coming army" that would democratize the nation. However, he broadly rejected White's thesis about compromise. The exchange frustrated White, who privately complained that Roosevelt did not understand that compromise was merely "taking what we can get and not getting what we demand." Western reformers such as La Follette and Stubbs recognized that there was an "educational value to martyrdom" when one was fighting for a strong agenda against daunting odds. A losing battle was an opportunity to educate the public about reform, and White knew that sometimes a "sacrifice hit at one point of the game beats a home run." White pronounced himself ready to "enlist under [Roosevelt's] banner and get licked if necessary" to defend progressive principles, but he was not sure whether Roosevelt was willing to assume the mantle.[11]

Roosevelt's unwillingness to commit to a presidential campaign or to adopt a more progressive posture left Senator La Follette as the leading contender for the Republican nomination. White wrote a laudatory article profiling the senator for *American Magazine*, and he accepted La Follette's subsequent invitation to join his recently formed National Progressive Republican League. The group aimed to unite leading Progressives around a common agenda, but it also served as a vehicle for La Follette's presidential aspirations. White joined La Follette's group while working to tamp down proposals that he felt were too radical, such as the group's call for direct democracy for all Americans. Direct democracy was a powerful weapon that White strongly supported in states such as Kansas or Wisconsin, which were dominated by his demographic of white Anglo-Saxon Protestants. However, he agreed with Roosevelt that the idea was unsuitable for racially and ethnically diverse states such as New Mexico, Alabama, or New York. Interestingly, White kept Roosevelt fully informed about the substance of his contacts with La Follette, and the former president entirely approved of the stands his friend had taken.[12] White was certainly aware of the intense rivalry between La Follette and Roosevelt, and perhaps he hoped to spur the latter toward a more assertive posture by very publicly flirting with the former.

Kansas's conservative Republicans extinguished any chance for the kind of intraparty collaboration that Roosevelt had advocated when they knifed the Progressive faction in 1911. The Progressives controlled the party apparatus and the governorship outright, and they controlled the legislature in alliance with progressive Democrats. The Republican platform called for direct democracy measures such as the initiative and referendum, and the outlook seemed favorable when the legislative session began in January. However, the Progressives' proposals languished after the Republican conservatives forged a tactical alliance with the Democrats to forestall progressive reform. White waged a ferocious last-minute campaign to save the Progressive agenda as the legislative session neared its end, arranging editorial support, visiting Topeka to coordinate strategy, and privately warning conservative legislators that the Republicans would suffer the voters' wrath if they broke their platform promises. The appeal failed, and the measures were defeated in the state senate. Meanwhile, rumors swirled that the conservative Republicans had secretly agreed to undermine a progressive Republican gubernatorial nominee in exchange for the Democrats nominating a weak candidate against conservative senator Charles Curtis. The rumored arrangement meant that the conservative Republicans preferred to stab their own party in the back rather than to allow the Progressives to have what they had won in the primary. White was utterly disgusted. The conservative Republicans' treachery was a blatant violation of his political code of honor, which required a man to take his licks when he was beaten fair and square. This, combined with the public's apparently lethargic mood, left White feeling that "a green scum is on Kansas politics right now."[13]

The political situation was so unpalatable to White that he seriously considered selling the *Emporia Gazette* and exiting the newspaper business in the spring of 1911. *A Certain Rich Man* had been a rousing success, and White planned to use his summer vacation

White on a working vacation in Estes Park, Colorado, around 1907. Courtesy of Emporia State University, Special Collections and Archives.

in Colorado to frame a new novel. As White began the exhausting task of preparing the *Gazette* for his absence, it occurred to him that he was "wrapping my one little old talent in a napkin" by neglecting his literary work in favor of politics. The time had come to choose between being an editor and a novelist, and White chose the latter on the theory that he could preach the Progressive gospel more effectively through fiction. To this end, he began searching for a buyer for the *Gazette* among his newspaper friends and a New York–based newspaper broker. Nothing came of the idea, and the family left Kansas in late August so that White could spend three or four months in Colorado "dead to the world" working on his novel. Once again, politics followed White to the Rocky Mountains, and he could not resist helping Colorado Progressives organize a campaign to replicate Kansas's progressive legislation. Overall, White's working vacation was a success: he completed a rough draft of a new novel whose thesis he summed up as, "There really are spiritual rewards for spiritual service and spiritual punishments for spiritual transgressions." He returned to Kansas on October 5 so that he could "revise at leisure," but political distractions kept him from producing a final draft for seven years.[14]

The fantasy of an exclusively literary career was persistent, but White's immediate reimmersion in politics on his return proved that he had chosen to be an editor. The political situation was stark in the fall of 1911. Taft was clearly unelectable, and White suspected that local Republican candidates would flee the unpopular president once they realized that his name on the ballot could cost them their own elections. Since Roosevelt remained on the fence about running in 1912, White believed that the national convention would be a battleground between conservatives supporting Taft and Progressives favoring La Follette. Although White liked La Follette and endorsed many of his ideas, he felt that the nation was not yet ready for the kinds of dramatic changes that La Follette was proposing. The conservative and progressive Republican factions would then compromise by nominating Roosevelt as a moderate, and White advised him to "prepare for the fireworks because it is coming." Roosevelt responded that he expected all of his friends to take any action necessary to prevent his nomination, but he also devoted most of his letter to attacking La Follette as a dangerous radical. Displaying his persistent desire to stand between Progressives and conservatives, the former president maintained that labor unions and socialists such as Eugene V. Debs were "quite as serious a foe to this country as the most conscienceless scoundrel of wealth in Wall Street." White conceded the point to keep the peace and promised to work against an unwanted nomination, while maintaining that "nevertheless, I think you are going to be."[15]

As much as White liked Roosevelt, his support for the former president was primarily strategic. Ideologically, White had moved significantly to the left since 1908. He spoke approvingly of the Socialist Party, praising its demand for political, social, and economic equality, "all qualified by the phrase 'equality of opportunity,'" and he evangelized on behalf of a socialist book depicting Jesus Christ as "a common working man, a rabble-rousing agitator." White could never join the Socialists himself because he believed that the party stood no chance of gaining traction under the American political system, but he admired its philosophy. Similarly, White liked Senator La Follette's ideas and believed that "with La Follette as President we should go further, much further" than any other candidate. However, he did not believe that the senator could win the nomination. Roosevelt's "weakness for compromise" was actually an advantage in the fight for the Republican nomination, and White speculated that he would find his way to the left if he was elected with a strongly progressive Congress.[16]

Senator Bristow disagreed with White's calculation that Roosevelt would become more progressive if given the chance, pointing out that he had established a far more conservative record than many of his supporters believed. The Progressive movement had reached the point where it needed to enact "constructive legislation," Bristow argued, and La Follette had outlined concrete proposals while Roosevelt had not. Furthermore, Bristow believed that La Follette would lead the nation through the kind of fundamental power transfer from the special interests to the ordinary people that would make American democracy real, while Roosevelt would not. Bristow's argument in favor of La Follette was persuasive, and he suggested that the two men work to squelch pro-Roosevelt chatter that might hurt La Follette's chances. The situation changed dramatically in February 1912, when Senator La Follette delivered a rambling, vitriolic, two-hour diatribe at the Periodical Publishers Association banquet in Philadelphia. La Follette was reportedly exhausted, frustrated, and angered by his faltering campaign, in addition to being preoccupied with his daughter's impending surgery for tuberculosis. Rumors swirled alleging that La Follette was mentally ill, an alcoholic, or suffering from a terminal illness. The damage was done. A shocked Bristow joined White in unequivocally endorsing Roosevelt.[17]

Having settled on Roosevelt, White began the work of organizing Kansas for the coming campaign. Early canvasses of the state's Republican county committeemen showed that Roosevelt had strong support, which validated White's thesis that local officeholders would spurn Taft to save their own skins from a Democratic sweep. The situation seemed to present an opportunity for the Progressive and conservative factions to collaborate, and White made overtures to his conservative friends. He argued that the two sides complemented each other: the Progressives provided the "steam" for forward movement, while the conservatives served as the "brake" that kept the train from going out of control. Conservative Republican leader Mort Albaugh responded favorably, and the two men agreed that the state party would hold an informal presidential preference primary in 1912. Under this system, the voters were allowed to choose delegates to the state convention based on the candidate's pledge to support a particular presidential nominee. White helped lead the progressive Republican campaign by fundraising, coordinating volunteer fieldworkers, and managing a clerical staff that sent literature to thirty thousand voters. The conservatives allegedly tried to pack the primary in several districts by admitting voters to the polls for only ten minutes, but Progressive electoral observers saved the day by demanding that the doors remain open until all voters were admitted.[18]

Roosevelt's Progressive supporters won the Kansas primary by a plurality of thirty-four thousand votes, giving them full control over the state convention and the right to name delegates to the national convention in Chicago. The result was bittersweet for White, who retained tremendous personal affection for Taft but felt that the president was too weak to stand up to the conservatives. The state convention subsequently elected White to replace Topeka's conservative machine boss, David Mulvane, as Kansas's representative on the Republican National Committee. White accepted because he wanted to make the GOP "definitely liberal," which could only happen after it had been purged of the "mercenary elements" that controlled its machinery. A secondary consideration was that National Committeeman White would be in the inner sanctum at the convention, where he could help keep Roosevelt from compromising too much.[19]

White was under no illusions about the enormous challenge the Progressives faced at the national convention. Taft and his conservative allies were certain to use "knucks and a jimmy" to try to control the convention's machinery, and White worried that they might have help from La Follette. The senator was to the left of the other Republican candidates, but his failed campaign left him bitter and angry at Roosevelt, White, and other Progressives. White took the precaution of writing to University of Wisconsin at Madison president Charles Van Hise, an early leader in the Progressive movement and one of La Follette's close allies, begging him to do anything in his power to calm the senator. A bolt was likely in any event, and White would have a front-row seat by virtue of his status as national committeeman-elect, his close relationship with Roosevelt, and his contract to cover the convention for the Adams Newspaper Service. White served on the subcommittee that wrote the strongly progressive platform that Roosevelt planned to present if he won the nomination, working alongside leading Progressives such as Roosevelt's former chief forester Gifford Pinchot, prison reformer George Kirchwey, and California journalist Chester Rowell. He was also in the front row at the Chicago Auditorium when Roosevelt gave his rousing convention-eve address demanding social justice, which concluded with the famous line "We stand at Armageddon, and we battle for the Lord!"[20]

Meanwhile, Taft's conservative allies were laying the groundwork to deny Roosevelt the nomination. The Republican credentials committee spent the days before the convention disqualifying Roosevelt's delegates and replacing them with Taft's men. Whether the Roosevelt delegates were disqualified justly or unjustly has been hotly debated by historians, but the relevant fact is that White and other progressive Republicans believed that they had been robbed. The conservative machine even took the precaution of wrapping barbed wire, concealed with bunting, over the handrail leading to the convention chairman's rostrum—a nasty surprise for any Roosevelt supporter who might try to rush the stage. Taft received the nomination, Roosevelt's forces marched out of the convention, and White resigned his RNC seat before returning to his hotel room to write his syndicated story. Dinner was next on White's agenda, but he had no idea that his leisurely meal cost him the opportunity to witness Roosevelt's speech founding the Progressive Party at Chicago's Orchestra Hall.

White only discovered his mistake when Roosevelt demanded an explanation for his absence at one of the seminal events in American history.[21]

Kansas's progressive Republicans returned from Chicago with a crucial decision to make about forming a third party. White naturally agreed with Roosevelt that his two-million-vote majority in the primaries gave him the strongest claim on the Republican nomination, while Taft's underhanded tactics had delegitimized his candidacy. Some Kansas progressive Republicans wanted to form a third party, but White argued that it was foolish to abandon the state GOP when they controlled its machinery. White's assertion was sound, but he failed to foresee that the conservative faction would seek to regain control of the state party at any cost. The conservatives sued to replace the Progressive slate of Roosevelt electors with a conservative slate of Taft electors on the August primary ballot, and the state supreme court ruled that both slates were entitled to call themselves Republicans in the election. The voters would be confronted with a long list of electors and no means of differentiating Taft's electors from Roosevelt's. As head of the Roosevelt Republican Committee, it was White's job to lead a massive voter education campaign in an attempt to teach Roosevelt's supporters how to vote for the right electors. The organization was headquartered at the *Gazette*'s offices, and its campaign staff booked speakers, organized volunteers, and mailed 750,000 pieces of literature. Roosevelt's electors defeated Taft's by a majority of sixty thousand votes, confirming White's view that Progressives ought to remain in the state party. At any rate, White very pragmatically argued that it was too late for Kansas's Progressives to form a third party because state law denied ballot designations to parties formed less than four months before Election Day.[22]

Progressive Republicans in other states found it more expedient to join the national Progressive Party, and White accepted a leadership role in the enterprise. The party held its first convention in Chicago from August 5 to 7, and White was elected to serve as both state party chairman and Kansas's national committeeman. White also helped write the national party's platform, which he described as a program of political, economic, and social reforms designed to eliminate the material causes of poverty. The convention delegates' enthusiasm was infectious, and White felt fully justified in asserting that "the Progressive party is here to stay as the definitely radical party of this Nation." The demands of politics allowed him only a brief vacation at the Colorado cabin he had recently purchased in Moraine Park with the $3,500 he earned reporting on the national conventions for the Adams Newspaper Service. He returned to manage the Kansas Progressive campaign in late August. The job was a "kettle of grief" for White, who had to juggle his campaign duties, the *Gazette's* daily operations, and his syndicated article assignments. Fundraising was always a difficult issue, but White refused to accept the national party's money because he knew that it flowed from Wall Street financier George Perkins. Roosevelt's three-day visit to Kansas was the highlight of the state campaign. The candidate spent a day and a half enjoying White's hospitality at his home in Emporia, culminating in one of Sallie's sumptuous fried chicken dinners.[23]

The Progressive campaign was well under way when the conservative Republican faction launched a successful coup to regain control of the state party. The opening shot came at the Republican postprimary council in early September, which assembled the party's nominees to formulate a general election platform. The conservative minority proposed a resolution that would have forced the victorious Roosevelt electors to promise to vote for Taft if the Republicans carried the state in November. The Progressives easily defeated the resolution, but the conservatives launched a second attack by persuading Kansas's Republican secretary of state to certify Taft as the only Republican candidate for president. Roosevelt's electors would appear under Taft's name on the ballot, giving the conservatives grounds for a lawsuit that would likely confuse the voters. White was outraged when he realized that the conservatives preferred to let the Democrats carry the state rather than tolerate a progressive Republican victory. The only solution was to persuade each progressive Republican elector to resign and reregister as an independent, allowing each to appear on

White and Roosevelt on the lawn of White's home in Emporia, September 1912.
Courtesy of Emporia State University, Special Collections and Archives.

the ballot without a party designation. White also supervised a massive publicity campaign to teach the voters how to pick through the mass of independent electors to find Roosevelt's electors.[24]

In spite of the conservatives' scorched-earth campaign, White was optimistic about Roosevelt's chances in Kansas. The Progressives had drawn large, enthusiastic crowds to their rallies, and Taft had never been a serious contender in the state. The real contest was between Roosevelt and Democrat Woodrow Wilson. White had met Wilson in 1910, when the latter was known as the pioneering president of Princeton University and the recent victor of the New Jersey gubernatorial election. Wilson was a strong progressive and White liked him, but he also believed that the Democratic Party was too "dominated by the old South which is really reactionary and by the Tammany bunch, which is always crooked" to be a home for progressivism. In the end, White believed that disdain for the Democrats' reactionary establishment and the strength of Roosevelt's personal magnetism would drive progressives of both parties toward Roosevelt. Ultimately, White knew that both Roosevelt and Wilson were progressives, and a victory by either man would be proof positive that the American people supported progressivism. As importantly, such a victory would prove that the United States had taken its place among the leading nations pressing for democratic social and industrial legislation. White was reasonably optimistic as Election Day loomed, and the teetotaling editor obtained "a special dispensation from Mrs. White to go out and get soused" if Roosevelt won.[25]

Wilson's victory in 1912 ensured that White would not have to face the temptations of the bottle. The Democrats won the White House, control of both houses of Congress, and Kansas's governorship, while the Progressives won more than 27 percent of the national popular vote and carried six states. The Taft Republicans came in a distant third. Kansas voters also approved an amendment to the state constitution giving women the right to vote in state elections, an issue that White held "very near to my heart." The most important political aspect of the election for White was that it spurred him to finally break with the Republicans and establish the Kansas Progressive Party. The response was generally positive, although Senator Bristow refused to join because he felt that the Progressives ought to focus on regaining control of the state GOP. In addition, Bristow warned White that his leadership role in the new party might place him "in the light of an arrogant boss." White had plenty of experience in dealing with party schisms after twenty years of rough-and-tumble Kansas Republican factional politics, and he held no grudges against those who did not bolt. The simple fact was that the Progressives had won control of the Republican Party at the ballot box, and the conservatives had used underhanded tactics to steal it from them in 1912. White reasoned that there was no point in trying to regain control of the state party when the conservatives had proven willing to burn it to the ground when defeated. Roosevelt strongly endorsed White's move, adding that the Progressives could only retain their momentum by expeditiously transforming their ad hoc campaign committees into a permanent party organization.[26]

The national Progressive Party established its foundations at a postelection conference in Chicago in December 1912, and White hoped the organization would seize the opportunity to become America's reform party. The Populist Party's failure had taught White that any third party faced a difficult task in finding its place in American politics, but he felt that the circumstances favored the Progressives. In White's view, the Democratic establishment was as likely to resist President Wilson's progressive reforms as the Republicans had resisted Roosevelt's, and the Progressive Party's job was to prepare itself so that it could capitalize on the resulting disillusionment. The Progressive convention began on December 10, and Roosevelt christened the new party with a speech calling for it to become the nation's only true reform party. White and other left-leaning Progressives were disappointed when Roosevelt also backed George Perkins to remain as the party's de facto leader. Perkins's Wall Street pedigree and his relatively conservative, probusiness ideology were a poor fit for the party, but Roosevelt defended him as the kind of efficient organizer that the circumstances required. The structure was a recipe for failure: the party's base was reform-minded, while its leadership was conservative. Kansas's Progressives convened their state convention at Topeka one week later, and White was elected to serve a full term as the state's national committeeman.[27]

White's only moment of party irregularity throughout his life was during the Progressive Party era, but his decision to bolt was neither rash nor uncharacteristic. The Progressive Party was led primarily by Republican political elites such as Roosevelt, Pinchot, and White, who were fighting against conservative Republican elites such as Taft. Strategically, White and the progressive Republicans had no reason to remain in the GOP, since they had fought fairly, they had won by playing by the rules, and they had been denied their due. From a moral perspective, White had even less incentive to remain a Republican. The conservative establishment had broken White's political code of ethics by resorting to underhanded tactics when they had been fairly and soundly defeated. To have adhered to Bristow's advice that the Progressives continue the fight under the conservative Republican faction's rules, which treated any progressive Republican victory as illegitimate, would have been folly. White knew that the Progressive Party faced a tough slog at best, but as he had often preached to Roosevelt, there were times when a principled defeat accomplished more than a compromising victory. As a Progressive, White came to experience both the pain and the exultation that flowed from that wisdom.

The Progressive Party's state and national foundations had been established, and White pronounced himself ready to "fade out and vanish" for the next two years. Both Mr. and Mrs. White had many reasons for wanting to disappear. White had devoted himself almost entirely to politics since early 1912, and he longed for "the Lord and the progressives" to give him a year's freedom to finish his new novel. Sallie was suffering from a chronic stomach condition that had left her bedridden and living on a strict milk diet. The family's doctors were perplexed by her illness, which eventually proved to be a duodenal ulcer, and they recommended a vacation in the hope that she would regain enough strength to undergo an operation at the Mayo

Clinic. The Whites traveled to La Jolla, California, at the end of December, where White toiled on his novel and his family relaxed on the beach. Unfortunately, Sallie's condition failed to improve, and White made little writing progress. Once again, White chose politics over literature. He abandoned the beach for a two-week speaking tour before Progressive organizations in Los Angeles, San Francisco, and Phoenix. The Whites returned to Kansas on June 4, 1913, but they remained only briefly before departing once again for their cabin at Moraine Park, Colorado. The family remained in the Rocky Mountains through mid-September, and White was finally able to make significant progress on his manuscript revisions.[28]

Ten months of rest and writing had restored White's taste for politics, and he returned to Kansas in September 1913 to begin preparing the Progressive Party for the 1914 midterm election. The situation was not encouraging, and White wrote Roosevelt a frank letter laying out the party's challenges. The base was composed of "men of the college professor, country lawyer, country doctor and country merchant type—men of considerable education and much more than the average intelligence of their fellows." Middle-class professionals were a valuable constituency because they often led opinion in their communities, but the party was in danger of losing the "clerks and the small farmer and the unskilled laboring" men who had supported Roosevelt in 1912. The drama and excitement of the bolt had originally attracted many of these working-class voters, but the novelty had since faded. Finally, White gauged that at least a quarter of the 1912 Progressive tally consisted of "Teddy votes" that would melt away without Roosevelt's name on the ticket. All told, White expected the party to lose at least half of its 1912 vote in 1914, and he warned that it would not survive the 1916 election unless Roosevelt ran for president.[29]

The Progressive Party's situation was even more depressing when it came to candidates for the 1914 state ticket, beginning with the party's nominee for US Senate. White hoped to recruit Senator Bristow for the position because Bristow had established a strongly progressive record in Congress and had actively campaigned for Roosevelt in

1912. Although Bristow had not joined other Progressives in bolting the Republican Party that year, White had good reasons for believing that he would do so in 1914. The senator had written White several letters suggesting that he was merely waiting for an opportune moment to join the Progressives, but he had also resisted White's pleas to make his decision public. Bristow's equivocation was a problem for the Progressives because it prevented them from recruiting their own candidate, while fueling rumors that the senator would not bolt because he knew that the new party was doomed. A frustrated White considered assembling the senator's closest political allies to pressure him to join the Progressives in the fall of 1913, but Bristow's former business partner, Henry Allen, persuaded White that the idea would be counterproductive. White hewed to Allen's advice, calculating that Bristow had no choice but to join the Progressive Party. Otherwise, the Progressives would run a candidate against him, the reform vote would be split between the Progressives and the Republicans, and the Democrats would take the seat.[30]

Bristow's indecision also hampered White's ability to recruit a gubernatorial candidate, since parties' gubernatorial and senatorial nominees generally constituted an informal ticket in Kansas. White's friend and fellow newspaper publisher Arthur Capper had nearly won the governorship as a progressive Republican in 1912, and White hoped to persuade him to run as a Progressive in 1914. The key to White's pitch was that Capper would share the ticket with Bristow, but the appeal failed because Capper saw that the Progressive Party's days were numbered. Capper replied that too many progressive Democrats were satisfied with President Wilson's performance to bolt their party as White had hoped, and too many progressive Republicans were tradition-bound to the GOP. The truth was that Wilson had skillfully managed Democratic conservatives and pushed numerous progressive measures through Congress, including the Federal Reserve Act and the Underwood Tariff. Capper's reply spurred White to beg Bristow to declare his intentions one way or another, on the theory that a positive decision might also nudge Capper into the party. In contrast, delay would encourage Capper to remain a Republican as a "harmony" candidate capable of bringing Progressives back into the fold, and White feared that he might succeed.[31]

White's letter to Bristow likely crossed paths with the senator's letter all but declaring his intention to remain in the Republican Party. Bristow echoed Capper's argument that President Wilson had succeeded at keeping progressive Democrats in the party, and he added that the conservative Republicans had co-opted enough progressive ideas to avoid further defections. Bristow concluded that the Progressive Party had been outmaneuvered, it had lost its constituency, and the reformers' only reasonable option was to try to make the GOP progressive. The senator promised that he was still a Progressive and that he would visit White soon to discuss the matter in person, but he expressed his intention to focus on the issues rather than on parties. White was disappointed but not surprised, and he forthrightly stated that he would have to support the Progressive Party's senatorial nominee in the election. An incredulous Bristow alleged that White was behaving like a machine politician simply because he supported his own party's candidate, which was a preposterous notion. White's former *Gazette* protégé David G. Hinshaw, now a journalist in Washington, DC, informed him several weeks later that Capper and Bristow had formed an alliance to forge a progressive Republican ticket for 1914. Capper had assigned Bristow the task of bringing White and his Progressive friends back into the Republican Party as part of the "harmony" movement.[32]

The harmony movement was gaining ground in Kansas, despite White's efforts to convince Capper and Bristow otherwise. Indeed, White admitted that he was willing to return to the Republicans if the conservatives made real concessions to the Progressives, and he attended a harmony meeting at Capper's insistence. The experience left White underwhelmed, and he wrote Capper that there was no way the Republicans could peddle harmony on the basis of "dish water" progressivism. As White put it, "the way to make the Republican National Committee give real concessions is not to talk harmony, but to talk war," and he argued that Capper was risking his progressive reputation by depicting "flim-flam" as sincere reform.

The Progressive Party was wasting away despite such tough talk, and White was dismayed to find that state party officials were quietly crafting local truces with the Republicans to help their office-seeking friends. He was reduced to filling the slate by begging men to accept nominations, culminating in a special Emporia conclave to draft candidates on May 8.[33] The need to resort to such methods highlighted the Progressive Party's dire straits.

Bristow's decision to remain a Republican made him a political rival, and White treated him as such while admitting that he still "loved him like a brother." White had the rare ability to remain on amicable terms with his political opponents, and the two men's friendship endured their disagreement. In the near term, as White remarked to Roosevelt, "this establishment of a new party is no old ladies' quilting bee. . . . It is a war of conquest," and he turned his formidable political skills against Bristow in the race. Congressman Murdock leapt at White's offer of the Progressive senatorial nomination even though White clearly stated that he was unlikely to win the general election. As for Bristow, White fully expected him to be defeated by conservative Charles Curtis for the Republican nomination. Shrewdly, White calculated that "as a martyr Joe [Bristow] will be worth just as much" to the Progressives, because his battered corpse on the battlefield would highlight the folly of collaborating with either of the two established parties. In a clever act of political gamesmanship, White leaked word that Bristow would run as a Republican three days before the senator's planned announcement. Then he issued Murdock's declaration of candidacy on the same day as Bristow's, causing the press to focus on the fresh news coming out of Murdock's camp rather than Bristow's stale news.[34]

The die was cast, and Senator Bristow became Capper's partner in the harmony movement. The pair planned to run as Republicans in exchange for the Republican establishment endorsing the Progressive platform, and they persuaded Progressive leader and former governor W. R. Stubbs to join their camp. Bristow dispatched Stubbs to offer White a leadership position in the harmony movement in exchange for convincing Murdock to drop out of the Senate race, a prospect White rejected as "something at which my conscience revolts." Instead, White used the opportunity to lobby Stubbs, arguing that it was indefensible to abandon the party without having made an honest effort to win in the coming election. He pointed out that the Progressives could return to the Republican Party at any time, and they would get more concessions from the Republican establishment if they returned with a record of electoral victories rather than defeats. White's telephone calls, letters, and a daylong conference with Stubbs persuaded him to delay publicly endorsing the harmony movement until the Republicans committed to a truly progressive platform.[35] Unfortunately, White's best efforts could not remedy the party's fundamental flaws.

The Progressive Party was clearly doomed, but White intended to do all that he could to see that the party went down fighting rather than by compromising itself out of existence. Progressives had compromised for years, and the result was that "America is behind the civilized world in social and industrial legislation, our political forces are more reactionary, and less responsive to public opinion . . . and with all our boast about being the land of the free, we are behind civilization in too many things." The Progressive Party had been formed because the two major parties' reform factions had been unable to convince their respective reactionary establishments to pass good laws. Unfortunately, the Progressives discovered that too many reformers were unwilling to break with their political parties. From White's point of view, the Progressives had to continue the fight if only to teach the nation's mindless voters to think. White was no idle dreamer, and he knew that the Progressives had lost what chance they had of becoming a permanent third party. Still, he knew that by fighting, "we shall see others reap where we have sown, which is all right. We don't care to reap, but we do care that there shall be a harvest."[36]

White and other western Progressives reacted to their party's decline by charging into battle, demanding a strong platform that would highlight the milquetoast reform agenda that both the Democrats and Republicans had embraced. Unfortunately, Perkins and his eastern conservative allies were determined to block what they considered to be radical proposals. Perkins solicited and then rejected all of White's ideas for the 1914 platform, including prohibition, woman suffrage, and government ownership of the railroads, and White chafed at the handcuffs Perkins's eastern elites had placed on the party. The Progressives were only truly viable in the western states, and it made no sense for wealthy easterners to dominate what White saw as a "middle-class, western movement." He quietly began to co-operate with a group composed primarily of western Progressives, led by Gifford and Amos Pinchot, which aimed to force the National Committee to replace Perkins. The Progressive Party was at death's door, and White argued that the times called for a "strong, rather ruthless, incorrigibly righteous, indomitable" leader. The group quietly circulated a letter highlighting Perkins's unsuitability, but the effort stalled after he discovered their activities.[37]

The Progressive Party continued to decline through the spring of 1914, which left White very discouraged. The party base was confused and demoralized, and many of its leaders had become "pussy-footers and political pickpockets" crafting secret deals with the Republicans to save their own hides. At best, White thought that the party could avoid complete annihilation in the coming election. The spectacle had all the attractions of an execution, and White preferred to take his family for a much-needed vacation in Colorado before the ax fell. He needed time to write, and Sallie was on doctor's orders to rest in anticipation of surgery for her continuing gastrointestinal woes. Once again, politics intruded. Former president Roosevelt returned from his expedition to the Amazon jungle during the summer, and White had hoped that he would side with the western Progressives against Perkins. Instead, Roosevelt wrote White full of praise for Perkins for having held the line against the western Progressives' supposedly radical ideas. White was further dismayed when Roosevelt betrayed the party by endorsing a progressive Republican instead of the Progressive nominee in a New York state race. The situation was bleak in Kansas as well. Bristow narrowly lost the Republican senatorial nomination to Curtis as White had predicted, but the Progressive nominees for senator and governor were feuding. White had to interrupt his vacation to restore peace between them, and to vigorously lobby Roosevelt to campaign on behalf of the state party.[38]

Roosevelt obliged White with a preelection rally in Wichita, but Sallie's medical condition prevented him from attending. Sallie had recovered enough of her strength to visit the Mayo Clinic for treatment, and the Whites departed for Rochester, Minnesota, in mid-September. The doctors found that Sallie's gallbladder was inflamed with several large stones and performed an immediate operation before the couple returned to Emporia in early November. White was pleased when Sallie seemed to make a dramatic recovery, and by January 1915 he reported that his wife was reducing her eating to avoid gaining too much weight. The Whites' optimism was premature. Sallie's gastrointestinal problems continued, forcing her to return to the Mayo Clinic for further treatment after developing an infected gallbladder the following year.[39]

It was merciful that White was not in Kansas for the 1914 election, which utterly devastated the Progressive Party. Not a single Progressive candidate won a major state or federal office in Kansas, with nearly all coming in a distant third. For example, the Progressives' candidate for governor, Henry J. Allen, tallied just 84,000 votes compared to 210,000 for Republican Arthur Capper and 160,000 for Democrat George Hodges. White's worst fears about the Progressives' demographic weaknesses in Kansas and around the country had been realized. The Progressives had won a "town vote—an upper middle class vote," and not "the clerk . . . the tenant farmer, nor the small farmer." The party's working-class vote was limited to the "engineers and conductors—the plutocracy of labor; but [not] the man at the forge or in the switch-shanty." In the end, the Progressives were decimated because "thousands of colorless people" voted Republican, convinced that the GOP was "ninety per cent progressive."[40]

White was sanguine about the outcome, which left him "cast in outer darkness politically" as a member of a dead party. The Progressives were defeated, but White firmly believed that "we have set the people to thinking whether they have voted their thoughts or not."

After many years in politics, he had learned that "the world goes ahead when we win, and when we lose, it still goes ahead. In the long run the thinking people rule. A man, or a party or a political idea is poured into the color pot of public sentiment, and a strong minority often sets the color of the times, as well as a weak and scattered majority." The only thing men, parties, and ideas could do given the pitiless fortunes of politics was "to persist; to keep vital; and to have faith that in the color of public sentiment no strong stain is lost."[41] White turned to this sage wisdom for support more often than he would have wished over the next thirty years, but it helped keep him engaged in reform politics while others in his cohort fell to cynicism.

The immediate turn of events was highly traumatic for Progressives, and Roosevelt outlined the many reasons for the failure in a clear-eyed, bitter, disappointed letter to White. First, Roosevelt attacked La Follette and other congressional insurgents who had spent years agitating for radical change only to shirk their duty by remaining Republicans in 1912. Second, he cited America's strong two-party system as having encouraged the Progressive base to troop back to their old parties once the excitement of 1912 had dissipated. Third, he criticized the Progressive Party's leaders for being too quick to return to the Republican Party, short-circuiting any chance of an alliance with the progressive Republicans. Most distressingly, Roosevelt believed that Americans were "sick and tired of reform." All the American people cared about was prosperity, and "they did not care a rap for social justice or industrial justice or clean politics or decency in public life." Roosevelt sensed that the public was tired of him as well, and he felt that he should retire from politics so that a new generation of leaders could begin training for the day when the pendulum swung back toward reform. One person Roosevelt did not blame was himself, and he remained blind to the fact that his decision to back Perkins had disgusted the party's activist base. Although White agreed with much of Roosevelt's analysis, he felt sorry for "the dear old soldier" who had "got a serious wound" from the turn of events.[42]

The Progressive Party was annihilated in 1914, and White characterized the party's postelection executive council meeting as "a 'wake' or a christening, or a 'pot latch' or a 'receiver's sale' or a bankruptcy proceeding." Perkins's proposal to cease all operations outside of a skeleton office was the main proposal on the agenda, which was designed to maintain the illusion of activity in case some unforeseen development changed the political dynamic. White promised to attend, although he grumbled that the Progressives had always been a western party saddled with eastern leaders who had embraced an easily co-opted conservative agenda. The western Progressives wanted to move beyond the party's setbacks, advance a more aggressive platform, and get back into the fight, but White complained that the party's eastern leadership seemed ready for an unconditional surrender. Perkins proved his point by completely misreading the letter as support for the idea that the party should lay low, and a steady stream of top Progressive leaders began filing back to the Republicans.[43]

White cast no stones at those who had fought valiantly and made an honorable surrender, since he knew that the battle had been spiritually exhausting and that elected officials needed to consider the best interests of their constituents. His own return as a prodigal Republican was yet to come, but he began setting the table for the day when he would "sit down and eat some fatted calf." As White told Morton Albaugh, a leader of the conservative Republican faction, "the wheel of fortune will roll around to the point where we can all get together within the next few years." In the meantime, White chose to remain in the Progressive Party for three main reasons. First, he wanted to "stay by the ship as long as there is a ship," if only because the war in Europe or an economic crisis might change the political equation over the next year. Second, he liked the Wilson administration well enough that he felt no urgency to return to the Republicans. Third, White knew that he had "banged the door after me so hard and then threw rocks at the house" when he bolted in 1912 that he would have little influence when he returned to the GOP.[44]

White remained a Progressive, but he did so with minimal engagement. The party had absorbed a tremendous amount of his time and energy, and he wanted time to work on the novel he had begun in 1913. The Whites were also occupied with the early stages of renovating their Emporia home, having commissioned a set of designs from noted midwestern architect Frank Lloyd Wright. White declared that he was not willing to play a more active role in what had become a lost cause, although he obliged Perkins's request for platform ideas with an assertive set of government measures to address the imbalances of capitalism. White departed in mid-June 1915 for his annual vacation in Moraine Park, Colorado, which had recently been incorporated into the newly established Rocky Mountain National Park. He was able to spend three blissful months focusing exclusively on his draft novel and on several short stories he was writing under contract during his summer in the Rockies.[45]

White returned from Colorado in September feeling like a man without a party, and by early 1916 he had decided to return to the Republicans. The only question was how to do so on favorable terms, and White recognized that the Progressive Party was still useful as a leveled pistol to obtain concessions from the GOP. Armed with the threat of an enduring party schism, Progressives could force the Republicans to nominate a Progressive-Republican fusion ticket on an unabashedly progressive platform. To make the threat more credible, White proposed nominating Roosevelt for president along with a full slate of Progressive candidates in every congressional district in the nation. As White put it to Roosevelt, the Republicans would only treat the Progressives fairly if the "fear of God" were put into their hearts. The party's 1916 national convention delegation ought to consist of reliable men who were cool-headed enough to stand firm until the Republican leadership agreed to a good bargain on fusion, without being so stubborn that they would not accept a fair deal at the proper time. Of course, returning to the GOP meant working with conservatives once again, but White still felt that conservatives and radicals needed each other. Ultimately, White had faith that the Progressives had already won the battle for public opinion, and that it was only a matter of time until the progressive electorate demanded progressive laws.[46]

The 1916 convention season held little allure for a politically exhausted White, especially since the Progressive Party's demise was finally at hand. He once again served as a reporter covering the Democratic, Republican, and Progressive conventions for the Adams Newspaper Service, but his main role was as Kansas's Progressive national committeeman. The Progressive and Republican conventions were held concurrently in Chicago from June 7 to 10, reflecting the two parties' impending fusion. The Progressives' only goal was to return to the Republican Party on the most advantageous terms, and the western Progressives believed that nominating Roosevelt and then adjourning their convention would force the Republicans to offer more concessions. In contrast, Perkins and the eastern elite aimed to curry favor with the Republican leadership by herding the wayward Progressives back into the GOP's fold with the fewest possible concessions. Perkins's strategy was to rig the Progressive convention to nominate the Republican candidate, but the western Progressives outmaneuvered him and placed Roosevelt's name in nomination. At the critical moment, Perkins revealed that Roosevelt had given him a letter before the convention absolutely refusing the nomination. Tears filled White's eyes as he watched the angry delegates storm out, strip their Roosevelt badges from their chests, and trample them as they passed.[47]

The Progressive Party was dead. The bitter ending left White feeling "as though I have had my face blown off," but he had no intention of mourning any longer than necessary. The fact was that there was little to mourn, because the party had always functioned as a small corps of sincere reformers hitched to masses of Roosevelt worshippers. The Progressives had never been a real party, and White decided that he would support the Republicans even though he found it impossible to gin up any enthusiasm for the ticket. The former Progressives could still influence Republican policy if they remained unified, and White exhorted Roosevelt to lead the Progressive remnant through the transition. To this end, White suggested that the Progressives withhold their endorsement of the Republican nominee, Charles Evans Hughes, until the party leadership made significant concessions. He also agreed with Gifford Pinchot and other leading Progressives that an informal, nonpartisan "Progressive League of agitators" ought to be formed to help the Progressive remnant continue the fight as an interest group.[48]

As much as White wanted to wage one last guerrilla campaign to leverage concessions, the Progressive Party's executive committee narrowly endorsed Hughes at its final meeting. White did not go, since he saw no point in attending a wake. An exhausted White wasted no time in departing for his annual summer vacation in Moraine Park, where he hoped to finish revising his new novel. Unfortunately, White had to request another extension from his publisher after Sallie's continued illness made it impossible for her to help with the revisions. Politics also intruded when Hughes visited nearby Estes Park, and the two men discussed the political situation on a riding excursion. Hughes had been a progressive leader in the early 1900s, but his political ideas were badly outdated by 1916 because he had spent years disconnected from politics. White did his best in a futile attempt to persuade Hughes that the American public was ready for the kind of advanced reforms that had once been mere fantasy. Naturally, White found it impossible to muster much enthusiasm for Hughes, but he gave the ticket token support by endorsing it on the *Gazette*'s masthead. Even this small act was merely a "sort of an alibi" that White thought would be helpful in establishing his Republican credentials in the intraparty battles to come.[49]

Wilson won reelection in 1916 without White's vote, but Sallie voted for him because she wanted "to get as far as possible away from the stink of the Hughes environment." Wilson had, in fact, performed a raft of progressive feats in 1916. He signed bills establishing taxes on estates, corporations, and munitions makers; the Keating-Owen Act, which sought to curb child labor; and the Adamson Act establishing an eight-hour workday in the railroad industry. White resisted Henry J. Allen's argument that the Republican Party needed "a reincarnation of the William Allen White that managed the Bristow campaign and headed the procession in 1912," rather than the man "who joined the 'don't giveadam' club in 1916 and shuffled when he marched." Instead, White shunned politics, having "had the everlasting daylights knocked out of me" in the Progressive Party's dizzying rise and tragic fall. The editor did act on his desire for a "Progressive League of Agitators" when he joined Harold Ickes and other former Progressive leaders in an informal group to fight for progressive ideas. The group began working in early 1917, but it dissolved when the United States entered World War I that April.[50]

In the end, White's faith that the Progressive Party had sown the seeds of future reform was vindicated, and the painful attempt to form a third party was worth the cost. The Republican Party's old guard had spent more than a decade fighting reform through means both fair and foul. When progressive Republicans began to win control, the conservative faction proved entirely willing to immolate the party in order to deny the Progressives their prize. Crucially, White and other former Progressives were able to leverage Republican fears of another party schism well into the 1920s to obtain concessions that they would not otherwise have received. White was absolutely correct when he stated that the best way for progressive Republicans to get conservative Republicans to treat them as Republicans was by fighting, not by surrendering.[51] In the long run, White came to see that the Progressive Party had written an important chapter in the history of American reform, and that they had written the preface to what lay ahead. In the near term, three doors to reform had been shut to White: the Progressive Party was dead, the Republican Party was led by conservatives, and, from White's point of view, the Democratic Party was an unsafe harbor.

CHAPTER FOUR

SAVING THE WORLD

World War I had been a constant backdrop to American politics ever since the conflict began in August 1914. Like many Americans, William Allen White was horrified by Europe's descent into barbarism, and he strongly supported President Woodrow Wilson's declaration that the United States would remain neutral in deed. Still, White found it impossible to abide by the president's appeal for Americans to maintain neutrality of conscience. The war was the product of Germany's soulless militaristic ideology, White argued, and he hoped that the British would build a stable postwar world order by putting the German "madmen into the madhouse." As much as White wanted the Allies to win the war, he felt that the United States could not become involved because it was occupied with advancing democracy at home. Just four months before the European war began, thirteen women and children were killed when mine company guards attacked a settlement of striking Colorado workers in the Ludlow Massacre. President Wilson ordered the American military to occupy the Mexican port of Veracruz a day later, and White editorialized that the United States should focus on the "civil war" between workers and corporations at home instead of the civil war in Mexico.[1] The worsening international situation and the Progressive Party's death spiral gradually spurred White toward the perspective that the United States had to help democratize the world system if it hoped to have democracy at home. Like many Progressives, White came to see the war as a new opportunity to continue the fight for democracy by reforming the world system.

Europe's battlefields were a long way from the Midwest, but the war soon found its way to Emporia. White's charity work for philanthropist Herbert Hoover's American Commission for Relief in Belgium marked his first direct contact with the war, and it helped the two men develop a lifelong friendship. Politically, White pointed to

European developments as a major factor in the Progressive Party's disappointing performance in the 1914 election. Four months of brutal European warfare had made voters "afraid of their own righteous judgments," and it had numbed them to the party's "plea of suffering and injustice." Calls for wages and hours legislation, workingman's compensation schemes, and old age pensions simply could not compete for the voters' attention against the mass slaughter on Europe's battlefields. The war also strained relations between White and Theodore Roosevelt after the latter savagely denounced Wilson for maintaining American neutrality. White had praised President Wilson for the same reason, and he remarked that Roosevelt "heard that I was speaking kindly of Wilson and Caesar's great heart broke."[2]

The German sinking of the British passenger liner *Lusitania* on May 7, 1915, triggered a slow evolution in White's thinking about America's role in the war. The attack killed 128 Americans and outraged the nation, but President Wilson coolly remarked that the United States would remain neutral because "there is such a thing as a man being too proud to fight." Wilson sent Germany a diplomatic note demanding respect for America's rights at sea, and he ordered a gradual expansion of the army and navy. In the meantime, an outraged Roosevelt denounced Wilson as cowardly and unmanly. White thought that both the Germans and the British had blood on their hands after learning that the *Lusitania* was carrying a cargo of munitions, and he continued to support Wilson's neutrality policy. In contrast, Roosevelt strongly advocated for a dramatic expansion of American military muscle on the grounds that the United States needed to be prepared for the possibility of conflict. White tried to spur Roosevelt to use his "preparedness" crusade for progressive reform. Germany's working-class soldiers fought tenaciously because their nation's advanced social welfare system gave them a stake in victory, White posited. He hoped Roosevelt would advocate for the kind of "preparedness in men" that would give American working-class conscripts a similar motivation in a potential conflict, but the former president was less interested in domestic reform than he was in foreign policy.[3]

Ironically, it was White who found himself embracing Roosevelt's call for a more assertive foreign policy, spurred by the ongoing European war and Germany's submarine attacks on neutral vessels in late 1915. White had praised Wilson's calm response to the *Lusitania* sinking in the spring, but now he wrote editorials applauding Roosevelt's argument that America needed to be more assertive. As White saw it, both Wilson and Roosevelt were patriots who wanted to advance the national interest. The difference was that Roosevelt was willing to show his guns in defense of America's neutral rights while Wilson was not, and the appearance of timidity was likely to cause war by encouraging Germany to push America's limits.[4]

Mexican revolutionary Pancho Villa's raid on the town of Columbus, New Mexico, on March 9, 1916, seemed to further validate Roosevelt's calls for a more forceful neutrality. The day after the raid, White remarked that it seemed unlikely that the Mexicans would have dared to attack the United States without an international backer. America had to "show a strong, courageous front to the family of nations" by defending its rights against foreign outrages. White now fully endorsed Rooseveltian preparedness, including a naval expansion program, a million-man ready reserve force for the army, and public ownership of the munitions industry to defuse the allegation that preparedness was a pretext for war profiteering. The Villa raid had shown White that "we must live in the world as it is and not as it should be." The German sinking of the French passenger liner *Sussex* on March 24, 1916, which injured several Americans, offered fresh confirmation that Germany was an imperialistic "wild beast" that only understood force. For the first time, White broached the idea that the United States might have to resort to war to defend its rights. Roosevelt had been proven correct from White's point of view, and he commented that Wilson's legalistic mind seemed ill suited to the war situation.[5]

War was averted when the Germans suspended their unrestricted submarine warfare campaign on May 14, but White was disappointed in his countrymen's lack of interest in the war issue during the 1916 campaign. Roosevelt was of the same mind, and White was pleased to learn that the former president planned to speak on the subject of preparedness in his Memorial Day address in Kansas City, Missouri. The speech fused Roosevelt's and White's ideas, and White watched the former president argue that America could only avoid the "lingering national decay" that came with selfish materialism and foolish pacifism by embracing a global mission. President Wilson's crime was that he had indulged in "visionary plans about world-action in the future" without taking action to resolve the present crisis, and Roosevelt called for bolstering America's military and economic infrastructure. White's ideas were reflected in Roosevelt's argument that preparedness also meant developing the kind of unified national spirit that could only be attained through democracy and social justice.[6] However, White was too occupied with the domestic political situation to focus on foreign policy until the Progressive Party died in the summer of 1916.

Germany's decision to resume unrestricted submarine warfare in early 1917 brought the war crisis back to the fore just as White's efforts to achieve reform through the domestic political process petered out. German submarines quickly sank three American merchant vessels, and the ideological path toward war was simplified when the autocratic Russian government was ousted by a provisional democratic regime in March. The war could now fairly be portrayed as both a defense of neutral rights and a conflict of democracy versus autocracy. White appealed to both justifications as the nation waited for Congress to debate the president's request for a declaration of war. First, White pointed out that Germany had fought a de facto war against the United States for two years, and it was past time that America fought back. Second, he argued that the war would reform the world by incorporating Germany into a democratic coalition to preserve world peace. Like many liberals, White urged Americans to rise to the occasion as "the champions of republican government in the beginning of the world's republic." Congress convened on April 2, and the president asked the body for a declaration of war both to protect America's neutral rights and to destroy autocracy in the world.[7]

Congress voted to declare war against Germany on Good Friday, April 6, 1917, which was a coincidence that White found significant. Three years of German crimes against humanity had proven that the European conflict was a war of Christian civilization against German barbarism, and White saw America as embarking on a holy crusade to defend civilization. The United States was making a sacred offering of American manhood to save the world, just as Christ had sacrificed himself to save humanity two thousand years before. White's messianic conception of the war as an engine for democratizing the world was widespread among reformers. He joined with his liberal allies in calling for the fundamental tasks of war mobilization to serve double duty by reforming American society. White, Ickes, and other progressive Republicans immediately canceled their plans for a "Progressive League of Agitators," but they used their final communiqué as a call for the government to adopt a vast program of liberal policies as war measures. The group proposed a draft of men and property, federal management of prices and wages, a graduated income tax, woman suffrage, prohibition, and labor reforms giving workers a right to participate in industrial management.[8]

The proposals White and his allies had outlined soon found expression in the Wilson administration's wartime economic regime. The administration established cooperative boards such as the War Industries Board to manage production and the National War Labor Board to avoid strikes by investigating labor disputes. Liberals such as White, journalist Walter Lippmann, and public intellectual John Dewey were united in their belief that the war was the vehicle that would finally democratize American industry. White had a particular connection with the Food Administration, which was led by Hoover with the assistance of White's old KU classmate Vernon Kellogg. The Food Administration was established to manage America's food supply, and White hoped it would make good on its promise by corralling the meat-packers, grain elevator operators, and other middlemen who had preyed on western producers for decades. He enthusiastically pointed to Wilson's measures as the crowning achievement of twenty years of European and American socialist and progressive efforts to "break down the evil system of capitalism in its ruthless control of opportunity." The editor argued that the nation had an obligation to prove that it believed in its own rhetoric about spreading democracy in the world by democratizing American society.[9]

After one year of war, the federal government had become established as the balancing force between labor's right to fair treatment and capital's right to a profit. The achievement was significant because the conflict between these two rights had driven the nineteenth century's social and political struggles. White was convinced that irresistible historical processes were bringing the nation into a new century of social justice. The wealthy had once dominated society and brought beauty in exchange for freedom, but they were replaced by the middle class, which contributed efficiency in exchange for the working class's mind-numbing labor. The workers of the world were asserting themselves in the war, and they would create a just peace at the expense of wealth. White disliked class consciousness, but it was clear to him that "there are certain class problems in labor that are not individual problems and the laboring class, it seems to me, must act as a class in considering and solving those problems." The war had forced permanent changes in America's economic structure, and White expected that class consciousness would wither away as the working class obtained middle-class living standards. He anticipated a short-lived period of antilabor reaction following the war, but he was certain that the project to use the war to effect lasting change at home had succeeded.[10]

Civil liberties were curtailed as a war measure as well, but White believed that this temporary sacrifice was a worthy price for democratizing the world. Congress passed the Espionage Act, making it a criminal offense to interfere in the war effort in any way, in April 1917. The law was so broadly written that individuals were convicted and sentenced to lengthy prison terms for innocuous crimes of conscience, such as expressing opposition to the draft. White was unsympathetic, arguing that attacks on the war's motives could not be tolerated because they might "justify all the molly-coddles and sapheads in their weak and wobbly attitude towards the war." Congress's role in wartime, he asserted, was to defer to the president's judgment and speedily approve the measures he deemed necessary. Furthermore, White applauded the government's campaign against socialists and draft resisters, although he hoped that this attitude would be extended to war profiteers and the obscenely wealthy. Freedom of speech was no defense because war was a community effort, and speech that worked against the community was not protected by the First Amendment. White cited anarchists, southern racists, and violent labor agitators as examples of groups that had used the First Amendment to shield their evil work. As he put it, "those who are not for us are against us . . . and should not be tolerated for a moment." Censorship thus allegedly served liberal aims because it protected society against those who exploited American freedoms in an attempt to subvert them during a time of national emergency.[11]

White normally spent the summers in Colorado, but he chose to remain in Emporia during the summer of 1917 for two reasons. First, he wanted to use his editorial pen for the war effort, and second, he wanted to heavily revise *In the Heart of a Fool*, the novel he had begun four years earlier. The thesis of the work was that the world was spiritual rather than material in nature, and that rewards and punishments were meted out on the basis of spiritual rights and wrongs. White feared that the work was outdated, gauging that the public was more interested in reading about the war than a progressive morality play. Still, he hoped that the book would be timely and relevant, positing that the war was similar as a "struggle of the world away from the gross materialism of Germany to a certain higher spiritual standard of life contained in the word, Democracy." Mr. and Mrs. White agreed that the story sagged in too many places, and he labored through the beginning of a hot, disagreeable Kansas summer to work it into shape. The work required more revision than could be accomplished in a summer, but White began his task with an eye toward improving the story while Macmillan, his publisher, reviewed the manuscript.[12]

A surprise invitation to visit the Western Front as part of a Red Cross inspection delegation happily disrupted White's plans. The

Red Cross drafted White as a writer who could humanize the war for a wide audience, and Macmillan gave him permission to postpone his work on *In the Heart of a Fool*. White was eager to use his "fresh eyes and country legs" to interpret the war for his American readers, and he sailed for Europe with his fellow delegate Henry J. Allen aboard the SS *Espagne* in mid-August. White and Allen visited the front lines in France, and they occasionally came under shellfire as they toured various Red Cross and YMCA facilities on the Western Front. White documented his experiences in a series of letters to Sallie over the succeeding six weeks, and he returned to the United States in late October 1917.[13]

He arrived in Emporia after a brief stop in Washington, DC, to discuss his experiences with the president, and he set himself to the task of turning the letters he had sent to Sallie into a marketable product. At first, he had believed that he could fashion the letters into an article, but Sallie persuaded him that the material was good enough to be forged into a larger work. The result was *The Martial Adventures of Henry and Me,* which Macmillan published in April 1918. The book was a lighthearted retelling of White and Allen's travels in France and Italy, although it included a few moments of solemnity as White experienced the horrors of war. Overall, *Henry and Me* struck an optimistic tone by arguing that the war's democratic goals made it worth the sacrifice. White hoped that the book would show Americans "that their very life was woven into the vast fabric of destiny that is passing over the loom of the fates in this war." Walter Lippmann, Senator Henry Cabot Lodge (R-MA), and other reviewers praised *Henry and Me* as a book that painted the war in distinctly American colors, without ever seeming to "have gone ugly or sour or blatant." Macmillan rushed to issue a second printing after the book's initial run of fifteen thousand copies sold out in less than a month, and *Henry and Me* became White's second-best seller behind *A Certain Rich Man.*[14]

The Martial Adventures of Henry and Me reached the market at the same time that the American Expeditionary Force was launching its first large-scale operations in the spring of 1918. As in the Spanish-American War, a fifty-year-old White commented that he could not

Touring the Western Front as part of the Red Cross inspection delegation. An unidentified man stands between White on the left and Henry J. Allen on the right, 1917. Courtesy of Emporia State University, Special Collections and Archives.

help but feel envious of the young men who were about to do battle for a grand cause. The war evoked vivid memories of White's childhood in post–Civil War America, with its "G. A. R. processions, the big reunions, and rallies, the tremendous emotional stir that still hung over the nation." White knew that the war was deadly serious, and his own eighteen-year-old son, Bill, Jr., was in a military training camp preparing for the trenches during the summer of 1918. Still, White advised one soldier who was about to sail for Europe to be excited for the epic adventure ahead. The young man would have the privilege of standing shoulder to shoulder with a host of men who were willing to fight and die to change the world. He gushed that the moment was as pivotal to the arc of human history as the birth of Christianity and the discovery of the New World. White was too old to shoulder a rifle himself, but he served his nation as a speaker for the Four Minute Man and Liberty Loan campaigns that sought to explain the war to the American people. The tour was a success and his speeches were well received, but the 1918 influenza pandemic forced the cancellation of several engagements. The flu soon struck Emporia and the White family, and Sallie was particularly hard hit because she had served as her neighborhood's nurse before falling ill.[15]

White had every confidence in the Wilson administration's ability to lead the military and diplomatic elements of the war effort, but he was increasingly concerned that the president was stumbling in his management of the home front by 1918. White had embraced Wilson's call for censorship when the war began, and the suppression of civil liberties for antiwar activists did nothing to diminish his support. However, White chafed at the restrictions put on journalists such as himself, particularly after an article he wrote for the Young Men's Christian Association was censored. The article examined the moral conditions facing young American soldiers overseas, but George Creel, head of the Committee on Public Information, felt that the piece unintentionally disparaged France. The official newspaper censorship was even worse, and White complained that every detail of the war was being withheld from the American public. He editorially scolded that "we should remember that democracy, like charity, should begin at home," but Congress restricted speech still further in May 1918 when it passed the Sedition Act, criminalizing any criticism of the government. Oswald Garrison Villard, White's friend and publisher of the *Nation,* was soon caught in the censor's net after publishing a piece deemed critical of American Federation of Labor leader Samuel Gompers. President Wilson ultimately reversed the censorship of the *Nation,* but the Wilson administration's decision to turn its censorship guns on journalists such as White and Villard helped turn many pro-Wilson liberals against him in 1918.[16]

The Wilson administration's aggressive assault on civil liberties coincided with other difficulties in managing the wartime economy, and White suspected that censorship was intended to conceal government incompetence. The Food Administration was a prime example of the government's struggle to manage the economy. White was thrilled when the agency seemed poised to democratize the food industry when it was established in 1917, but he felt that it had been captured by business interests by early 1918. The agency's local boards were supposed to regulate the prices of basic staples with the interests of both producers and consumers in mind, but Kansas's board members came entirely from the ranks of wholesale and retail grocers. By excluding consumer representatives, food merchants were able to fix prices at levels that gave them a 40 percent profit on staples such as flour, sugar, and rice. In Emporia, residents had addressed the problem by persuading their local board to replace half of the grocers' representatives with consumer representatives. By working through Food Administrator Hoover's assistant, Vernon Kellogg, White was able to convince the agency to start applying the concept nationally.[17]

The Wilson administration's missteps spurred White to resume his project to reform the Republican Party, beginning with Kansas. The state's Republicans united behind Henry J. Allen's candidacy for governor even though Allen had remained in Europe to pursue charity work with the Red Cross and YMCA. White served as Allen's publicity director and chief spokesman, and one of his duties was to help bridge the gap between the state party's progressive and conservative wings. White held a luncheon at his home with twenty leading Republicans drawn from both factions in a bid to unite the party in March 1918. Several prominent conservatives were given leadership positions in the Allen campaign, and White was pleased to find that many were eager to help because all Republicans would benefit by capturing the governorship from the Democrats. In the end, Allen's reluctance to leave his charity work, the difficulty of obtaining westward passage, and a last-minute bout of paralytic diphtheria prevented him from returning before the general election. White led an army of proxies who waged a successful campaign for their absent nominee, which also helped restore his position as a leading Republican in the state.[18]

At the same time, White was working for a progressive reconciliation with the Republican National Committee through newly elected chairman Will Hays. White, Ickes, and other western Progressives regarded Hays as a man they could work with, and they were encouraged by Hays's initiative to reorganize the RNC. White wrote to Hays to encourage his efforts to unite the party by giving the Progressives more say on the RNC, and Hays invited White to join him on a "scouting, harmonizing trip" through the western states. White eagerly accepted, and he proved his goodwill by writing Roosevelt and other progressive friends to ask them to support Hays's efforts. The best way for Progressives to win fair treatment, White argued, was to show Hays and the RNC that the Progressives were decent men fighting for a good cause. Conservatives did not have to agree with the Progressives' ideas, but White understood that reconciliation could not succeed until each side regarded the other as honorable.[19]

Hays canceled the harmonizing trip three days later, explaining that he feared it would be interpreted as playing politics on the eve of the Liberty Loan campaign. He proposed rescheduling the trip to midyear, and White accepted because he wanted the party to have a conversation about its policy on postwar economic reconstruction. Specifically, White wondered whether the Republicans would acknowledge that the war had transformed America as profoundly as it had changed the world. Men of great power and wealth had to recognize the necessity of yielding some of their privileges, or they would lose them entirely under some more radical form of government. The Bolshevik revolution in Russia showed White that the time was not yet right to "inject social and economic problems into active politics," but he felt that it was important for the Republican Party to begin an internal discussion about these issues. The GOP would not get very far politically if it contented itself with being the "party of criticism and delay and reaction." Instead, the Republicans had to be "a constructive forward moving party" advocating an active role for the federal government in public affairs. White did not pretend to know exactly "how far and how fast" the Republican platform ought to go, but he believed that it was imperative that responsible Republicans begin considering the shape of a "liberal constructive platform" that would give America a moderate course of reform.[20]

White was angered when he discovered that Hays had actually gone on the trip alone several days later, remarking that "Hays got cold feet on me." Although he conceded that Hays had every right to go on his trip alone and to run the RNC as a conservative organization if he desired, White saw no reason why he should serve as a "side show to their circus." He dashed off a letter to Hays explaining that while Progressives believed he was a fair-minded man, they feared that the Republican organization was ultimately unwilling to share access to the party machinery. The Progressives had no desire to re-fight the battles of 1912, and White noted that World War I had placed new issues on the table. America needed a party that "believes in a strong central government that shall be for the purpose of construction and not for the purpose of checking the progress of things." In particular, White called for strong federal action that would recognize that "labor must have a new voice in the management of industrial affairs." It was essential that the federal government enact measures providing meaningful protection for collective bargaining, such as guaranteeing a union's right to examine the company's books during negotiations. The Republican Party would be defeated if it remained focused on the "rights of capital" while trying to "dam the moving current of the times," and White asked Hays to call a conference of conservatives and Progressives to discuss an agenda suited to the age. Roosevelt persuaded White that the letter was too radical to send, but many of the ideas White articulated in 1918 were later realized in the New Deal.[21]

Outside of politics, the other major project that kept White occupied in 1918 was revising *In the Heart of a Fool*. He excised more than fifty thousand words from the draft by May, and he and Sallie agreed that the manuscript was tremendously improved. Still, they both felt that publication should be postponed until after the war because the public had little appetite for fiction. The work needed more revision, and White planned to further streamline its prose and plot during the family's annual summer vacation in Moraine Park. Finally, after years of writing and rewriting, the manuscript was finished in the summer of 1918 and the book published in the fall. The plot revolves around the tension between a town's business-minded middle class and its working class. The conflict intensifies when union organizer Grant Adams arrives in town, organizes a strike, and is murdered by a mob of vigilantes. Adams's death spurs both sides to discover the need for understanding and cooperation, and White ended his book on an optimistic note. Overall, White knew that the war had changed the world so much as to make the story an anachronism better suited to 1912 than 1918. Still, he did his best to salvage the work, and he emphasized its "labor novel" aspects in an attempt to make it relevant to the era. The book sold poorly in spite of White's efforts, and he later called *In the Heart of a Fool* "a real disappointment" that had foundered in the cynical postwar environment.[22]

The national political situation was similarly disappointing for White, who returned to Emporia in September to find that the Republican leadership was not interested in discussing the new economic realities the war had created. Instead, White complained that the party's leaders regarded the wartime economic regime as temporary, while looking "longingly back to the good old days before the war." The electorate was undeniably drifting toward the Republicans, but White argued that the party was needlessly alienating Progressives and the working class with its reactionary talk. It was perfectly obvious to White that "after the war some readjustment, relatively socialistic, will have to be made," and he wrote Hays that the Republican leadership would lose the Progressive vote if it tried to bring America back to "the Laissez Faire days before 1912." The former Progressives had not returned to the Republican Party because they opposed Wilson's policies, such as a federal role in managing the economy or industrial relations. The Progressives sided against the Wilson administration because "it is doing badly, things that should be done well," and White warned that Progressive support for the GOP could not be taken for granted.[23]

President Wilson committed a tremendous political blunder when he demanded that the voters send him a Democratic Congress on the eve of the 1918 midterm election, which appeared to violate his own springtime declaration that "politics is adjourned." Actually, Wilson had been referring to a temporary political truce to allow Congress to address war matters that summer. Political battles had raged unabated since the declaration of war, but Wilson's demand enraged White. The president had, in White's view, demonstrated that he did not trust the people to make the right decision at the ballot box. The war was a bipartisan effort, and White overlooked his apprehensions about the Republicans by calling on every American voter to prove his manly independence by sending Wilson a Republican Congress. In spite of his criticism of the Wilson administration's domestic performance, White remained a believer in the war's larger goals and defended the president as a man who "functions as a leader of world democracy remarkably well."[24]

The Republicans won a tremendous victory in the November election, including capturing both houses of Congress. The outcome pleased White, who observed that Wilson's call for a Democratic Congress had done more to unite the warring Republican factions than any other development in the preceding two decades. Still, he put Chairman Hays and the nation on notice that the election results did not constitute a mandate for reaction. It was clear to White that

> we are not going back to the old order. The railroads never will be what they were a year ago; labor will not be sold again in the open market; the society of nations never again will be a free-booter's paradise. Price making of necessities like wheat, meat, fuel and cloth will never again be left to speculators on exchange. Life for the average man after this war will contain more than it held before of creature comfort, of civilized amenities.

White called for the Republican Party to lead the development of a permanent postwar economic plan addressing these realities. World

War I had taught the working class its value to society, and he warned that potential American Bolsheviks could capitalize on workers' apprehensions of being "returned to their former economic status of low wages and bad living conditions." The worst thing Americans could do was allow society to drift.[25] The democratic revolution White believed the war had unleashed seemed more powerful to him than any short-term political movement, but both political parties interpreted the Republican victory as a green light for a probusiness, antilabor agenda.

World War I ended by armistice on November 11, 1918, and White assessed the outcome just days after the GOP's smashing electoral victory. The rise of democracy in Europe was a definite win for America, and White interpreted the spread of Bolshevism as a temporary reaction against militarism. The most autocratic European nations were the ones that were "trembling with the fear of revolution," proving to White that democracy was the best antidote to Bolshevism. The war against plutocracy still raged at home, to be fought at the ballot box, in the schoolhouse, and in the court of public opinion. White applauded the fact that women were increasingly active in the workforce and that their wartime service had placed them on track toward the right to vote. He similarly cheered the fact that workers had gained class consciousness, but he preferred class compromise to class dictatorship. Liberal reform was the key to avoiding class warfare, "not so much to thwart and suppress the movement as to prevent its culmination by intelligent discussion and by earnest consideration of [its] causes." To this end, White prescribed an active agenda of the eight-hour day, government management of transportation, a federal farm labor employment bureau, cost of living adjustments to wages, and other measures designed to make the promise of American democracy real.[26]

The looming international peace conference to be held at the Paris suburb of Versailles left little time to ruminate on the consequences of victory or the means by which it had been achieved. White was among the scramble of journalists vying for an opportunity to attend the Versailles Peace Conference, which was scheduled to begin in January 1919. He had lobbied for a secretarial position on the bipartisan delegation he assumed Wilson would select to negotiate at Paris, but it was soon evident that the president would not appoint any Republicans. Instead, White sailed for Europe as a syndicated reporter for the Wheeler Newspaper Syndicate on December 7, bringing along his eighteen-year-old son, William, as secretary. White's columns appeared in almost a hundred American newspapers, earning him an annual salary of $25,000 plus expenses, or nearly $350,000 when adjusted for inflation. Since the peace terms Germany had accepted in the armistice were vague, White took it on himself to disseminate his interpretation of the president's peace plan: freedom of communication, a fair economic policy for workers, and, most importantly, a league of democratic states. The war's democratic promise seemed on the verge of realization. White was elated, but his joy was tempered when he arrived in Paris to learn that Theodore Roosevelt had passed away on January 6, 1919.[27]

The conference's first session proved to be an enormous disappointment for the assembled journalists, and White was amused to find Villard sound asleep on a sofa during the opening ceremony. The first session had the virtue of being open to the press, but the conference was soon closed to journalists. Walter Lippmann was in Paris as an assistant to President Wilson's chief advisor, Colonel Edward House, and he argued against secrecy on the grounds that the press should be employed as a partner in molding public opinion at home. Lippmann's advice went unheeded, and he was sidelined with White at the press corps' Paris office. The American journalistic contingent was naturally disgusted by the turn of events, and White reportedly surmised that the European diplomats had demanded secrecy so they would have a free hand to eviscerate Wilson's proposals. White, Villard, and the rest of the American reporters failed in their effort to persuade the diplomats to reverse their decision for secrecy, and they began to cast about for other opportunities.[28]

An exciting possibility immediately presented itself to White in the form of an unexpected diplomatic assignment. Russia had been mired in civil war since the Bolshevik Revolution began in October 1917, and American troops had been deployed there as part of an Allied intervention force. President Wilson proposed a conference that would aim to resolve the Russian civil war at the island of Prinkipo, in the Sea of Marmora, on February 15, 1919. White had made his interest in the Russian situation known to Wilson in early 1918, when he asked a mutual friend to suggest his name to the president as a member of a rumored fact-finding commission to Russia. Nothing seemed to come of the idea, but Wilson surprised White a year later by appointing him to join Russian expert Professor George Herron as the conference's two American delegates. The pair played the diplomatic game skillfully. On their own initiative, they organized dinner parties for representatives of the anti-Bolshevik Russians and the Baltic nations, overcoming their initial reluctance to attend the conference. The Bolsheviks agreed to send a delegation as well, but the French sabotaged the conference by announcing that they would give military support to the anti-Bolsheviks regardless of the meeting's outcome. White was incensed, correctly deducing that the French government preferred a military solution to the Russian situation. To White, it seemed as if France had adopted Germany's militaristic ideology and become "a great Nation drunk with victory, turned reactionary, blind with materialistic philosophy, and going to hell in a handcar."[29] The Russian Revolution had begun as a democratic movement before it was commandeered by the Bolsheviks, and White always believed that French interference had cost the world its opportunity to save Russian democracy.

The doors of two major conferences had been shut to White, who was left to comment on the general European situation. He was disgusted as he watched Europe's diplomats try to use the peace conference to restore the discredited balance of power system, establish large standing armies, guarantee British naval supremacy, contain Bolshevik Russia, eviscerate Germany, and settle all territorial questions through a secret commission of the Great Powers. European diplomats seemed openly contemptuous of President Wilson's liberal peace terms, and in many cases they succeeded in forcing Wilson to compromise his principles. Although he laid most of the blame for this mischief on Europe's diplomats, White correctly identified two crucial mistakes that President Wilson had made. First, Wilson refused to delegate responsibility for the negotiations, which were more involved than any individual could competently manage. Second, the president had not properly consulted the American people about the role he was embracing on their behalf. Still, White had faith that America would not reject its duty to the world by retreating to isolation. In the meantime, he used his time in Paris to educate himself about international relations and to enjoy the sumptuous feasts staged by the delegations that highlighted their national delicacies.[30]

By far, the most controversial issue that emerged from Paris was American membership in Wilson's proposed league of democratic states, which became the League of Nations. The league was an international organization that aimed to contain war through collective security, and American debate over US participation in the league began while the conference was still under way. White used his pen to advocate for Wilson's vision while he was still in Europe. He capitalized on Americans' anxiety by calling Bolshevism "one big awful unmistakable reaction" and a successor to German militarism, since both ideologies were based on nations obtaining what they wanted by force. The only difference was that Germany used force to achieve its political goals, while Bolshevism used force to achieve political, social, and economic goals. White argued that the League of Nations would challenge both militarism and Bolshevism by ending the "old world of nationalism, of individualism, of *laissez faire* at home and abroad, the old world that was not its brother's keeper" and replacing it with an internationalism based on democratic values. America had become "chief defender of the new faith," although White acknowledged that reforming the world system would take decades. In the meantime, America ought to cooperate with like-minded nations against the dual threats of Russian Bolshevism and a resurgent Germany through the League of Nations. Finally, he explained that Wilson's idea of national self-determination had filtered to every corner of the globe, and "the little peoples of the world" were rebelling against imperialism. The newly independent nations faced a choice between liberal democracy and Bolshevism, and White argued that the United States had a responsibility to ensure that the world's former colonial subjects found their way to democracy.[31]

White returned to the United States just before the Treaty of Versailles was submitted to the Senate for ratification on July 10, just as the domestic debate over the peace plan reached a fever pitch. The opponents of American membership in the League of Nations were known as the Irreconcilables, and they launched a national speaking campaign against the proposal. Many internationalists who had originally supported Wilson's proposals, including Villard and Lippmann, turned against the treaty when they learned about the concessions President Wilson had made to the vengeful Allies. The tide of public opinion had begun to turn against the treaty, and White estimated that roughly 60 percent of Kansans were against it by midsummer. White did what he could, penning articles and editorials in support of the league, joining the League of Nations Association, and delivering speeches in support of the treaty around the Midwest on his own dime. Meanwhile, the treaty stalled in the Senate Foreign Relations Committee after Wilson stubbornly refused to compromise on its terms. Instead, Wilson decided to counter the Irreconcilables with a whirlwind speaking tour of his own beginning on September 3. From the left, Wilson argued that America had a global mission to help prevent war through free trade and the league, and from the right, he portrayed the league as the only real firewall against Bolshevism. Wilson's efforts were too little, too late, and the strain of his exhausting speaking schedule likely contributed to the crippling stroke he suffered on September 25 at Pueblo, Colorado.[32]

The Treaty of Versailles's most prominent advocate had been struck down, and many of White's friends who had once argued passionately for Wilson's ideas had turned their back on the agreement. The treaty faced daunting prospects since the Constitution requires a two-thirds Senate majority to ratify treaties. White remained true to the cause. He noted that an odd alliance of senators, including "Knox and Johnson, the arch-standpatter and the progressive of progressives; . . . Borah and Sherman, men of middle way; . . . every kind and class and kindred of Republicans . . . are united in this attitude of protest against the League of Nations." White professed optimism that the Senate would pass the treaty with mild alterations, in part because he believed that the consequences of rejecting it far exceeded the risks of ratification. For example, the United States would have to maintain a large, expensive military defense since it would not have access to the league's promise of collective security. The public's "hen-minded" inability to recognize such consequences was tragic, particularly since White expected the league to function as an alliance of English-speaking, peace-loving, democratic nations that would be friendly to American interests. Furthermore, White argued that the league was exactly the kind of body that should be used to reverse the bargains Wilson had made with Old World imperialism at Versailles.[33]

The Senate voted to reject the Treaty of Versailles on the final day of the first session of the Sixty-Sixth Congress, November 19, 1919. Wilson had consistently failed to compromise with his Senate opponents, destroying any chance of ratification. White blamed both sides for the failure. President Wilson had been a poor champion for the cause because he had failed to explain what his ideas meant in practice, and he had stubbornly refused to accept the Senate's minor revisions despite swallowing significant compromises at Versailles. Then Wilson had scurried about the nation in a futile campaign, only to have the strain force him to his sickbed. The Senate was also to blame for allowing itself to be held hostage by a small group of senators who were unalterably opposed to the treaty. White made no attempt to push for ratification in his editorials when the treaty was revived for the second congressional session in early 1920.[34] The Treaty of Versailles was finally defeated in the Senate on March 19, 1920, by a vote of 49 in favor versus 35 against, which fell short of the two-thirds majority required for ratification. The United States would never adopt the Treaty of Versailles, and it would never be a part of the League of Nations.

White immortalized Woodrow Wilson's role in the treaty debacle in a fitting epitaph the following day:

He didn't know it was loaded. He meant well; he pointed the gun of self-confidence, gaily, blithely, wantonly, at his elders and betters in American politics; pulled the trigger of his stubborn, implacable will, and—
BANG!
Went the hope of the world.
Woodrow Wilson killed it.[35]

Whether Wilson was right or wrong in refusing to compromise was irrelevant, because as White put it, "by stubbornly refusing to compromise upon things which are right, one may often do a vast wrong." Wilson was a tragic figure in White's view. The president was "a man of lofty motive, of high ideals, of great courage and of more than ordinary wisdom. But he has the faults of a tyrant. And it is definitely too bad." Wilson's personal flaws killed the treaty, and the nation would pay the price. As historian Thomas Knock observed, Wilson himself had wielded the knife that eviscerated his 1916 coalition through his complicity in wartime repression and his failure to safeguard liberal reforms. Instead of democracy and security, the postwar world was one of repression and fear, and it was clear to White that America was "going through a long, dark corridor from one world to another, from the old order to the new. And I am blind as a bat. The only thing that I know is that we must walk carefully and not hurry, and trust to God. After that, I give it up." Although he admitted that "these are days of disillusion," White still believed "sincerely that in the next decade, or perhaps the last half of this decade will see a justification for our view in those shining days of autumn, 1918."[36]

Like many progressive reformers, White had spent sixteen long years fighting to lead Americans to the promised land of democracy by 1920. He had fought for reform as a progressive Republican, as an insurgent Republican, and as a Progressive Party leader, only to see the way to reform barred. World War I had given him a new chance to remake the world along democratic lines. Once more, White enlisted in the fight to change the world and America along with it, and he accepted the cost in terms of lives, national treasure, and civil liberties. The peace Woodrow Wilson negotiated at Versailles was an imperfect step forward in White's view, and he was sorry when the president's refusal to compromise killed the treaty in the Senate. White's arc from machine politics to crusading reformer was one shared by many in his cohort. Not every reformer who had enlisted during the Progressive Era would remain in the ranks long enough to see the triumph of liberalism in the 1930s, but they could all say they had tried to change the world. In the end, the war was like the Progressive Party. Neither offered any promises of victory; they only offered a chance to change the world. Neither campaign developed as White had hoped, but he found a new purpose as one of the few who kept the flames of reform alive during the conservative 1920s.

CHAPTER FIVE

A HARD-BOILED WORLD

William Allen White was fifty-two years old in 1920, and the world he found was far different from the one he had imagined when the doughboys marched to war in 1917. The US Senate had rejected the Treaty of Versailles, and with it President Woodrow Wilson's progressive vision of America as a democratizing force in the world. Congress also repealed the wartime economic measures that White had praised as one of the war's real accomplishments, such as the labor-friendly War Labor Board. The move was part of an aggressive retrenchment as businesses sought to return to prewar, antiworker policies such as the open shop, spurring more than 20 percent of American workers to go on strike in cities from Seattle to Boston. Labor's assertiveness, a wave of unsolved terrorist bombings, and the rise of Bolshevism around the world convinced many that the foundations of American society were under attack. Opportunistic politicians such as Seattle's mayor, Ole Hanson, and business organizations such as the National Civic Federation used anti-Bolshevik hysteria to bludgeon labor, and the press eagerly joined in with sensationalized propaganda about "radicalism." Meanwhile, President Wilson called on Congress to enact a permanent version of the wartime Sedition Act making it a criminal offense to criticize the government, which thankfully fell short of approval. White had seen the war's sacrifices as the necessary cost of establishing a democratic world order, but it seemed as though America had succumbed to "the materialistic philosophy, the philosophy of Nietzsche, against the philosophy of Christ." There was no telling how long the national fit of conservatism would last, and it proved to be far more enduring, virulent, and irresistible than he had feared.[1]

White had predicted that there would be a reaction against the progress that had been achieved during the World War, but he was stunned by the breadth and power of the Red Scare. Federal agents working for Attorney General A. Mitchell Palmer arrested four thousand suspected radicals, and the New York state legislature suspended five officeholders merely because they were socialists at the peak of the hysteria in January 1920. White was outraged, privately remarking that Americans had become so panic-stricken that they were "liable to out-Herod Herod" in their hunt for "Reds." He courageously denounced Palmer in the *Gazette* as "un-American" for targeting individuals who had merely exercised their constitutional right to advocate for a better world. In addition, he worked with other liberals to lobby President Wilson to pardon socialist leader Eugene V. Debs and the hundreds of other individuals who had been imprisoned for crimes of conscience during World War I. White cleverly turned the Red Scare to his advantage, claiming that the prisoners ought to be released because "a martyr in jail is worth more votes than ten soap box orators out of jail to the cause of radicalism." Wilson was deaf to such pleas, but they found a more receptive audience with his successor, President Warren G. Harding, who pardoned Debs and twenty-three other federal political prisoners in December 1921. Hundreds more remained in custody, and White continued lobbying on their behalf for several years as the tide of Red Scare hysteria receded.[2]

The tide of conservatism did not recede as quickly as that of the Red Scare, and liberals such as White had to persevere as voices in the wilderness much longer than they had hoped. Some liberals, such as Oswald Garrison Villard of the *Nation,* spent the 1920s as outcasts in hair shirts crying out for Americans to repent. White was not cut out for exile, and he began accommodating himself to the new conservative reality after a period of mourning. The Progressive Party's failure and the disappointing outcome of the war had taught him that slow change was preferable to no change, and he embraced his role as a liberal guerrilla. As White put it, "The world needs reforming. The curious thing about reform is that the fellow who has one idea or two or three ideas doesn't get forward with any of them but the fellow who dumps a basket full into the hopper gets a few of them out." He was able to make reasonable progress in a conservative age by engaging with conservatives on a personal level, by strategically leveraging public opinion, and by confining his policy efforts to a few issues, such as labor policy and US foreign policy.[3]

The political culture of the 1920s was considerably different from that which White had known, and not merely because the dominant ideology was conservative. For two decades, White had operated under a political dynamic that was driven by two exceptional people: Theodore Roosevelt and Woodrow Wilson. The curtain descended on both men in 1919. Roosevelt passed away on January 6, depriving White of a friend who had long inspired him with his dynamic political courage. Wilson survived the debilitating stroke he suffered on October 2, but he became ideologically rigid and incapable of exercising competent leadership. Neither the Democratic nor the Republican Party fielded a leader of even remotely comparable stature to the two fallen giants. Like many in Roosevelt's circle, White initially sought a successor in Roosevelt associate general Leonard Wood. He invested considerable effort in an attempt to nudge Wood toward a moderate platform, but the attempt failed after Wood strongly embraced the Red Scare. White was aghast, warning that "this crazy notion to hunt 'em down and shoot 'em, and see red, and all that sort of thing is going to pass during the Spring, and leave you high and dry."[4] Wood's candidacy fizzled as White had predicted, and White entered the 1920 presidential election cycle without a viable candidate to support.

Instead of backing a candidate, White focused his efforts on influencing the Republican platform. The Republican National Committee still feared that White and other disaffected reformers would bolt, and it sought to buy peace by including them in the party apparatus. RNC chairman Will Hays offered White a position on the newly formed Committee on Policies and Platforms, which was assigned to recommend platform planks to the Resolutions Committee at the national convention. White and other former Progressives complained that the committee's preliminary roster overemphasized conservatives who "haven't had an idea since the fall of Babylon and who, while they agree with the general justice of the fall of Babylon, think it was hasty and ill considered." He wrote Hays that midwestern reformers would fight if "the horse thieves of the Chicago Convention of 1912 are at all conspicuous." The implied threat of another bolt was effective. Hays expanded the committee and reserved more seats for former Progressives, and White accepted his appointment while working to coordinate the reform-minded members' activities. Ickes and several other former Progressives refused to do the same, and White might have been better served had he also declined. The committee workload and the emotional strain of the antiliberal political climate induced another bout of "nervous exhaustion" that caused him to "go to pieces" when he attempted to write.[5]

As usual, White attended the Republican National Convention as both a syndicated reporter and a delegate. White had editorially opposed Senator Harding's nomination in the months before the convention, but he served as part of a committee of internationalists who interviewed the dark-horse candidate about his foreign policy positions. Harding persuaded the delegation that his declared support for American participation in an "association of nations" was code for joining the League of Nations under certain conditions. White knew that Harding was a conservative and that he had been fiercely anti-Roosevelt in 1912, but White was a pragmatist who accepted Harding's inevitability given the political climate. White's friend and fellow delegate Ickes refused to do the same, citing Harding's harsh attitude toward the Bull Moose Progressives. Ickes rejected White's pleas to "be a sport" and tolerate the nominee, retorting that Harding was "a platitudinous jelly-fish" whose lack of "backbone" made him ripe for manipulation by business interests. While the nomination of a spineless machine politician like Harding left White "heart broken about politics," he noted that the Democratic candidate, conservative Ohio governor James M. Cox, was merely "Harding in Democrat terms." The choice was between two conservatives, and White found what solace he could in the fact that he had helped inject reform elements such as support for collective bargaining into a platform that was otherwise totally reactionary.[6]

The nation was in a "wallow of reaction," and White looked forward to making his summer escape to Colorado as soon as he had met his journalistic obligations. The Harding campaign took White's lack of enthusiasm seriously, and the candidate worked to build a rapport with White by asking him to visit Marion, Ohio. The invitation arrived during the short interval between White's return from California on July 10 and his departure for Colorado one week later, and he declined the offer. Instead, White cautioned Harding against misinterpreting his inevitable November victory. Americans would vote Republican because they opposed Cox, disliked Tammany Hall, and rejected the Democratic Party's stance on cultural issues such as Prohibition, not because they strongly agreed with the conservative Republicans. Reformers were angered by Republican boasts that the nation was heading "back to McKinleyism," and White asserted that they would abandon the GOP unless they saw progress. Still, he was persuaded that Harding sincerely wanted to treat the former Progressives fairly, and he was encouraged by the possibility that Hoover might be appointed to the cabinet. In the end, White believed that reformers would have to "hold our nose and take our medicine and bide our time" until a liberal savior emerged. He did his partisan duty in a preelection editorial by declaring that the contest was not about Cox or Harding, but whether the anti-Prohibition Democratic Party could be trusted with the White House. White's heart was not in the race, and he privately confessed that he was "low in my mind politically, but am coming through supporting the Republican ticket with about as much enthusiasm as a man has when he puts on his evening suit and goes out to usher at his best girl's wedding."[7]

White joined the sixteen million Americans who elected Harding overwhelmingly, but he took no pleasure in the victory. Although he congratulated Harding, White privately forecast that the conservatives would blockade necessary changes until the pressure became so great that the dam burst, resulting in real, permanent, and monumental progress. Harding owed his victory to the electorate's foul mood and anti-Wilson sentiment, a fact laid bare when White declined to help Franklin D. Roosevelt, the 1920 Democratic vice presidential candidate, raise funds for the newly established Woodrow Wilson Foundation. White had accepted FDR's request that he serve as state fundraising chairman for the Lighthouses for the Blind project, but he declined the Wilson Foundation job on the grounds that he could not ask donors to contribute to two different campaigns. Weeks later, White admitted that his main reason was that the public was in a "mean rattlesnake disposition" against Wilson that would make it difficult to solicit funds for a project bearing his name. The second anniversary of the armistice ending World War I occurred nine days after the election. White took the opportunity to decry the fact that Americans seemed to be "living in a hard boiled world" in which selfishness and greed replaced the hope, idealism, and national purpose of the war years. Liberals had "prayed to the living God for the fire to fall upon our altars, and they are cold. The prophets of Baal are triumphant. How long, O Lord, how long shall we await thy coming!"[8]

The pain of Harding's inauguration on March 20, 1921, paled in comparison to White's soul-crushing torment at his sixteen-year-old daughter Mary's death in a horse-riding accident on May 13. Mary had grown into a tomboyish teenager who shared her father's impish streak and poor grades, and she was both a handful and a joy to her parents. In contrast, White's twenty-year-old son, Bill, Jr., had become a student at Harvard University, inheriting both his mother's serious demeanor and his father's writing talent. White loved his daughter as dearly as he loved his son, but he had a special place in his heart for Mary because he had always wanted a daughter. Mr. and Mrs. White were naturally devastated, and White proposed taking Sallie for a vacation to the Rocky Mountains. Vacations in the Rockies had helped both of the Whites through many periods of mental and physical difficulty, but Sallie was too emotionally distraught to make the trip on this occasion. The pain of Mary's death lingered, and White confessed seven months later that the couple still spoke about their daughter often, mixing tears with smiles. As White explained to Hoover, Mary was "an exceptional child. Full of gaiety and joy and quip and persiflage, and of wisdom far beyond her years."

Victor Murdock played a crucial role in the Whites' emotional recovery when he sent his twenty-five-year-old daughter Marcia to stay with them that September. The mere presence of a bright, young, vivacious girl in the home was the best medicine for the Whites' malaise.[9]

White returned to something approaching normality within six months of Mary's death, but Sallie remained distraught over the loss of her daughter for many years. Vacations in the United States and overseas failed to cure her chronic depression. Murdock once again applied the salve of a young woman around the house in the summer of 1923 when he sent his seventeen-year-old daughter Katharine to stay with the Whites in Emporia and Colorado. Katharine was "a source of pure delight" for both Whites, but Sallie slipped back into a "nervous condition" as soon as she departed. Sallie's depression could be quite severe, as White discovered after returning from a two-week business trip to New York City in May 1926. He was horrified to find Sallie bedridden and extremely depressed, and he confided to Henry Allen that "every day she grieves, being alone, and uses up her nervous energy." The incident left White so fearful for his wife's safety that he declined an invitation to visit Allen in nearby Wichita because it was too dangerous to leave Sallie alone for even a few hours. Sallie's doctor in Emporia found nothing physically wrong with her, and the Whites traveled to the Mayo Clinic in Minnesota in the futile hope of finding a medical solution for her psychological condition. Time proved to be the only treatment, and Sallie spent most of the 1920s in mourning.[10]

White's emotional recovery was one prerequisite for his reentry to political life, but he also had to come to grips with the fact that he was a liberal in a conservative age. The strategies White had employed during the Progressive Era had to be modified, and by 1922 he had settled on a strategy that employed personal engagement with conservative leaders combined with efforts to shape public opinion. The strategy took shape after White had observed Harding for a year, and he presented his observations in a *Collier's* article. White argued that the president had abandoned the Roosevelt and Wilson leadership style of powerful, ideologically driven chief executives working in

The Whites' two children in 1910: William Lindsay White, born in 1900, and Mary Katherine White, born in 1904. Courtesy of Emporia State University, Special Collections and Archives.

close collaboration with public intellectuals. Instead, he emphasized Harding's background as a machine politician and as a member of a "Senatorial syndicate" of allied politicians. Harding was like any other machine politician with legislative rather than executive experience, in that he was guided by the practical need to balance public opinion and triangulate between various interest groups. Consequently, Harding had no organic interest in new ideas. White postulated that those who wanted change could go directly to the people, generate pressure on the administration through public opinion, and spur action. Furthering this dynamic was the fact that both political parties were heavily fragmented. As White succinctly put it, the Democrats were "held together by fear of negro domination in the South and by fear of Puritan rule in the great cities, while the other party is held together by the property-minded agricultural voters of the West, who desire to make the big Eastern industrial captains disgorge, and those same big Eastern industrial leaders who wish to make the Western farmers disgorge." The politics of fragmentation meant that great things could be achieved by a relatively small group of liberal guerrillas skilled at leveraging public opinion, and White became adept at using this tactic to achieve outsized influence in a conservative decade.[11]

White had found an outsider's strategy to effect change, and he refused to chase chimeras such as another bite at the apple of a liberal third party. As a pragmatist, White knew he was "classed as a liberal Republican, more liberal than Republican" in a period dominated by conservatism. The Senate's reform-minded members were reelected in 1922 despite facing conservative challengers, and White suggested that the liberal senators establish an informal, bipartisan bloc to advance reform. However, he rejected a suggestion from Villard and other members of the "New York intelligentsia" that the 1922 election showed that the time was right for another attempt at a third party. Wistfully, he editorialized that "whenever a Bull Mooser hears talk of a third party he whistles softly and sadly and remembers that it was the last straw vote [at the 1916 Progressive Party convention] that broke the camel's back." In a conservative era, White felt it most productive to tack toward the moderate policies that he felt that

Commerce Secretary Hoover and Senators Arthur Capper (R-KS), George W. Norris (R-NE), and William E. Borah (R-ID) embodied.[12]

The fact that White had accommodated himself to the reality of the decade's conservative politics did not help mitigate the highly frustrating nature of the experience. The occasional moments of electoral rebellion against the conservative order, centered primarily in the Upper Midwest, reminded White of the periodic protest movements that characterized the region in the late nineteenth century. Farm movements such as the Grangers and the Greenbackers had been "little isolated dust storms on the desert, whirling spitefully, but meaning little except as evidence of a gathering storm which is not yet even upon the horizon." It was obvious to White that "the nation has not yet been shocked out of its materialism," because the "little isolated dust storms on the desert" erupted when times were hard and disappeared as soon as prosperity returned. The popularity of conservative politicians such as Harding or Calvin Coolidge helped deflect the kind of national shame that the lack of social justice in America might have stimulated, according to White. In particular, he noted that Coolidge was "a tremendous shock absorber. His emotionless attitude is an anesthetic to a national conviction of sin which must come before a genuine repentance." It was tremendously frustrating to White to "sit in my office and write unimportant editorials and go to my house and write unimportant books," when he wanted to "get out and raise hell for righteousness!"[13]

Of course, White's editorials, books, and articles were far from unimportant, and his ability to offer sincere advice to those with whom he disagreed politically meant that his friendship was valued even in a conservative White House. Harding and White shared a common background as small-town, midwestern newspaper publishers of approximately the same age. Indeed, Harding's ability to commiserate about his own *Marion Star* and White's *Emporia Gazette* gave him the opening he needed to overcome White's initial reluctance to engage. The two men gradually established a real friendship, and White was occasionally able to present his reform ideas to the president. As much as Harding wished White would come around to his way of thinking, the president expressed his gratitude for the fact that White gave him his honest opinion about political developments. White also provided Harding with trustworthy companionship as members of the administration became immersed in scandal and corruption. It was White to whom the president famously bemoaned his "Goddamn friends, White, they're the ones that keep me walking the floor nights!"[14]

President Harding's sudden death in 1923 elevated Vice President Coolidge to the Oval Office, and he also sought and received White's friendship. Like many Americans, White knew little about the famously colorless Coolidge when he took office, but he was inclined against the new president because he was worshipped by the conservative Republican establishment. Once again, a conservative president recognized White's value as a friend and advisor, and the administration cultivated him soon after Harding's death. White ultimately endorsed Coolidge for reelection in 1924 even though he saw the president as a "whirling dervish of business" who was "candidly, and with a certain amount of vanity, proud of his belief that property should rule." The facts were that the electorate was conservative, that Coolidge's puritanical persona allowed him to ignore structural inequality, and that the average man during the decade "imagines himself politically a rich man going down a dark road on a rough night with thugs in every corner." The Democratic nominee, John Davis, was also a conservative, and White pragmatically accepted Coolidge as "the best that the times will permit." Coolidge's reelection would not change the fact that the Republicans were divided into two factions: Senator Charles Curtis (R-KS) led the conservatives, Borah led the liberals, and White believed that reformers still had a say in public affairs because Coolidge needed both factions to govern.[15] In essence, White had devised an inside-outsider strategy: he was simultaneously whispering into the ears of presidents and helping rally the crowds beyond the gates by molding public opinion.

The strategy White devised was employed in three main areas during the 1920s: Kansas's industrial policy, American foreign policy,

Aboard the presidential yacht Mayflower, *1924. President Calvin Coolidge stands on the left, and White is the second man on the right. Courtesy of Emporia State University, Special Collections and Archives.*

and the 1920s culture war. The issue of Kansas's labor policy was closest at hand and the first to emerge, making it the first area where White deployed his ideas about advancing change in a conservative age. White was supportive of organized labor even at the height of the Red Scare, editorially endorsing the Boston police officers when they went on strike in September 1919. Public safety, education, and communications workers ought to operate under a grand bargain in which they gave up their right to strike in exchange for recognition as "a distinct industrial class" with generous compensation, White argued. The editor had hoped that President Wilson's attempt to address labor unrest with his 1919 Industrial Conference in Washington, DC, would craft an accord of this nature for America's largest industries. Instead, the conference ended in failure, violence erupted in the national steel strike, and a national coal strike loomed at the end of October. White was shattered, remarking that America was going through "the worst case of social belly ache" he had ever seen. The chill of winter was already in the air when the threatened coal strike erupted on November 1, and White blamed both sides for the dire energy shortage. The mine owners were "a rather contemptuous and cynical group of labor baiters," but he also felt that the coal miners had harmed the public by striking. The plain fact was that labor and capital were at war, and "under the war-like policies of both, the public suffers." Like many Progressives, White enshrined his own middle class as "the people," and he held them up as "neither capitalists nor laborers, but consumers of the products of both before they are supporters of either." Since both labor and capital were "running amuck," White believed that the time had come for the people's government to settle industrial unrest in the interest of the supposedly neutral, consuming public.[16]

Coal supplies were quickly exhausted throughout Kansas by late November, and the strike became a life-and-death issue as hospitals starved for heat in the paralyzing winter cold. Both White and Kansas's governor, Henry J. Allen, were convinced that the state needed to force both labor and capital to bend to their definition of the public good. The governor commandeered the state's coal mines, called for citizen volunteers, paid them five dollars per day, and operated several strip mines for three weeks until supplies were replenished. The national coal strike was settled on December 10 after the Wilson administration began prosecuting United Mine Workers officials, but unrelated wildcat strikes persisted in Kansas. Although he defended labor's right to strike and criticized those who called every striker a "mad Bolshevist who wants to destroy government," White thought that labor was harming its cause by striking at a time when antiunion hysteria was at a fever pitch. Liberals were generally disheartened by the government's role in repressing labor, but White's faith in government's ability to craft a fair resolution to the labor question was undiminished. First, he believed in Governor Allen, and second, he believed that both labor and the public would come to their senses once the hysteria of the Red Scare had subsided.[17]

Governor Allen, with White's active collaboration, responded to the industrial situation by proposing a state "industrial court" empowered to investigate and adjudicate disputes in the public interest. The court would have broad jurisdiction over businesses in five essential industries: food, clothing, mining, utilities, and transportation. Primarily, the court was designed to cultivate voluntary settlements between disputing parties based on an impartial investigation of the facts, but it also had the power to compel obedience from recalcitrant parties. Specifically, the law banned lockouts, strikes, boycotts, and picketing. The idea embodied White's vision of a grand bargain where workers surrendered the right to strike in exchange for fair wages and treatment, while capital surrendered its absolute control in the workplace in exchange for a fair return on its investment. White testified before the state legislature that the court would civilize labor relations, but Kansas's unions were fiercely opposed to it because they did not trust government to protect their interests. The measure passed nearly unanimously on January 23, and White celebrated the idea that labor had been recognized as "a partner and not a slave." The Kansas idea soon attracted national attention, and the liberal journal *Nation* called it a "contagion" that threatened to spread from state to state. Both Allen and White were tireless proselytizers for a national industrial court, and Allen even publicly debated the idea with American Federation of Labor president Samuel Gompers. Meanwhile, the US Supreme Court issued a ruling in the 1921 Tri City case that allowed states to all but ban peaceful picketing.[18]

Organized labor denounced the Industrial Court as "slavery" because it stripped unions of their right to strike, and a mystified White regularly used his editorials to try to persuade labor that the court was a friend. For example, White pointed to one of the court's rulings granting workers higher wages as proof that the law was prolabor. The court's decision was based on the law's mandate that workers receive a fair wage, but White was oblivious to the fact that the court's concept of a fair wage was highly subjective. The Industrial Court examined factors such as the type of work involved, the inherent dangers of such work, the prevailing wages in the industry, and the cost of living, but it also included an assessment of "the fidelity of the individual employee." The ruling explained that "the worker who is faithful to his trust . . . is entitled . . . to a greater reward than the worker who thinks only of his wage and not of the interest of his employer and of the public." The idea was very progressive, because Progressives believed that rights ought to be based on obligations. Labor's wages were to be set by upper-middle-class judges based in part on ambiguous standards that could be exploited to force the workers into a subservient position. White's blindness to this fact was based on his optimistic view of human nature. Basic humanity would spur the Industrial Court's judges to side with the rights of workers who had to toil to survive over the rights of business owners who already had plenty. Furthermore, he argued that labor needed a powerful government body to protect its right to organize against "highly organized and ruthless capital" seeking to crush unions through the open shop campaign.[19]

Ironically, capital also viewed the Industrial Court as a middle-class "usurpation—government without the consent of the governed," but White saw business's opposition as proof that the law was needed. The "Associated Industries," an organization of approximately six hundred Kansas businesses, represented the Wolff Packing Company in a legal assault on the Industrial Court beginning in January 1921. The Associated Industries' argument was that the court confiscated capital because it forced industries to operate under wages and operating conditions set by the government. White saw this attack as the most serious threat to the court, and he accepted an invitation to explain the measure in the Chamber of Commerce's publication the *Nation's Business,* which he described as "a hard-boiled, reactionary magazine." The court's objective was not to establish industrial peace, he explained, because "the right to peace depends upon the establishment of justice." Justice was the Industrial Court's only goal, and White expressed his support for the institution "not for what it has done, though it has done well, but for what it must do."[20]

The Great Railroad Strike of 1922 finally eviscerated White's progressive illusions about industrial conflict. The strike had its origin in cuts to wages and working conditions for employees in the railroads' rolling stock repair shops. The railroad companies could only enact such changes with the consent of the Federal Railway Labor Board (RLB), which President Harding's administration had stacked with antilabor representatives. The various unions that represented railroad workers united in defense of the shopworkers when they called a strike for October 30, 1921, and White agreed that the workers' cause was just. However, he advised them not to strike because he believed that they could earn more support by presenting their case to a just public than they could by holding the public hostage through a strike. The strike threat evaporated because the RLB promised to shelter the four biggest railroad workers' unions from the cuts, and the shopmen refused to strike without the "Big Four." The stars were aligned against the shopmen when the RLB approved another wage cut on June 6, 1922, based on the railroads' plea of financial distress, even as their profit margins soared. The shopmen's union called a strike for July 1, but the powerful Big Four once again refused to participate because the RLB had not cut their wages.[21]

The RLB's action outraged White, who exclaimed that the board had "buried the hatchet in the back of labor" by breaking its 1920 promise of a living wage. He solemnly declared that "that guarantee was a contract" and warned that there would be violence in this "nasty little civil war called a strike." Two miners and nineteen strikebreakers had recently been killed at Herrin, Illinois, in a coincidental national coal strike, and White printed both the Associated Press and the labor press accounts of the massacre. Governor Allen entirely blamed the miners for the violence, and he was dismayed that White had reprinted what he deemed to be labor's "exultant note over the bloody victory of the miners." White was unapologetic, retorting in the *Gazette* that "we have civil war in this country, and now we're going to have reprisals and poison gas, and shooting of prisoners of war, and mopping up and all the rest of it, and until the public is prepared to establish justice it can't have peace." Justice meant paying a living wage while guaranteeing business a fair profit, but White complained to Allen that "capital wants your court merely to establish peace and to take away the right to strike."[22]

The Great Railroad Strike began when four hundred thousand shopmen walked off the job on July 1, and White focused on the injustice the workers faced in pursuing their cause. The RLB declared that the strikers were no longer employees two days later, which freed the railroads to use strikebreakers and impose company unions. Emporia was home to a Santa Fe Railroad repair shop employing about a hundred of the nearly ten thousand shopmen in Kansas, and White asked his neighbors to remember that both the striking workers and the railroad were pillars of the community. However, he clearly sympathized with the strikers, and he was indignant that the RLB had broken its compact with labor, refused to hear their appeal, and declared them "outlaws" with lightning speed, while the railroads had paid no penalty for habitually ignoring the RLB. White advised the governor to remember that "labor is human beings" and not a commodity, and he wrote an editorial on July 8 pointing out that the striking railroad workers had hungry families to feed. The men did not have the luxury of waiting for a government board or public opinion to force capital to provide fair treatment. The governor circled a passage in which White stated that when their funds ran out, the strikers "will not be polite. Whereupon some of us will be shocked; forgetting that in his place we would do the same thing. Next week will see developments."[23]

Allen wanted to maintain order at all costs, and White's prolabor editorials were published precisely as the governor was dispatching troops in response to reports that violence was imminent. For instance, the mayor of the town of Parsons, Kansas, was a former shopman who armed sixty strikers, deputized them, and allowed them to harass railroad operations. Governor Allen guaranteed state protection to the railroads and issued felony warrants against a number of strikers for violating the Industrial Court law's picketing ban, which yielded the railroads' tremendous appreciation. The governor also rebuked White for his July 8 editorial, which he felt was sure to encourage the strikers in their violent designs. Allen warned White that there was "murder in the hearts of some of them. Don't get too far over." Although White sympathized with his friend for the difficult choices he faced as governor, he retorted that either of them would "tip over a few cars and burn them and snipe a few scabs" if they found themselves fighting an injustice while worrying about feeding their children. Allen rejected White's claim that the workers were in dire straits, instead choosing to believe the railroads' old data purporting to show that the shopmen were overpaid. He warned White that his editorials were making him "dangerous at a time like this when given a double action typewriter . . . and I think you are more dangerous at that than you realize." White reduced their disagreement to the fact that "I think the men ought to win and you think they ought to lose."[24]

White got "too far over" on July 19, after the governor invoked the Industrial Relations Act's antipicketing provisions to outlaw union-distributed placards that many town merchants had hung in their windows reading "We are for the striking railroad men one hundred percent." The Industrial Court's judges interpreted the term "picketing" as "any form of action which tends to prevent the orderly and efficient operation of a business enterprise," and more than two hundred labor leaders were arrested under this interpretation. Angered, White hung a union placard in his window that he had altered to read "We are for the striking railroad men forty-nine percent," intending to add one percent for every day that the strike lasted. His support invigorated the workers. One local union leader exclaimed, "Three cheers for William Allen White," and another stated, "It is refreshing to see a man of Mr. White's prominence come out for the fundamental principles upon which this government was founded." Strike committees circulated copies of the *Gazette* to local merchants to persuade them to replace their placards, and many did. Governor Allen ordered White's arrest on July 22 for "entering into a conspiracy to encourage strikers to interfere with transportation," and White appealed for all sides to pursue their goals peacefully. The law's antipicketing provisions were the central issue for White because they

The sign that got White arrested for "picketing" when he hung it in the Gazette's window during the Great Railroad Strike of 1922. Courtesy of Kenneth Spencer Research Library, University of Kansas Libraries.

denied workers a voice to counter the press's antilabor propaganda. Allen allowed White to place another sign in his window declaring that the governor "believes that peace is more important than justice, and I believe that justice is the only thing that will bring peace."[25]

White won the 1923 Pulitzer Prize for Editorial Writing for his piece "To an Anxious Friend," which summed up his position as "you say that freedom of utterance is not for time of stress, and I reply with the sad truth that only in time of stress is freedom of utterance in danger." The editorial was widely reprinted, and White published responses from the *New York World* and other major newspapers endorsing his stand. Letters of support followed from national groups and figures such as the American Civil Liberties Union, Senator Borah, and Harvard law professor Felix Frankfurter, who wrote White exclaiming, "Thank God we've got some people left with old fashioned guts!" Frankfurter and Borah also pledged to write amicus briefs on White's behalf if the case reached the Supreme Court. Many Kansans supported the governor because they saw no reason for defiance of the law, and White was inclined to temper his words when he discovered that his middle-class neighbors "immediately shrink from freedom and call it license." For his part, Allen complained that many out-of-state newspapers were "jumping at the conclusion that Kansas has assaulted free speech." The governor felt that White's action had obstructed the right to work, which he called "a freedom that ought to be as precious as the freedom of speech." Allen grumbled that White had allowed his heart to overtake his head, and he complained to one correspondent that "Will . . . always had a tendency towards socialism and this has very much affected his attitude in this strike."[26]

The strike persisted through the summer, and President Harding made a genuine effort to use the government as an "honest broker" between the warring parties. He directed Commerce Secretary Hoover to work to arrange a settlement, but after weeks of impasse the president turned to Attorney General Harry Daugherty to end the strike by force. Daugherty was fiercely antilabor, and he obtained a federal injunction in September that prohibited the shopmen's union from interfering in railroad operations. The attorney general promised to "destroy the unions" if necessary to crush a supposed labor conspiracy against the American government and the open shop. Meanwhile, Governor Allen proudly noted that his enforcement of Kansas's antipicketing law had undermined the strike by allowing the railroads to use "Kansas as a sort of mobilization point in which their engines are repaired and their personnel selected for the entire system." Disturbingly, White's twenty-two-year-old son, Bill, following in his father's footsteps as a cub reporter during his summer vacation from Harvard, noted that Emporia's middle-class merchants had begun to see the strikers as "radicals" who ought to accept the railroad's terms as soon as the workers began asking for credit to buy staples.[27]

The Great Railroad Strike was speeding toward its conclusion, and White had learned a great deal about labor relations in America. For the first time, he acknowledged that "the strike is labor's only weapon" because society had allowed it no other means of obtaining fair treatment. Government could play an important role in helping resolve industrial disputes, but only after it was given enough power to force capital to obey the law. Strikes were justified because they were part of the conversation between labor and capital about wages, and a striking worker had an "inherent right to the job while he is discussing with his employer the wages which his job should pay." Crucially, White acknowledged for the first time that the middle class had "just one attitude toward labor: down with it, spit on it, to 'ell with it." The working class was increasingly isolated because the middle class was inconvenienced by strike disruptions and bombarded with sensationalized newspaper propaganda about labor's supposed radicalism. There was much truth in this statement. As Walter Lippmann explained, newspapers assigned qualified men to report on sports, politics, and business, but "wage questions and matters of industrial relations are handled by almost anybody, very frequently by the person who normally reports riots." White's theories about the Industrial Court were based on the idea that the middle class could be trusted to stand between labor and capital, and his admission that the middle class was capable of acting unfairly meant that the court idea was bankrupt.[28]

Daugherty's injunction broke the strike, and the shopmen were left with no other choice but to make what agreements they could with the railroads on September 13. However, the case of *Kansas v. White* still had to be resolved. Many observers wrongly concluded that White and Allen had staged the affair because the two men remained friends, and they appeared together at an event at Emporia State University to avoid the "entirely erroneous impression" that they were at personal odds. Allen and White agreed that his case would be brought before the Kansas Supreme Court to clarify what "picketing" meant under the law. The governor interceded to prevent the attorney general from dropping the charges on the grounds of triviality, and he arranged a meeting in his home between White and a Kansas Supreme Court justice to discuss legal strategy. However, Allen ultimately concluded that the law was likely to be overturned, and he convinced the trial court to dismiss the case on December 9. The *New York Times* quipped that "a Kansas court is the only place in the universe where [White] can't make himself heard," but White was aghast. Although White and Allen's personal friendship endured, the developments ended their political alliance. White remained bitter that Allen had "ditched me on the test of the anti-strike law. I was never so deeply hurt in all my career in politics as I was by his ruthless behavior at that time."[29]

The Industrial Court carried on in the meantime, but White's prediction that capital would kill the court was correct. The US Supreme Court invalidated the Industrial Court's wage-fixing powers as a violation of property rights on June 11, 1923, although the Industrial Court retained the power to suppress strikes. White observed that the court, stripped of its power to protect labor, was now "merely a labor baiting agency." Labor had played by society's rules in an attempt to obtain justice, and its only reward was to be attacked as "radical." The strike was the only weapon in labor's arsenal, and he now saw organized labor as the vital "balance wheel of our politics. Vastly safer

On campus at Emporia Normal, which was later renamed Emporia State University. White appeared with Allen at this event to prove that the two men were not at personal odds. Left to right: college president Thomas Butcher, White, and Governor Henry J. Allen, July 19, 1922. Courtesy of Kenneth Spencer Research Library, University of Kansas Libraries.

than organized capital." The US Supreme Court finally eviscerated the remainder of the Industrial Court as a violation of property rights in April 1925, but the Great Railroad Strike had dispelled White's progressive illusions nearly three years earlier.[30]

The Industrial Court was the apogee of Progressive Era thinking that envisioned a conflict-free society where "special interests" were made to bow to an all-encompassing "public interest." The court was a distinctively progressive attempt to resolve the labor question, but like many reformers, White was blind to the fact that industrial disputes could not be resolved through simple adjudication. The Great Railroad Strike forced him to recognize that capital controlled the machinery of the state, the middle class disdained the working class, and both preferred industrial order through repression over industrial peace through justice. White realized that labor could not be denied its only means of obtaining full citizenship when society would not treat it fairly, and he no longer saw courts as a substitute for strikes. The middle class was capable of endorsing a profound government role in the economy so long as it was persuaded that it stood to benefit from such measures. It was White's mission to enlighten his middle-class neighbors around the country to the fact that their prosperity was entwined with that of labor. Ultimately, the crisis of the Great Depression spurred White's vision of an industrial policy that sought to channel rather than dam conflict. The Wagner Act of 1935 codified White's values by unambiguously guaranteeing labor's right to organize, bargain collectively, and picket, and the "inalienable right to strike if necessary, . . . without the interference of police, militia or boss."[31]

Foreign policy was a second area where White was able to use his guerrilla strategy to exert outsized influence in a conservative era. The Senate's rejection of the Treaty of Versailles had not changed the fact that America was more involved in world affairs than ever, and White remained a strong internationalist. He likened the world to a small-town American neighborhood writ large, with each "nation [a]s somewhat like a family." Each family naturally saw itself as the best on the block, but it also had to accept the goodness of other families if it wanted to be accepted as part of the community. Similarly, White felt that America ought to "develop according to our own customs, our own blood, our own traditions," without treating other nations as if "we have the only customs, the only blood, the only traditions worthy of being preserved." Fortunately, the Harding and Coolidge administrations had little interest in foreign policy, and on such matters they tended to defer to their secretaries of state, Charles Evans Hughes and Frank B. Kellogg. The fact that foreign policy was decentralized gave White and his allies an opportunity to use public opinion to advance international cooperation by small degrees.[32]

Disarmament was the most important issue reformers addressed in the immediate aftermath of the Senate's refusal to ratify the Treaty of Versailles. The naval arms race had been one of the causes of the war, and many nations still had warships under construction after the armistice. No nation was willing to be the first to reduce its construction program, and some feared that the naval arms race would lead to a second world war. Senator Borah acted boldly by introducing a Senate resolution on December 14, 1920, that authorized the president to invite Great Britain and Japan to a conference to limit warship construction for five years. The incoming Harding administration resented Borah's interference and resisted his proposal in Congress for several months, but the idea had broad appeal. White strongly supported it as a first step toward the inevitable banding together of the world's democracies. Other reformers embraced disarmament as an antiwar proposition, and the business community supported it as an austerity measure that would lead to lower taxes. The Harding administration finally bowed to public opinion, and the State Department invited Britain, Japan, Italy, and France to attend a conference in Washington, DC, to begin on November 11.[33]

The Washington Naval Conference cheered the liberal ranks, and White proclaimed that the reduction of arms would be one of the greatest imaginable advances in human history by freeing nations to reallocate defense funds to social spending. Privately, he wondered whether disarmament was achievable, but Borah assured him that it was as long as reformers led the way. White attended the conference as a reporter when it opened on November 12, 1921, as he had the Versailles Peace Conference in 1919. The two conferences could not have been more different, beginning with the delegations' attire: the Versailles conference was a European-style top-hat-and-coattails affair, while White observed that the Washington conference was dominated by enterprising Americans in business suits. Another key difference between the two conferences was that Versailles had been closed to the press, while the Washington conference was open. Third, White favorably contrasted Secretary of State Hughes's willingness to build consensus by rubbing elbows with foreign delegations with Wilson's aloof style at Versailles. The Hughes approach paid off when the conference endorsed his proposal for a ten-year naval construction holiday that included scrapping many of the world's newest and most powerful warships.[34]

The Washington conference produced several treaties, but the most important were the Four Power and Five Power Treaties that were announced in mid-December 1921. The Five Power Treaty mandated a naval tonnage ratio of 5:5:3:1.7:1.7 between the United States, Great Britain, Japan, France, and Italy, respectively. The Four Power Treaty committed the United States, Great Britain, Japan, and France to maintain the status quo in Asia, and the signatories pledged to confer in the event of war. The treaties were an important first step toward further disarmament and internationalism in White's view, although he conceded that the treaties functioned as an "Anglo-Saxon Alliance to underwrite the safety of the white man against the yellow and brown." By this, White meant that the Washington treaties would insulate the West against war in the developing world by resolving Great Power colonial disputes before they could escalate into larger conflicts.[35]

A second impact of the Washington conference was that White and other liberals discovered that they had a shared agenda with business Republicans such as Hughes, who wanted to establish international legal structures that would facilitate commerce. White strongly supported the Harding administration's 1923 proposal to join the World Court, a legal tribunal created by the Treaty of Versailles to settle international disputes. Countries could join the World Court without joining the League of Nations, and the administration explained that membership would aid American businesses by codifying the rules of international exchange. White embraced the World Court for the same reason he embraced the Kansas Industrial Court: both were attempts to create civilized forums where disputes could be adjudicated in the light of impartial law. Borah and the other senators who had opposed the Treaty of Versailles also opposed the World Court, but White argued that the body was a fair compromise between giving America a say in world affairs and avoiding entangling obligations. Regardless, White hoped that President Harding would not allow "a few malcontents in his own party who have no plan for world peace, but American isolation" to control his foreign policy.[36] Despite the administration's and White's support, Borah and the Senate's isolationists were able to ensure that the United States never ratified the World Court protocol.

Coolidge shared Harding's disinterest in foreign policy, and the same dynamic that had allowed White to exercise influence on foreign policy continued under the new administration. White used his friendship with Coolidge to ask him to work with Borah, who had risen to the chairmanship of the Senate Foreign Relations Committee in November 1924. Although White disagreed with Borah's opposition to American membership in international organizations, he was pleased by the senator's ascension because he still held him in high regard on other foreign policy questions. Despite White's request that Coolidge "endeavor to work out some kind of a definite foreign policy" with Borah, the president's disinterest in foreign policy matters prevented any such collaboration. White observed this dynamic firsthand as a guest at one of the president's frequent White House breakfasts, which were Coolidge's idea of an outreach gesture. Unfortunately, the president never made a serious attempt to interact with his guests, and many congressmen came to regard them as a waste of time. Borah and several members of the Senate Foreign Relations Committee gave a detailed presentation on American foreign relations during the breakfast White attended. He was astounded when Coolidge's only response was, "Were the crullers all right this morning?"[37]

America's relationship with the developing world was the foreign policy issue that absorbed White's interest the most during the mid-1920s. White had opposed the Spanish-American War of 1898 partly on anti-imperialist grounds, and he had embraced the Wilsonian concept that nations ought to have the right to determine their own destinies during World War I. His extensive travels in the developing world during the 1920s strengthened his sympathy for nations asserting their right to national self-determination. The Whites' two-month Mediterranean cruise was a particularly transformative experience. The couple embarked aboard the RMS *Mauretania* from New York City on February 7, 1923, partly motivated by a desire to escape the crushing emotional burden of Mary's tragic death in 1921. The *Mauretania*'s ports of call included the Azores, Spain, North Africa, Italy, Greece, Turkey, Palestine, Egypt, Corsica, Portugal, and England, giving White an opportunity to visit several Middle Eastern nations under European imperial control. White observed that "the intelligent Mohammadian sees how far Christianity falls short of its ideals," and it struck him as "insanely odd that Christendom should still insist upon force rather than reason" because Muslims far outnumbered Westerners in the world. He observed Turkey undergoing a dramatic modernization under secular nationalist Mustafa Kemal, and he praised Kemal's wife, Latife, as "a miracle of modernism" who "speaks in public and Turks listen." The Christian Church of the Holy Sepulcher in Jerusalem offended White as a gaudy architectural "horror," but the Islamic Mosque of Omar struck him as the city's most beautiful building. In Egypt, White talked politics with four middle-class Egyptian professionals who "looked for all the world like a group of Bull Moosers" except for their brown complexions and their fezzes. The issues they discussed revolved around sovereignty, such as the capitulations giving Britain the right to administer justice for foreigners and "dissatisfied minorities."[38]

Of course, White also had his critique of the Middle East. For the most part, White found that Muslim women were treated poorly, as if they had "no souls, and they are tolerated for breeding purposes chiefly." The region was a bubbling cauldron of racial and religious animosities, but so was America during the 1920s. White was careful to qualify his criticism by stating that "hate based on fear is at the bottom of a lot of political movements. And cowardice taking a highly moral ground also has its place in history as the inspiration of moral causes." He sarcastically described Egypt as a paradise for conservatives. Anyone who thought that "there is too much government in our life" ought to visit "the sweet realization of his blessed ideal" with its "low taxes, high rents, cheap labor, little government, and

White in pith helmet, Sallie, and Mr. and Mrs. Victor Murdock at Giza, Egypt, during their Mediterranean cruise in 1923. Courtesy of Emporia State University, Special Collections and Archives.

native justice for those who have the price." Palestinian Arabs made an unfavorable impression. To White, they were cousins to America's Mexican American population as groups who had "come about so far along the road of progress and have stopped to snooze." All in all, White felt that British occupation of Palestine and Egypt was not all bad because it would help civilize, modernize, and develop what would otherwise remain a backward region. White's Middle Eastern visit was the first of many to the developing world, and he also subsequently engaged in a variety of conferences, delegations, and other activities designed to cultivate international relations.[39]

White's anti-imperialist tendencies and his sympathy for revolutionary nationalism drove him to directly challenge the Republican foreign policy establishment on US–Latin American relations.

American troops had occupied Nicaragua on several occasions beginning in 1909, and President Coolidge ordered another deployment
after civil war erupted in mid-1926. American forces were sent to
strategic points in the country, where they allowed free movement
to the side the State Department favored while denying the same to
their opponents. Secretary of State Kellogg justified the intervention
by telling Congress that the Nicaraguan crisis was the product of
a vast Soviet-inspired Mexican conspiracy to control Latin America.
The Mexicans were aiding their chosen side in Nicaragua just as the
Americans were, but the proposition that Mexico was the cat's paw
for a massive Soviet conspiracy was widely ridiculed. White had been
on vacation overseas for much of late 1926, and he returned to the
United States just as Kellogg was giving his testimony to Congress in
January 1927. White straddled the question of blame in the *Gazette*
while upholding the concept of national self-determination, criticizing both Mexico and the United States for meddling in Nicaragua's
right to determine its own destiny. Since both were guilty, White
called for Mexico and the United States to cosponsor free elections
in Nicaragua, although he posited that the State Department would
never agree to the proposition.[40]

The public pressure generated by White and his congressional allies, including Senators Borah, Norris, and Hiram Johnson (R-CA),
helped spur the Coolidge administration to change course. The administration brokered a power-sharing arrangement between the
warring factions that most Nicaraguan forces accepted in April 1927.
The conflict continued on a lesser scale because a small group of
soldiers led by Nicaraguan general Augusto Sandino rejected the
settlement, and White continued to denounce the occupation in the
Gazette. Unfortunately, interest in Latin American affairs waned after
the administration's settlement, and White complained that developments that had once produced a chorus of condemnation now yielded
from "the liberal press only an exhausted ripple of sympathy."[41]

White and his liberal allies enjoyed much greater success in their
campaign for a qualified candidate to replace the retiring US ambassador to Mexico, James Sheffield. US-Mexican relations had been

strained since the Mexican Revolution, and the status of American oil and mining claims in Mexico was a significant problem. Ambassador Sheffield was an abrasive man who was openly contemptuous of the Mexican people, whom he regarded as an inferior race, and his aggressive efforts on behalf of American investors only magnified tensions between the two nations. President Coolidge shared Sheffield's view of the Mexican people, but the latter's retirement created an opportunity for liberals to advance a more suitable man. Foreign Relations Committee chairman Borah asked White if he would allow his name to be considered for the post. White believed that America's interventionist foreign policy naturally conflicted with revolutionary nationalism, and that American mantras of property rights and contractual obligations had blinded many to this truth. Americans needed to accept that their cousins to the south had every right to define their own culture, even though White saw many aspects of Latin American culture as inferior. Nevertheless, he declined Borah's invitation on the grounds that he could not be effective in the post, since the diplomatic corps was filled with "a lot of property minded, routine bound young sons-in-law with the diplomatic tradition encrusted upon them so heavily that they . . . would regard me as a wild ass of the desert."[42]

Ironically, White and other liberals who had railed against the influence of Wall Street in American foreign policy found their ambassadorial candidate in an executive at the House of Morgan, Dwight Morrow. While the oil firms demanded a hard line toward Mexico in order to protect their drilling claims, the interests of Wall Street financiers and American exporters were better served by stable relations with Latin America. Morrow had a reputation as a fair, amiable, public-minded individual, and he was one of President Coolidge's classmates at Amherst in the 1890s. Senator Borah's support was crucial if Morrow expected to be confirmed for the position, but Borah was initially suspicious of Morrow's Wall Street connections. Morrow was friends with Walter Lippmann, who lobbied Borah on his behalf and likely asked the candidate to write to White as well, given the latter's friendship with the senator. White and Morrow corresponded prior to the confirmation hearings, and they agreed that American relations with Latin America constituted the most important foreign policy question facing the United States. He eagerly explained to Morrow that financial imperialism and cultural misunderstandings were at the root of the United States' incessant conflicts with Latin America, and he hoped to infuse the candidate with liberal sympathies for "the semi-backward people" of Latin America and Asia. Liberal support for Morrow helped persuade Borah that he was a good choice to improve relations between the two nations, and he was confirmed. The new ambassador presented his credentials in Mexico City in late October, and Lippmann informed Morrow that Borah had become one of his strongest supporters in Washington by December.[43]

Ambassador Morrow was immediately effective at reducing tensions with Mexico, which White interpreted as a strong repudiation of Kellogg's confrontational approach to Latin America. According to White, the tragedy of Kellogg's policy making was that he believed his own propaganda about Latin America's supposed Bolshevism. In contrast, Morrow worked to cultivate good relations with Mexico by learning Spanish, befriending Mexicans, and participating in local cultural events on his arrival in Mexico City. Morrow reached out to Mexican president Plutarco Elias Calles, and the two agreed to a settlement under which the United States conceded that Mexico owned all mineral rights while Mexico allowed American oil operations to continue. The outcome validated White's assertion that the dispute was better settled in a court of law or at a negotiating table than on a battlefield. A satisfied White noted that the hysteria of a "Red Menace of the South" had been dispelled, having existed nowhere but "locked in the state department's archives . . . and the ultra-Republican press."[44]

Liberals faced a tough row to hoe during the reactionary 1920s, and White suffered the same pains and outrages as other liberals as they watched the nation travel a path with which they vehemently disagreed. However, White soon found his footing and was able to rejoin the battle for his vision of democracy. He built real friendships with conservatives such as Presidents Harding and Coolidge, and he positioned himself to give them a view of the world from a liberal, midwestern perspective. White, Harding, and Coolidge all knew that reformers remained a force in American politics, albeit one that found itself to be at a distinct disadvantage during the 1920s. At the same time, he was not afraid to fight when the terrain favored his side. In labor policy, the debate over disarmament, and the effort to end the imperialistic policies toward Latin America, White showed that he was willing to put on his armor, strap on his shield, and stand his ground, spear in hand, against the reactionary tide. Midwestern cultural concepts such as "community" and "neighborliness" were his most effective weapons in his fight to explain reform, which he cast as both necessary and fundamentally American. Ironically, the same midwestern cultural concepts that fueled White's liberalism during the 1920s also made him susceptible to the decade's illiberal culture war, and he eagerly enlisted as a culture warrior in the fight against urban, ethnic America during Herbert Hoover's 1928 presidential campaign.

CHAPTER SIX

MAIN STREET

CULTURE WARRIOR

Sinclair Lewis's breakthrough novel *Main Street* was published in 1920. The work revolves around an idealistic young woman from Saint Paul, Minnesota, who moves to the small town of Gopher Prairie after marrying a local doctor. The woman soon discovers that Gopher Prairie is a drab and listless provincial village, and her efforts to reform the town end in failure. *Main Street* was written during the 1910s, but it resonated with the cultural battles being waged in America during the 1920s. In particular, the book spoke to the conflict between America's rising cosmopolitan society and its waning rural civilization. William Allen White was asked for his opinion of the work as one of America's leading voices of midwestern liberalism. He replied that he liked the work and its author so much that he had ordered copies to send to his friends. *Main Street* was a valuable tool for reform because it "makes us see our uglinesses, which are obvious, but often because they are so obvious, are overlooked," and he praised both *Main Street* and its successor, *Babbitt* (1922), as "splendid, poetical things, dramatizing the struggle of the human heart toward the ideals." White wrote Lewis admitting that the Midwest had plenty of dull towns, typically those with fewer than five thousand residents. In larger towns, one would find communities with "some civic spirit" that were "striving consciously to be just and beautiful." White pointed to Emporia, with its ten thousand residents, as an example of a town with a vibrant cultural life that had evolved "into the Country Club stage."[1]

The struggle between America's cosmopolitan and rural civilizations that *Main Street* had dramatized was at the forefront of the culture war that raged during the 1920s, and White's reaction to the novel aptly illustrated his role in this debate. White fought on both sides of the culture war. He was a vigorous champion of liberal tolerance in an age when the revived Ku Klux Klan, powered by a membership roster in the millions, controlled towns, counties, and whole states. White used his journalistic pen to attack the Klan, but he also proved willing to act on his rhetoric by running an independent campaign for Kansas's governorship as an anti-Klan candidate in 1924. Four years later, White joined the fight for Herbert Hoover against New York governor Al Smith during the 1928 presidential campaign. The 1928 election was a pitched battle between cosmopolitanism and rural civilization, and White fiercely defended the latter as the only true form of Americanism. White's dual roles as a liberal warrior in 1924 and a reactionary culture warrior in 1928 might seem to be a paradox, but both are consistent with his worldview during the 1920s. Simply put, White saw midwestern values as the core of American culture, and he was willing to plant his flag alongside whichever army stood against the cultural forces he found most threatening.

Like many midwesterners, White's cultural ideology during the decade centered on two basic concepts: the Midwest was the heart of American civilization, and it was under attack by outside forces. To White, Kansas seemed particularly important as the home of American reform because it reflected the nation's economic diversity. Kansas was an important producer of agricultural commodities, fossil fuels, and manufactured goods, including approximately 25 percent of the nation's nascent aviation production. The state was a laboratory for Progressive Era experiments in active government, including state-owned enterprises, regulations on freight and utility rates, pioneering labor laws, and a public university system that guaranteed admission to all high school graduates. White was proud of these innovations, which he attributed to the same midwestern "country values" and "neighborliness" that he argued constituted the foundation of American liberalism. For example, White asserted that no midwesterner would allow his next-door neighbor's children to toil in unsafe conditions at unfair wages, and he explained the effort to enact industrial reforms as a logical extension of midwestern values. To White, liberalism itself was merely "the application of a neighborly, village-minded aspiration to our national life."[2]

Naturally, White pointed to his own hometown of Emporia as a model of the thriving, neighborly community that America ought to emulate. The town was an important regional hub that boasted two colleges, a bustling retail district, and vital repair shops for the Santa Fe and MKT railroads. The economic depression of the early 1920s had yielded to renewed prosperity that disrupted Emporia's traditional living patterns. Emporians were building better housing and buying a myriad of consumer products, which was part of a trend playing out in small towns across America. The *Gazette*'s pages reflected the tension between the old and the new, with Bible features and tales of farm life appearing next to advertisements for cars, radios, movies, and other luxuries that were increasingly within the grasp of average consumers. Although White was racially tolerant by the standards of his day, he explained that Emporia's success was due in no small measure to the fact that 95 percent of its fourteen thousand residents were native-born whites who traced their lineage to New England's "old revolutionary stock." The 1920s were the decade in which small-town America began to lose its dominance over American culture to the cosmopolitan civilization rising in the cities. White reacted to this trend by vigorously defending the small-town civilization he loved, proudly declaring that anyone who wanted to "belong to the governing classes" in America had to be an Emporian in spirit.[3]

Cultural chauvinism was the dark side of White's faith in the supremacy of midwestern civilization, especially his belief in Theodore Roosevelt's idea that race was an important component in national identity. The crime, corruption, and moral failings associated with America's large cities outraged White, who penned an article warning that southern and eastern European immigrants "from the low breeds of Europe" posed a dire cultural threat to American democracy. The article, titled "What's the Matter with America?" claimed that urban disorder was the product of the new immigrants' defective cultures, which lacked "Anglo-Saxon political taboos" against selfishness, corruption, and graft. He likened millions of urban immigrants to rapidly reproducing "political bacilli . . . tearing down the tissue of our institutions" with their alien culture. In contrast, White claimed that rural society had avoided the problems afflicting the nation's cities because country children were taught proper American values in the home, around town, and in church. White spoke volumes when he pronounced all other national issues "subsidiary to [the] fundamental clash of ideals" between those of rural America and those of the new immigrants, which he suggested might be genetically ingrained. The only hope for the survival of liberal democracy in America was to try to teach the new immigrants that "our ideals are better than theirs, or their ideals will overcome ours."[4]

White's provocative article generated a great deal of reader mail, which broke approximately half in favor of and half against his position. The article proposed education as a remedy for the cultural infection menacing American democracy, but many of his midwestern neighbors turned to violence in defense of traditional civilization through the reactionary Ku Klux Klan. The KKK enjoyed a resurgence during the early 1920s as an organization of "respectable" Americans that embraced violence as a necessary and proper tool for defending "traditional" values against "immoral" urban elites, immigrants, and the working class. The Klan thrived in small towns dominated by native-born white Protestants, and its members were most often middle-class professionals, small businessmen, and skilled workers who felt threatened by the rise of large-scale corporate capitalism.[5] Kansas neatly fit this demographic profile, and White was blind to the fact that his own rhetoric of native-born, white, Protestant cultural superiority paralleled that of the Klan. A Klan organizer arrived in Emporia in the summer of 1921, and White was proud of the fact that none of the men invited to join accepted membership. He was confident that Kansans had rejected the KKK because the group was un-American, antidemocratic, cowardly, and unneighborly, but perhaps the fact that the Klan charged a membership fee of ten dollars at a time when the economy was emerging from the 1920–1921 depression played a greater role. The Klan soon fielded approximately forty thousand members in Kansas, and it became a potent political force in cities and states across the country. By 1923, White's Emporia neighbors had elected a Klan mayor, Klansmen infested the town's police department, and the *Gazette*'s exposés of Klan activities were met with a campaign of intimidation.[6]

The Whites gained a more complete understanding of the international nature of the Klan phenomenon during their two-month Mediterranean cruise in the spring of 1923, which included several stops in fascist Italy. Prime Minister Benito Mussolini had recently risen to power in Italy and was well on his way to establishing a dictatorship, giving White an opportunity to observe fascism in action. White admitted that Mussolini had brought order and "put people to work," and he could not help but feel impressed as he described a fascist Blackshirt parade as "here was the militant individual; here was the rambunctious unoppressed." Ultimately, White disapproved of Italy's turn toward fascism, recognizing that "fear of losing their money has made [Italians] forget that they may lose their liberty." White saw the Klan phenomenon for what it was: Italian fascism on American terms. He was disgusted to discover on his return that the Klan had conquered Emporia. The whole Western world seemed to be afflicted with "a spiritual epidemic" that manifested itself as the Klan in the United States, "the Fascisti of Italy and the Die-Hards of England and the military party [the *Reichswehr*] of Germany." Rural America's "rage and a sort of Fascisti hatred and suspicion and a paralyzing poison of supernatural patriotism" was what made it susceptible to the Ku Klux Klan, and White was disappointed that his neighbors had fallen to the group's appeal.[7]

The Klan found fertile soil in Kansas, but it did not go unchallenged. Corporations doing business in Kansas were required to obtain a state charter, and Governor Allen accused the group of being a corporation in violation of the law at the end of his second term in 1922. The case was to be heard by a state board consisting of three elected officeholders, two of whom were opposed to the Klan. The case proceeded slowly and had not been resolved by the time the anti-Klan board members stood for reelection in 1924, which meant that the Klan's fate in Kansas turned on the election's outcome. Democratic governor John M. Davis stood for reelection with the Klan's support that year, and the Republican nominee, Benjamin Paulen, publicly refused to denounce the group. White, Allen, and other anti-Klan Republicans were outraged. Not only would the voters be forced to choose between two Klan-friendly candidates but the lack of an anti-Klan alternative for governor threatened to affect down-ballot races such as those for the charter board. Former governor Allen asked White to join the gubernatorial race as an anti-Klan independent, but White was reluctant to break his journalistic vows by entering politics. He instead tried to persuade others to join the fray, but no one was willing to stand up to the Klan.[8]

White finally threw his own hat into the ring as an independent in early September 1924, declaring that he would defend American culture, small-town values, and the Constitution against the Klan. The KKK was a "hooded gang of masked fanatics, ignorant and tyrannical in their ruthless oppression" of Catholics, Jews, African Americans, and immigrants. The group's doctrine of intolerance was an assault on the fundamental ideology of the Constitution, which White summarized as a rurally inspired "charter of freedom, under which men may live with one another under the rule of fraternity and neighborly consideration." He asserted that the Klan subverted the Anglo-Saxon notion of the rule of law by aiming to impose a shadow government that employed "force instead of reason, terror instead of due process of law, and [that] undermines all that our fathers have fought for since free government has been established." White cast his candidacy as an opportunity for Kansans to defend the American political tradition and neighborly tolerance by voting for a "governor to free Kansas from the disgrace of the Ku Klux Klan."[9]

White's run for the governorship immediately became a national sensation. Walter Lippmann of the *New York World* called it "the most inspiring campaign being waged in the United States," and the newspaper published editorials and political cartoons to support his effort. *Time* placed White's portrait on its cover, and a *New York Times* reporter shadowing the campaign likened him to "a middle-aged, rosy faced, baldish St. George" heroically battling the Klan dragon. White crisscrossed Kansas in his Dodge touring car, and he explained to his

White poses with his Dodge touring car in front of the Gazette *building during his campaign for governor in 1924. Courtesy of the Kansas State Historical Society.*

audiences that he was fighting for "the principle of American freedom that these imperial gizzards, nightly nobility and cow-pasture patriots are out to betray." He asked Kansans to join him in defense of "law and order under law not under force, for an American civilization—tolerant, neighborly, kind, fundamentally democratic and everlastingly against the wicked reactionary imperialism of the invisible empire." The survival of the republic was at stake, because "America cannot remain half empire and half democracy." White campaigned across two-thirds of the state, put 2,700 miles on his car, delivered

104 speeches, and addressed tens of thousands in crowds ranging from several hundred to seven thousand in the Klan stronghold of Topeka. In every speech, White also urged his audiences to vote to reelect the charter board's anti-Klan members.[10]

Kansas's political establishment united in what White called an "unholy alliance" against him. Klansmen burned a small cross in downtown Cottonwood Falls shortly after White had finished his candidacy announcement on the steps of the Chase County courthouse. Hooded Klansmen ominously interrupted services at Cottonwood Falls's African American church in a bid to coerce the congregation to vote for Paulen. White's campaign banners were vandalized in one town, and they were removed by law enforcement acting on the mayor's orders in another. Organized labor was allied with the Klan and the Democratic Party, and the head of the Kansas Federation of Labor denounced White as a false friend to workers despite the editor's long record as a union advocate. Paulen left much of his campaigning to Republican surrogates such as prominent attorney John L. Dean, who embodied the fusion of the GOP, the Klan, and business interests. Dean gave speeches on Paulen's behalf, he defended the Klan in its case before the state charter board, and he was counsel to the Kansas "Employers' Association," which included the state's largest packing houses, railroads, and insurance companies. A labor-baiting judge smeared White as a glory hound, a racist, and a demagogue, while another surrogate exhorted Kansans to defeat "William Allen Whiteism and the other isms which come from Russia."[11]

Although Paulen won the governorship with a total of 323,000 votes in the Republican landslide of 1924, White's relative outperformance showed that Kansans could be receptive to the liberal rhetoric of tolerance. Almost 150,000 voters supported White, while 183,000 voters cast their ballot for the Democratic candidate. Running a close third was an amazing result considering that White had campaigned for less than six weeks as an independent on a shoestring budget of just $476.60. Many Catholics and African Americans voted for White, but organized labor overwhelmingly favored the Klan because it supported white Anglo-Saxon Protestant nativism. White's protégé,

Alf Landon, reminded him that many working-class voters hated the Catholic Church just as strongly as they hated the Klan, and White displayed a flash of his own bigotry by replying that the Catholic Church was not much better than the Klan. All in all, White saw the outcome as a moral victory because it had exposed the KKK as a sham, proven that ordinary citizens could stand against it, and taught Paulen that pandering to the Klan was politically costly. Individuals who had suffered Klan oppression wrote White thanking him profusely for his efforts, and one supporter expressed his hope that the group's "swaggering boldness is permanently reduced. I think from now on we can live in peace."[12]

White's high-profile campaign helped the charter board's anti-Klan majority win reelection, which ruled in January 1925 that the KKK was an out-of-state corporation operating illegally. The decision and the Klan's own missteps contributed to its collapse in the state, and White exalted that "the Ku Klux Klan in Kansas [would be] a busted community" within a year. Eastern liberals such as Harvard law professor Felix Frankfurter, Lippmann, and Villard saw White's effort as a ray of hope in an age of conservatism, and the latter two solicited his insights on the Klan phenomenon for their urban readers. White's fight against the Klan was a heroic campaign against one of the most formidable fascist groups in America during the 1920s. His liberal allies were right to celebrate his stand, but the fact was that White had not abandoned his belief that America was a white Anglo-Saxon Protestant country. He made this point abundantly clear in his editorial celebrating the 1924 National Origins Act, which established an immigration quota system that functionally excluded southern and eastern Europeans. White saw the measure as a move to preserve American democracy by maintaining "the infusion of clean, white blood," by which he meant western Europeans. Southern and eastern Europeans, White maintained, could only be allowed to immigrate gradually in order to prevent their inferior rootstock from infecting America.[13]

White continued to make headlines in the eastern press through his opposition to some of the more ludicrous expressions of the culture war during the mid-1920s. He editorialized that "nothing is as dynamic as suppressed desires" in ridiculing a local mayor's attempt to enact laws curbing dancing. In the same breath, however, White endorsed laws such as Prohibition as reasonable measures to enforce "the decent instincts of a civilized majority against the barbarism of untaught minorities." White defended evolution to a friend who he thought had adopted fundamentalist Christianity, pointing out that "the Bible is shot full of mistakes" and rejecting the idea that God was "a man who sits around with a pointer and says to the winds do this and to the waves do that." He believed in God, but his view was that God was "a spirit and should be worshiped in spirit and in truth and not as a graven image." White chuckled at Emporia's churchmen after they denounced him for the sacrilege of inviting the town to watch the World Series scores being tallied in front of the *Gazette*'s offices after Sunday services in 1926. He mocked the president-general of the Daughters of the American Revolution for adding his name to a blacklist of dangerous radicals for his support for civil liberties, attacks on literary censorship, and opposition to the Ku Klux Klan. Dozens of mainstream individuals and groups were named on the list, including defense attorney Clarence Darrow, the Young Men's Christian Association, and the National Catholic Welfare League. White observed that the list's targeting of Jews, Catholics, and liberals paralleled the Klan's, and he joked that the DAR president had "allowed several lengths of Ku Klux nightie to show under her red, white and blue."[14]

Ironically, the same midwestern cultural factors that fueled White's liberalism also spurred him to embrace conservatism when he felt that his own rural middle class was under attack during the late 1920s. Cosmopolitan America's rejection of Prohibition signaled the erosion of rural America's cultural dominance, and White fiercely contested any whiff of repeal as a serious threat to American democracy. The rural middle class had prescribed Prohibition as a remedy for the industrial inefficiency and social waste caused by liquor, White claimed. He scolded Prohibitionists who characterized the issue as a

moral question, insisting that "in the west the dominant prohibitionists were not the churchmen . . . but the business men" who wanted
a reliable workforce. Nevertheless, White's rationales for Prohibition
relied on an assortment of moral judgments. Liquor was a "constant
breeder of poverty" because the poor were too weak willed to resist
spending their limited resources on alcohol, leaving society to clean
up the wreckage. As long as liquor was legal, it did "little good to
talk about child labor, or an eight-hour day, or a minimum wage, or
any other measure intended to improve the present capitalistic order." White also denounced "the rich boozer" whom he described as
"a rebel—a militant, insistent lawbreaker" whose scofflaw behavior
encouraged the rest of society to disregard the rule of law. Although
he allowed that reasonable people could disagree about the policy of
Prohibition, White saw urban society's tolerance of liquor in violation
of established law as an adolescent rebellion against the rural majority's sober wisdom.[15]

The contest between rural and urban culture was foremost in
White's thinking as the 1928 presidential campaign got under way.
The Republican National Convention was held in Kansas City, Missouri, from June 12 to 15, and a sixty-year-old White played an especially important role in the proceedings. Senator Borah had fallen
short in his campaign for the Republican presidential nomination
in 1928, and one of White's tasks was to soothe his friend's bruised
feelings to avoid a messy convention fight. The two men collaborated on the Republican platform committee, and White helped Borah craft planks supporting two of his pet issues: the outlawry of
war and a law banning federal injunctions in labor disputes. In farm
policy, White helped turn the Kansas delegation against the McNary-
Haugen Bill, which was a perennial proposal to use government action to help support falling prices for agricultural commodities. The
idea was wildly popular in the West, but White agreed with Republican conservatives that the proposal would not be effective. All in
all, he felt that reformers had been reasonably accommodated in the
Republican platform of 1928.[16]

Herbert Hoover was the front-runner for the 1928 Republican

nomination, and White gave his campaign more support than he had any presidential candidate since Theodore Roosevelt in 1912. Hoover actively sought the nomination and understood the value of cultivating good press relations. For instance, White happily obliged Hoover's request that he host a newspapermen's dinner in Emporia on July 18, 1927, to introduce Hoover to the region's press corps and spark a western boom. White penned campaign propaganda once the stumping began in earnest, including a *Collier's* biography that depicted Hoover as the best that small-town midwestern America had to offer. Hoover was a hero from West Branch, Iowa, who had made a fortune for himself and fueled prosperity at home through his career as a mining engineer installing American-made machinery overseas, according to White. While abroad, Hoover had helped bring order to a chaotic world and demonstrated the virility of American manhood by defending white women during the Boxer Rebellion in China. Finally, White described Hoover as a fine example of American neighborliness as the humanitarian who led the Belgian Relief campaign that fed occupied Europe during World War I. Hoover's main flaw was that he was overly "sensitive to personal criticism" and lacked political instincts, but White sought to turn these weaknesses to his advantage by portraying him as an ordinary American untainted by politics.[17]

Hoover's biography contrasted sharply with that of the Democratic nominee, Al Smith, who was the son of immigrants raised in the heart of New York City's vibrant ethnic culture. Smith rocketed through New York's Tammany Hall political machine to eventually reach the governor's mansion, launching an audacious campaign of labor, education, and public utility reforms. White admired Smith as an intelligent, courageous, and sincere reformer who had distanced himself from the Tammany machine that bore him. At the same time, he acknowledged Smith as the nation's most prominent symbol of a new, urban civilization that marked a "challenge to our American traditions, a challenge which . . . will bring deep changes into our American life." Although White admired Smith as a keen politician with a "national size" character, he rejected Smith's urban culture and

Herbert Hoover's Emporia dinner party, July 18, 1927. White and Hoover are seated at the head table in the far background, near the ivy-covered tree trunk. Courtesy of Kenneth Spencer Research Library, University of Kansas Libraries.

his Tammany pedigree. As Lippmann presciently observed, Smith's fate in 1928 would turn on whether he could convince rural voters that he was culturally qualified for the White House, or at least to set their prejudices aside long enough to vote for him. As one of rural America's most prominent midwestern liberals, White highlighted the difficulty of this task when he depicted a procession of urban delegates at the Democratic National Convention as a circus "filled with Sullivans, Murphys, O' Tooles and Guadellis and Greeks, with names that sound like a college yell."[18]

Governor Smith's biography alone made him unpalatable to the Democratic Party's rural constituencies, but his stance as an unapologetic "wet" who had ended New York State's enforcement of Prohibition posed a potentially insurmountable obstacle to party unity. The Democrats managed to finesse the issue with a platform plank

calling for an "honest effort" to enforce Prohibition, but Smith reig-
nited the controversy when he stated in his nomination acceptance
note that he intended to enforce Prohibition while pressing for its
modification. "Drys" such as White were astounded. The editor noted
that the candidates were both honest men with similar platforms,
and Smith's action had made Prohibition the campaign's central issue. He launched an editorial fusillade that ranged far beyond the
liquor question by claiming that Smith had served Tammany Hall
by voting for bills that favored liquor, gambling, and prostitution as
a New York state legislator. Tammany Hall had launched Smith's career, and White claimed that rural Americans opposed him because
"his record shows the kind of president he will make—a Tammany
president" willing to sacrifice his principles for political gain. A
President Smith would, White asserted, "menace American ideals
and threaten the institutions of our fathers. Smith must be beaten if
America remains America."[19]

The editorial went unnoticed nationally until White reprised his
comments in a speech launching Hoover's Kansas campaign at
Olathe on July 12. Senator Borah congratulated White for his speech,
which he noted had received attention well beyond Kansas. The press
focused on White's charges that Smith's record on saloons, gambling,
and prostitution made him a threat to America's "whole Puritan civilization," and Smith responded that "Mr. White has brains and ought
to know better." The *New York Times* chirped that ending Prohibition
was the best way to restore "Puritan civilization" because the Puritans
were heavy drinkers by modern standards. White retorted that the
Puritans had also persecuted Quakers and hung witches, but their
positive contribution was "an orderly individualistic civilization" that
"moralized its economic issues," as he claimed Americans had with
Prohibition. Although he conceded that Smith was courageous, intelligent, and audacious, White alleged that these attributes were dangerous unless tempered by midwestern morality because they made
it possible for Smith to "chloroform the people so that the Tammany
chain will be forged upon them." He wrote one local Democrat that
he could have supported a man like Smith if he had "been born out

here in our country. I wish he did not have the sour beer smell of Tammany in his clothes." A disappointed Felix Frankfurter wrote White lamenting that the latter had "joined the blind forces of Phariseeism so rampant in America today," and White's own son, who stood to the left of his father, concurred.[20]

White had planned to spend several days in New York City before sailing for a much-needed vacation to Europe that August, and he longed for the opportunity to give Smith "another wallop" on his home turf. The RNC and a church group provided White with research aides to dig into Smith's record, and the editor released their report reiterating his charges on arriving in New York City on July 29. However, White withdrew his allegations pertaining to gambling and prostitution the next day after Lippmann, their mutual friend, informed White that Smith had sound reasons to vote against the measures in question. Lippmann believed that White had seen the light, and he assured another mutual friend that the Kansan was merely guilty of "carelessness, an attempt to make good on his carelessness, an amateur investigation and muddle-headedness. He's a sweet fellow and I think he was very contrite." White saw things differently, explaining that he had withdrawn the charges as "a chivalrous gesture" after Lippmann told him that Smith's "wife and daughter were weeping" about the allegations. The controversy subsided after White sailed for six weeks in Europe aboard the SS *DeGrasse,* but it flared again after Henry J. Allen, now the RNC's publicity director, leaked a private letter from White reasserting the charges. The editors of the liberal journal the *Nation* were amused, quipping that "what Mr. White plainly needs is a rest cure in some Swiss resort, until he recovers his ordinary political judgment, not to say sanity."[21]

The presidential campaign intensified in White's absence, and the *Nation* observed that his allegations against Smith lived on in the form of vicious pamphlets titled "William Allen White Says" that were distributed anonymously in the Midwest. The pamphlets used a brief excerpt of White's charges to mask the pamphleteer's own denunciation of Smith as a member of "the Catholic so-called Religion" that "represents the downward slant of moral principles." White's charges had become part of the "whispering campaign" that, as the *Nation* pointed out, used rumors and innuendo to tar Smith with "two prejudices—those against Catholicism and against Tammany Hall." Smith's candidacy opened the solidly Democratic South to Hoover's appeals, and both sides employed vicious tactics while jockeying for advantage. Pro-Smith Democrats claimed that Hoover would put African Americans in charge of the South if the Republicans won, while Hoover's supporters spun lurid tales of Catholic domination, ecclesiastical immorality, and urban vice in denouncing Smith. Anti-Catholic bigotry was particularly effective in the South, but negative attitudes about Catholicism were so widespread that even pro-Smith liberals fully accepted the idea that the Catholic mind was incapable of independent thought. Both the Prohibition and Tammany Hall issues fit neatly into this anti-Catholic narrative, and Hoover's campaign wielded all three against Smith in the South.[22]

The same midwestern ideas of neighborliness and orderly government that had inspired White's anti-Klan run in 1924 motivated him against Al Smith in 1928, and he obliged Hoover's request to return to the battle on returning from Europe in October. Although White never mentioned Smith's Catholicism, he did not need to because his rhetoric about Tammany and Prohibition played into widespread cultural biases against Catholics. Indeed, White declared that "Tammany is like the Ku Klux Klan in robbing a man of his individuality and deadening his conscience" as soon as he disembarked in New York City. Many flung the same charges against the Catholic Church. Speaking requests quickly poured in, and White focused his energies on a southern tour attacking Smith as the enemy of rural neighborliness and America's founding principles. White's stump speech acknowledged that both candidates were exceptional men, but he claimed that Hoover was "a farm boy" with "the American mind" while Smith was imbued with "the Tammany Mind." Americans ought to vote for Hoover because American civilization was built on rural values, which White hyperbolically summarized as "orderly, moral, healthy, neighborly, kindly, with just and equitable relations between all citizens rich or poor." White's brief argument for Hoover was that the Republican was best suited to preserve the nation's founding principle of millions of voters casting free ballots as well as its cultural "ideals of probity, of neighborly kindness."[23]

The vast majority of White's speech was dedicated to attacking Smith and his "Tammany Mind." The Democratic machine challenged the American doctrine of political independence by operating a rival system that demanded strict obedience from its lieutenants and block voting by the lower classes, with votes paid for with "charity rather than justice." The elevation of a Tammany man such as Smith to the highest office in the land threatened to "infect the Nation" with the Tammany rot. White summarized the question before the voters as "shall the government of free men exalting a free conscience in government survive on this continent, or shall we Tammanize America?" Prohibition was merely "the symbol which dramatizes the issue," because the rural majority had enacted it as an economic measure to improve society. Tammany rejected Prohibition because the law represented "a conscience in politics, the rule of the majority, the obedience of the minority, [and] fundamental rights" without favor. White reasserted that Smith had stood with Tammany on the saloon question in the New York legislature on every occasion, straining credulity by claiming that this recapitulation was intended to show "how Tammany perverts its followers," not to "pretend that any moral turpitude lurked in these votes." Smith would "stand in the White House as he has stood in Albany," and White begged his rural audiences to "save the America of our constitution, a free unbought, unbossed America," from the "gang of Tammany hoodlums" that would ride Smith's coattails into the White House.[24]

Smith was the visible embodiment of an America that was increasingly ethnically, religiously, and culturally diverse, and that was increasingly urban. Anti-Smith hysteria helped elect Hoover by an overwhelming margin, and the shock of this divisive campaign reverberated through the liberal ranks. Villard severed his friendship with Senator Borah after the Republican Old Guard paid Borah's expenses to campaign for Hoover. The GOP shunned White's liberal friend Senator George W. Norris (R-NE) for having actively campaigned for

Smith. Lippmann spoke for many eastern liberals when he stated that Hoover's win was a "victory of economic conservatism and of political and religious fundamentalism," although he and other observers acknowledged that Smith was an economic conservative. The *Nation* noted that "from the beginning of the campaign there has been a group to which he emphatically owes his success: Prejudice, Bigotry, Superstition, Intolerance, Hate, Selfishness, Snobbery, and Passion." The "whispering campaign" against Smith had shown Villard that the attitudes of "dense ignorance and prejudice of the Scopes case in Tennessee, which we had flattered ourselves was limited to backwoods districts, are in reality to be found in every American community." Villard cited the fact that Hoover had not felt compelled to sound a single note of disapproval against this bigotry as proof that a wide swath of the population was not considered to be fully American.[25]

The most egregious examples of racial and religious bigotry that had been used against Smith during the campaign disturbed White, but he was blind to the inherent intolerance in his rural triumphalism. Instead, he exalted that the presidency had been saved from Tammany Hall, although he conceded that he had reservations about Hoover's thin skin and his deification of prosperity. Ever the optimist, White cited the president-elect's prosperity mantras as heralds of his blossoming liberalism because they reflected a desire to advance social justice by lifting all boats. Lippmann was in Kansas City two weeks after the election delivering a speech on the American people's complacent attitude about prosperity, and he took the opportunity to visit White. Lippmann reported that he "found the experience extremely depressing. White surely is about the best thing that the Middle West and the small-town in the Buick-radio age has produced. And judged by any standard of civilized liberalism it's a pretty weedy flower. He made me feel as if defeating Al Smith had in it an enterprise about equivalent to heaving a stray cat out of the parlor." Lippmann saw the beauty in midwestern liberalism with its impulse toward political and economic democracy, but he also felt that it was severely marred by its cultural conservatism. He consoled himself with the observation that Hoover liberals such as White were anti-Smith rather than pro-Hoover, and he hoped that they would see the light after Hoover began to implement his agenda.[26]

White had played a vital role in defeating Smith in 1928, but the outcome also laid the foundation for the New Deal liberal coalition. While Lippmann mourned the defeat, he recognized that Smith had "started something" by tallying a greater share of the popular vote than any Democrat since Woodrow Wilson. Smith contributed to the coming of the New Deal by winning the cities for the Democratic Party, which provided the foundation for Franklin D. Roosevelt's New Deal coalition of labor, the cities, liberals, and the Solid South in 1932. Several of White's midwestern liberal Republican friends became New Dealers after campaigning for Smith in 1928, including Harold Ickes and Senator Norris. Midwestern liberals of both parties continued to play an important role in the New Deal coalition for the next fifty years. Al Smith was no liberal on economic questions, but the key issues in 1928 were cultural rather than economic. The 1920s culture war scrambled the usual liberal and conservative battle lines, and the 1928 campaign was a cathartic episode that set in motion events that would refocus liberals on economic and political reform. New Deal liberalism could not rise as long as liberal midwestern reformers such as White were distracted by cultural issues. Herbert Hoover's 1928 victory epitomized the culture war, and the stage was set for a realignment when midwestern liberals such as White realized that Hoover's cultural values alone were not an answer to the devastating economic and political crisis of the Great Depression.[27]

The crisis that shattered the Hoover myth was not long in coming, because the patina of everlasting prosperity that Lippmann had discussed in Kansas City concealed a deadly rot. Even White, who openly admitted that the vagaries of banking and economics were Greek to him, noted in May 1929 that the American economy was built on a "foundation of sand." He wondered, "When will the sleeper awake?" The crisis soon arrived, and Lippmann was stunned when White wrote him frankly admitting that Prohibition, the issue that White had claimed epitomized rural superiority and the American way, had been a "sort of stalled car in the road" that had wrecked liberal cooperation and had to be repealed as soon as possible.[28]

Was White's midwestern liberalism "a pretty weedy flower"? He had spent a conservative decade fighting as a liberal guerrilla on behalf of labor, disarmament, and an enlightened foreign policy, and he had enjoyed more success than might reasonably be expected. His reform ideology was based on midwestern values, and these values spurred him against both the Ku Klux Klan in 1924 and Al Smith in 1928. Both the Klan and the Tammany Hall system that produced Smith functioned as machines that subverted American values by demanding obedience to a hierarchical organization. The Klan pursued its goals through intolerance and terror, while Tammany Hall used favors and corruption to achieve its agenda. Both violated White's midwestern affinity for neighborliness, individualism, and good government, but White was just as much a product of the machine system as Smith. Good government was not the factor that motivated White in this case. Smith's great crime was that he triggered White's cultural apprehensions about the rise of urban America. Liberalism could not "flower" as a coherent political movement as long as cultural issues spurred its adherents to make war on each other, but Lippmann was mostly correct. White realized his mistake once he discovered what Hoover *would not do* during the Great Depression. The emergency forced White to set aside his cultural fears, revive the embers of his alliance with eastern liberals in support of efforts to grapple with the Depression, and evolve into a New Deal liberal.[29]

CHAPTER SEVEN

RELUCTANT NEW DEALER

William Allen White and Walter Lippmann had both sensed that America's apparent prosperity was an illusion during the late 1920s. By a twist of fate, the two men dined together in New York City on "Black Tuesday," October 29, 1929, when panicked investors overwhelmed the New York Stock Exchange with a tsunami of sell orders. The day's dramatic events almost certainly provided interesting fodder for their table conversation. Fully one-third of the value of the Dow Jones Industrial Average was wiped out within weeks, and analysts offered a variety of explanations for the catastrophe. White shared the prevailing wisdom that crashes were a positive aspect of capitalism that trimmed economic fat and stimulated business to behave more responsibly. The innocent would suffer along with the guilty, he editorialized, but depressions were an inevitable part of the economic cycle, and the nation would endure this one before emerging stronger and wiser. Both White and Lippmann rallied around President Herbert Hoover as an act of patriotism in a moment of national emergency, but Hoover soon squandered this support by failing to rise to meet the crisis.[1] The resulting social and economic collapse ironically forced White to accept the liberal reform he had always wanted from a Democrat he felt he could not fully trust: Franklin D. Roosevelt.

Paradoxically, although the sixty-year-old White had vigorously campaigned for Hoover in 1928, he enjoyed relatively limited influence with the new president. His first inkling that Hoover was not as open to advice as other presidents he had known came when a battle erupted over a vacancy on Kansas's federal district court shortly after the inauguration. The region's federal judiciary had long been dominated by conservative judges whom reformers regarded as creatures of the corporations. Kansas's congressional delegation rallied around reform-minded state attorney general Richard Hopkins to fill the vacancy, and the delegation's backing normally carried overwhelming weight. White was horrified when President Hoover announced that he intended to get politics out of judicial appointments by refusing to accept congressional recommendations. He privately complained to Lippmann that Hoover was a second William H. Taft in that both men were political neophytes who were prone to potentially fatal blunders. Hoover seemed to prefer businessmen for judgeships and other offices, but White thundered that "it is better to have bad politics under even remote democratic control than it is to have good politics by divine right for the ukase of big business." Kansas's conservative establishment alleged that Hopkins was corrupt, since he had accepted reimbursement for expenses incurred while delivering political speeches to the Women's Christian Temperance Union when he was attorney general.[2]

The president summoned White to Washington to discuss Hopkins's possible nomination, and he was dismayed to find that Hoover also shared former president Taft's unwillingness to fight the conservatives. Instead, Hoover wanted White to save him from the controversy by persuading Hopkins and the Kansas delegation to step aside. White accepted the apparent defeat gracefully, pledging to give Hopkins the bad news personally if Hoover felt that the nomination was impossible. However, he also presented a strong case for Hopkins, refuting the allegations of corruption and countering that the corporations opposed him because he was not in their pocket. Finally, White added that Kansas's two Republican senators would be politically weakened if they failed to deliver on a nomination they had publicly endorsed. The appeal succeeded, and Hoover finally nominated Hopkins in October 1929. The Senate Judiciary Committee was the nomination's next stop, and White immediately went to work lobbying his committee-member friends, Senators George Norris (R-NE) and William Borah (R-ID). The committee voted in Hopkins's favor despite some misgivings, and Borah admitted to White that "nominally, I voted for him. In fact, I voted for you. I would not have voted for Hopkins if it had not been for you." The full Senate voted to confirm Hopkins by a vote of 49–22 in late December, but the fight had begun souring White on Hoover.[3] White admired leaders cast in Theodore Roosevelt's crusading mold, and Hoover's willingness to surrender at the first sign of opposition left a distinctly unfavorable impression.

The fight over Hopkins only hinted at the leadership crisis that was soon to overwhelm Hoover's presidency. The pain of the stock market crash quickly spread from Wall Street to Main Street, and 4 million Americans were out of work by the spring of 1930. President Hoover's initial response to the Depression included voluntary stabilization agreements, public exhortations for calm, and assertions that the economy was poised for a rebound. The support the president had enjoyed began to evaporate as his efforts failed to halt the economic free fall. White tried to rescue the president by channeling advice through one of his former *Gazette* protégés who was now a White House staffer, David Hinshaw. The president's problem, White explained to Hinshaw, was that had he proven incapable of "stir[ring] people emotionally, and through the emotions one gets to the will." Hoover's inability to rally the public meant that he could "plow the ground, harrow it, plant the seed, cultivate it, but seems to lack the power to harvest it and flail it into a political merchantable product." Hinshaw became White's conduit to an Oval Office that he felt was dominated by conservatives determined to shield the president from liberal advice.[4]

The national leadership vacuum was partially filled by a bipartisan group of congressional liberals that included Senators Norris, Borah, and New York's Robert Wagner, all of whom bombarded the president with impassioned pleas for government action. White offered Hoover his services in helping broker a legislative collaboration with the liberal Republicans, advising that the president needed to "mollify those progressive Republican leaders" if he hoped to be reelected in 1932. Instead, the administration chose to obstruct them in Congress, and the Republican establishment tried to purge Borah and Norris in the 1930 primaries. The GOP was particularly underhanded in its campaign against Norris, bribing a Nebraska grocer who shared Norris's exact name to run for the Republican nomination in an attempt to muddle the vote. White campaigned vigorously for both Norris and Borah over the summer, and he noticed a rising tide of anti-Hoover sentiment that he attributed to "a state of dubious expectation that he will do something to help the situation." Norris and Borah won their primaries, which proved to White that the Republican Party's liberal wing was alive and well. On the whole, however, he knew that the national reaction against Hoover would allow the Democrats to triumph in the national midterm election, and he was doubtful that his thirty-year-old son, Bill, would succeed in his campaign for a seat in the Kansas legislature.[5]

Bill White won his campaign, but the 1930 midterm election was a disaster for the Republicans overall. The Democrats won a slim majority in the House of Representatives, and they gained six seats in the Senate, which remained in Republican hands. Once again, White tried to use Hinshaw to warn the White House, writing that Hoover increasingly resembled "Harrison and Taft: A good man surrounded by bad advisors." The GOP's use of dirty tricks against Norris was "a beautiful case in point" that had enraged the West, and White pointed out that Hoover was doomed if he lost the region's support. He warned another friend and Hoover confidant, conservative newspaper publisher David Lawrence, that the ship of state was "listing" because "the quarter deck seems to be manned by a lot of brass collared, congenital idiots who do not see that we are hell bound . . . if we cannot do anything to restore justice in this country." Although he continued to support Hoover publicly, White confided to another protégé that the president lacked the political skill required to lead the nation, and "unless a miracle happens in national politics Hoover will not succeed himself. And he may not be succeeded by a Democrat."[6]

One factor shaping White's increasingly pessimistic outlook was the extreme drought gripping the Midwest in the summer of 1930. White helped lead public and private relief efforts in Emporia that winter, working himself to the point of exhaustion in the process. The observation that the people were beginning to lose their fundamental faith in the American system troubled him, and he felt it was imperative that the federal government act to relieve the people's suffering immediately. Broader structural problems such as income inequality needed to be addressed as well, since "too much of the gross income of the world is paid for superintendents and salaries and too little for wages." America risked a Bolshevik revolution unless it found a way to give all citizens a stake in society, he warned. Borah and the Senate's liberals proposed meeting the midwestern drought crisis with an appropriation of $25 million to the Red Cross in January 1931, but the Hoover administration attacked the measure as a "dole." Instead, the administration countered with a wholly inadequate $20 million farm loan program, spurring Borah to remark that he "never realized the hold that property sentiment has on this country . . . until this controversy came up on drought relief." Hoover's decision to fight drought relief shocked White, and he abandoned his idea of serving as "a sort of liaison person" between Hoover and the Senate liberals.[7]

White had once praised President Hoover's strategy of "voluntarism," which emphasized private sector initiatives to achieve public goals, but the drought emergency highlighted the inadequacy of this approach. The problem with voluntarism was that it was contrary to human nature, and White pointed to Hoover's Farm Board program as a prime example. The Farm Board aimed to help prop up the price of farm products by encouraging farmers to voluntarily reduce planting, but White pointed out that anyone would react by planting more while hoping that their neighbors would plant less. Another strategy the Farm Board used was to buy wheat and store it for sale at a later date, but White correctly predicted that the scheme would fail because the market would factor the stored wheat into supply until it was consumed. White proposed that the government sustain farm prices and simultaneously help address starvation by purchasing wheat, baking it into bread at US Army bakeries, and giving the bread to the unemployed. The fundamental "function of any civilization, capitalist or communist, is to provide its people with either work or free bread," White argued. He condemned the Hoover administration for having failed to provide either work through publicly funded construction programs or bread to feed the hungry, despite having had "ample opportunity to foresee the present emergency which confronts us this winter."[8]

In addition to failed policy, the nation was suffering from failed leadership. In White's opinion, Hoover's problem was that he approached the presidency with the sterility of a corporate administrator when the office's real power lay in its potential to inspire the public. The people needed a leader "in the greatest adventure ever undertaken on the planet. For without leaders the people grow blind and without vision the people perish." White had not shied from telling presidents the hard truth in the past, but he knew better than to try to explain this to President Hoover directly "because I know Hoover is Hoover." The president was notoriously thin-skinned, and White had learned that he "doesn't want advice. He is not interested in public opinion from the liberal standpoint." It was perfectly clear to White that Hoover never even glanced at the correspondence he received regarding pending legislation. By the summer of 1932, he had abandoned hope that Hoover would overcome his inability to inspire the citizenry or master the art of politics. The president was an able administrator, but he "simply can't explain it to the people. He is atrophied, dead and petrified on that side of his nature." Walter Lippmann reached the same conclusion. The parallels between Hoover and Taft were eerie for White, who recalled having once tried to get Hoover to address the public about an issue. Hoover echoed Taft's sentiments twenty years before when he turned to White "half peeved and half frightened and said 'Oh I can't be a Roosevelt. I am not built that way.'"[9]

The fact that the Democrats now controlled the House of Representatives and the liberal Republicans had survived the GOP's purge attempt spurred Hoover to finally begin taking serious action against the Depression. However, his newfound policy urgency was not paralleled by a newfound ability to inspire the American people. White began to consider other presidential alternatives, and he found one in

New York's Democratic governor Franklin Delano Roosevelt. White and Roosevelt had become loosely acquainted when they collaborated on charity fundraising during the early 1920s, and White wrote the governor in 1930 gravely concerned that America's wealthiest men would resist necessary change. The resulting economic deterioration would then squeeze the lower middle class into the ranks of the poor, and White feared a reactionary revolution as the poor joined a mob of "the credulous, the suspicious, the bigoted, the ignorant, led by the crafty and the fools." Editorially, White praised Roosevelt as a liberal of presidential stature who had bravely challenged the New York state power trust, and he accepted the governor's invitation to visit Albany to discuss farm policy in April 1931. The only concern White expressed was that the issue of Prohibition might sink FDR as it had Al Smith in 1928, highlighting his shift away from the cultural politics of the 1920s.[10]

White felt honor-bound to stand by Hoover despite his flirtation with Roosevelt, and he sought to avoid any move that might imply otherwise. White's reaction to Senator Norris's bipartisan conference in March 1931 was a case in point. Norris assembled a number of leading liberal lights in an effort to craft a legislative response to the Depression, and White supported the effort editorially. However, he declined to attend himself because he had "asked and received favors" from Hoover, such as the Hopkins appointment. White was careful to preserve his access to the White House by informing Hinshaw that he had declined to avoid being linked with "an anti-Hoover" position. However, he also took the opportunity to protest Hoover's veto of Senator Norris's bill creating an experimental public power plant at Muscle Shoals, Alabama. The veto had alienated Congress and thousands of "mild progressives" with the stroke of a pen, he warned. Nevertheless, Hoover remained a constant obstacle to congressional liberal efforts, chanting the mantra that government intervention was not required to address the emergency. White left-handedly complimented Hoover's position as the "sound, sane pronouncement of

a great American" that would probably become the Republican platform of 1932, while noting that it was unlikely to save the nation in
its hour of crisis.[11]

The Depression worsened in mid-1931, and White suffered as well
in the form of another medical crisis. The illness began after he gave
a luncheon for Martin Insull, brother of infamous holding company
magnate Samuel Insull, in Emporia on March 12. The two men re-
tired to the *Gazette*'s office after lunch, where they began arguing
about politics "at the top of our voices for two hours when I was fairly
mentally drained. And I blew up." The symptoms were "miserable
attacks of vertigo and nausea," and White visited the Mayo Clinic in
Rochester in the hope of a medical solution. The doctors diagnosed
an inner ear pressure imbalance, but the symptoms could have been
another one of his periodic mental breakdowns or a harbinger of the
diabetes he eventually developed. They prescribed six months' rest,
and Mr. and Mrs. White began a vacation in northern New Mexico
followed by Estes Park during the spring and summer of 1931. Bill
White took over daily management of the *Gazette,* and the elder White
chuckled that his liberal son regarded him "as a moss-bound conservative." Although Bill wrote the editorials, he managed to accurately
capture his father's sentiments. Americans were starving in a land
of plenty, and those who wanted honest work were being driven to
desperate measures to survive. The *Gazette* editorialized that Americans had trembled in fear at the idea of mobsters and Communists
overthrowing society, but the real danger lay in ignoring the plight of
the poor and hungry. The world did, in fact, owe a living to every person who was willing to work for it, and the *Gazette* expressed concern
that social and political revolution would ensue unless the American
system was adapted to suit modern economic realities.[12]

Rest helped improve White's condition, and he was able to return to Emporia in September to accept Hoover's appointment to
the President's Organization for Unemployment Relief (POUR). The
organization was a voluntarist attempt to coordinate private relief efforts, and it was Hoover's attempt to silence critics who called for
government action to help the people. White was pleased to accept

the position despite his persistent medical problems, because it offered him "a real opportunity to serve" the nation in its hour of need. President Hoover had given White ample notice about his impending nomination, allowing him to begin framing his ideas on unemployment and relief in several summertime letters to Hinshaw from Moraine Park. White envisioned an expansive program that better resembled the New Deal than anything Hoover would ever support, including a government-operated unemployment insurance system financed with contributions from employers and workers, an effective farm policy, utilities regulation, a tariff reduction, reduced land taxes, and stronger civil service measures. The Depression also demanded unprecedented, immediate relief measures because "there is no normal economic solution of the present acute emergency in American industry." The crisis called for a "national emergency relief corporation" funded by a public subscription, which would help farmers by purchasing produce that would be fed to laborers in exchange for work on public projects. Hinshaw put White's idea to President Hoover, and he reported that the latter was "open minded" about trying it if authorized by Congress. A wide gulf still separated White and the president. Hoover was determined to "defeat the dole," and White was willing to try it if jobs were not forthcoming. Ultimately, he rightly noted that "we cannot afford to be squeamish with self-respecting men and women who are hungry."[13]

Two weeks of additional rest in Emporia gave White the impression that he was fit enough to begin his work for POUR, and his first task was to try to foster collaboration between the ten out of sixty committee members he saw as reform-minded. He counted American Federation of Labor president William Green among the reformers, and White wrote Green strongly advocating government action to address joblessness. Unemployment and relief had to be remedied even if it meant the dole, or the nation would see "barricades in the streets this winter and the use of force which will brutalize labor and impregnate it with revolution in America for a generation." White traveled to Washington and New York to meet various captains of industry in connection with his POUR duties that fall, and the conditions he found were utterly demoralizing. Business leaders were terrified and befuddled, and they shared White's concern about "military rule of the streets, barricades in the streets, and they are trying to work out some kind of a scheme for the future that will prevent this." Unfortunately, the debilitating symptoms that had forced White to his sickbed in the spring returned with full fury, and he was unable to play a significant role in POUR. By October, White complained to his Mayo Clinic doctors that "I am not much stronger than I was when I put on my coat and walked out" of the *Gazette* six months earlier. He had little choice but to abide by his doctors' orders that he drop everything and devote himself entirely to rest.[14]

Illness kept White sidelined as President Hoover began to take a more active approach to the Depression, spurred by the liberal Republicans and Democrats in Congress. The Seventy-Second Congress opened on December 7, 1931, and Senator Robert La Follette, Jr. (R-WI) proposed creating jobs with a $5.5 billion program to build infrastructure. Hoover short-circuited the idea with his own request for a $500 million program to help stabilize the economy by lending money to governments and private enterprises, which became the Reconstruction Finance Corporation. Hoover's new willingness to act gave White cause for hope that the president was finally beginning to grapple with the Depression, and he traced Hoover's evolution editorially. The president had believed that the Depression was an ordinary recession in 1929, the next year he stated that it was a contagion from Europe, and his RFC proposal was an admission that America was "in the midst of a world wide economic catastrophe." The Constitution made it very difficult to give aid directly to individual citizens, White explained, so the president was operating on the theory that aid given to corporations and the wealthy would trickle down to the broader population. The administration suggested that the RFC would do just that. The measure received widespread praise from political commentators such as Lippmann, but it was too little, too late. White noticed that Kansas banks were failing at an increasing rate as conditions worsened in early 1932. The crushing economic situation meant that the Republican Party was likely to suffer punishing defeats in the West that year, and White felt that his "tenuous" standing at the White House left him powerless to help the party avoid its fate.[15]

The prospects seemed good for a change in presidential leadership, but White was troubled by his sense that liberals as a whole were not "thinking in terms of a better tomorrow, but merely trying to make a bridge back to yesterday." He was heartbroken that liberalism "ha[d] sounded no note of hope, made no plans for the future, offered no program" that would result in "some sort of permanent peace of mind and economic security for the average man." White dreamed of a twenty-year campaign to extend the "security line" to the working class, giving them the economic peace of mind that had allowed middle-class Americans such as himself to take risks and prosper. Such a program would include unemployment relief, national economic planning, a supportive farm policy, public regulation of utilities, old age pensions, and an acknowledgment that those who were willing to work deserved a decent living. There remained the slightest possibility that the Hoover administration might recognize that "we have gotten to the bottom of the barrel," and White argued that "the time has come to liberalize the [administration's] policy" by using government spending to create jobs. Funding would be provided by a confiscatory inheritance tax, which White argued would be the "most powerful agency for social justice guaranteeing equality of opportunity as nothing else can do."[16] Unfortunately, it appeared that no liberal of either party was willing and able to advance the agenda White envisioned.

The 1932 campaign was soon under way, but White never seriously considered endorsing anyone except Hoover. His was an act of personal loyalty rather than ideological conviction. White had long understood that the president had no chance of reelection, which made it easier to endorse him because there was no real danger of a second term. Still, White put up a good front by defending the president as a reformer at heart on the eve of the Republican national convention, albeit one "considerably to the right of The *Gazette*." Hoover had a talent for alienating his allies, and he managed to outrage the ever-loyal

White by declaring that it was acceptable for the government to lend money to profitable businesses because business was more efficient than government. White politely disagreed with Hoover in the *Gazette,* while fuming to Senator Arthur Capper (R-KS) that business's recklessness had caused the Depression. Considering his diatribes against urban political machines during the 1920s, it was shocking that White stated that machine politicians "Jimmy Walker, Big Bill Thompson, [William] Vare and their kind are better, wiser, and more efficient than [financiers] [John] Raskob with his inside pool manipulating the markets, the crooks whom [Robert] LaGuardia uncovered, [Samuel] Insull with his pyramid of larceny, and [Ivar] Kreuger with his till-tapping, bond-snatching manipulations." The people had starved and frozen and suffered during the winter of 1931, and White reminded Capper that "when the hungry and cold call in the armed gangsters and are directed by the ruthless Communists, we are going to have a kickup which will give us a most disagreeable time." Ultimately, White argued that any man who was willing to work ought to have it, even if the government had to do the hiring.[17]

White attended both parties' conventions in 1932, but he found the Republican event unremarkable compared to the excitement of the Democratic National Convention. Roosevelt impressed him as a representative of the Democrats' liberal wing, complete with what White saw as a call for "a platform promise to wipe out the depression in the Jeffersonian manner by beginning at the bottom rather than by beginning at the top as the Republicans have begun." Roosevelt's acceptance speech struck White as the first "unterrified liberal note" by a presidential candidate since Theodore Roosevelt in 1912. Reformers had been blockaded since World War I had pushed aside progressive issues in the 1916 election. The Democratic and Republican Parties had both reacted to the postwar world order by nominating conservatives in 1920 and 1924, and cultural struggles had torn the liberal movement apart in 1928. White was pleased that Roosevelt's speech had transformed American politics by offering the nation its first real opportunity in a generation for a "clear cut contest between left wing liberalism and right wing conservatism."[18]

As much as White admired Roosevelt's liberal war cry, both he and Sallie agreed that it was best to support Hoover "on the general ground that we cannot afford to rock the boat." Roosevelt had not been tested in a national role, and many liberals, including White's Democratic friends Lippmann and Villard, regarded FDR as a genial but shallow politician. White confessed "a terrible fear of what will happen if Roosevelt wins. I fear panic and catastrophe," and Hoover was promising nothing more than to "keep the ship afloat and that is something." Publicly, he editorialized that both Roosevelt and Hoover were offering good medicine, but White endorsed Hoover on the theory that the real difference was one of parties rather than candidates. White knew the Republican Party and he trusted it more than the Democratic Party, which he still regarded as hopelessly divided between liberals, southern racists, reactionaries, and urban machines. Privately, White conceded to Harold Ickes that he would be pleased if Roosevelt were elected and managed to enact the measures he had outlined in his acceptance speech. Understandably, he wondered whether Roosevelt could "go the distance" after watching the Democratic convention divide between its liberal wing demanding strong government intervention and its conservative wing insisting on a balanced budget and laissez-faire economics.[19]

White had sided with Hoover even though he knew that the president had only "one chance in a hundred" of prevailing, and he pitched in as best he could for his friend. The Hoover campaign was eager for anything White would write in favor of the administration, and he obliged even though he disliked writing "under orders." The RNC distributed his editorials by the hundreds of thousands during the campaign. In one piece, White argued that President Hoover was a diligent worker who lacked the publicity skills required to educate Americans about his efforts to fight the Depression, such as balancing the budget or sponsoring the RFC. In a radio address, White credited Hoover for having been a steady hand on the helm during the existential crisis of the Depression. Roosevelt had offered masterful speeches, but White alleged that they were devoid of specific proposals and that the Democrats could not make good on their promises.

Actually, Roosevelt had campaigned on a coherent vision of America as an interconnected society that needed government regulation to ensure equality of opportunity. In contrast, Hoover had stood on rugged individualism. For White, the contest was simple. "Herbert Hoover is the issue in this campaign" because he lacked charisma, but White claimed that the president had risen to meet the challenge of the Depression. He implored the voters to demonstrate their faith in America, in democracy, and in Hoover by giving him a second term.[20]

Franklin Roosevelt won a landslide victory on November 8, and White immediately called on all Americans to stand with the president-elect in his efforts to confront the Depression. Although he felt that "the sinister influences of Tammany, Hearst and the hillbilly Democracy surrounded Governor Roosevelt in the campaign," White conceded that many of his old Bull Moose allies supported FDR because they believed in something Hoover would never support: a government safety net for all citizens. White declared that he would throw his endorsement to Roosevelt as well if he made good on his promises, although he doubted that FDR had the strength required to resist the "New York slickers" who would bamboozle him for their own personal gain. As for Hoover, White likened his defeat to the long-anticipated passing of a terminally ill patient: death was merely being "put out of his misery and into a better world." The loss was a bitter pill for Hoover, whom White described as "groggy" after he and Sallie spent three postelection nights at the White House.[21] In the end, Hoover was defeated because the Depression was a fundamental crisis of the American psyche, and he was utterly incapable of leading the nation through the darkness.

Fear was palpable as the nation's banking system verged on the brink of collapse during the four-month-long lame-duck period between the Hoover and Roosevelt presidencies. As White observed, banks slashed credit, feelings of "unrest and insecurity" abounded, and the crisis seemed likely to worsen to the point of catastrophe. Given the dire situation, White wrote Senator Capper that President

Hoover needed to do whatever it took to create inflation as a means of breaking the "impasse between debtors who are broke and creditors who will soon be broke." Hoover might not want to foist policy on the incoming Roosevelt administration, but White pointed out that it was unfair to leave Roosevelt with "a crumbling commerce in the throes of economic revolution." Senator Capper read White's letter aloud to the president, who instead sought to ram his conservative policies through the lame-duck Congress in early 1933. Meanwhile, White was forced to contemplate laying off employees at the *Gazette*. Action was desperately needed, and White observed that no nation in the world was safe and prosperous: China had been attacked by Japan, and there were riots in Spain, rumors of revolution in Cuba, skirmishes between Nazis and communists in Germany's streets, and civil unrest in Ireland. The best summary of the situation came from an Emporia farmer, whom White quoted as having remarked that President-Elect Roosevelt needed to "do sumpin'." White was thrilled when early reports indicated that Roosevelt intended to create what amounted to state-directed capitalism, which the editor applauded as "a complete about-face in the American attitude towards government."[22]

By Inauguration Day, March 4, 1933, a sixty-five-year-old White had joined Lippmann and many other journalists in calling for the president to be given nearly dictatorial powers to deal with the crisis. The economic situation was most acute: the national income had dropped by 50 percent since 1929, 13 million were unemployed, and the American banking system was utterly paralyzed. As White observed, "no president has come to the White House since Lincoln's day facing such national peril as confronts this man." All Americans had to stand with the new president and trust that "no matter what he urges, it may be presumed to be wise." Roosevelt immediately declared a bank holiday while the administration feverishly developed a plan to present to the special session of Congress that was set to open on March 9. Congress passed the Emergency Banking Act stabilizing the banking system on the first day of the special session. Within weeks, the president signed a raft of legislation to relieve the people's suffering, stimulate recovery, and reform the nation's economic superstructure.[23]

Roosevelt's flurry of activity restored the American people's morale during the first hundred days, and White was pleased to admit that he had been wrong about the president. He gushed to Ickes, now secretary of the interior, that on "March 4, the American people did not care what a man did so long as he did something. And since March 4, there has been something doing and mostly something doing in the right direction. . . . These are grand days, worth living for!" White had once thought that Governor Roosevelt was a good state politician who was not "Presidential size," but the activity of the first hundred days had shown that he had "developed magnitude and poise, more than all, power." To another friend, White wrote that Roosevelt had proven his mettle but he "still remain[ed] a puzzle to me. . . . His qualities never came out, never were revealed" during the campaign. White planned to depart for an extended trip to Europe to attend the London Economic Conference in mid-1933. He pledged to Ickes that he would eat the words he had uttered against Roosevelt with such zeal that "I shall smack my lips as my Adams Apple bobs" if the recovery was still under way when he returned. Secretary Ickes proudly forwarded a copy of White's letter to the president, who naturally approved of the editor's stance.[24]

White embarked on his five-month-long European tour as a syndicated correspondent on May 31, but the London Economic Conference dissolved after the Roosevelt administration withdrew. Still, he profited tremendously from his time in Europe, which once again helped him develop a fuller understanding of the international situation. The Whites quit London and joined former YMCA official Sherwood Eddy's Russian-sponsored tour of Leningrad and Moscow, where they spent "two weeks—two gorgeous weeks—and saw the world turned upside down." The scale of the Soviet experiment impressed White, who recognized that the Russian people had "no liberty . . . and probably don't want it, preferring other things, security and peace." The Whites next visited Vienna, a city he saw as "starving to death, wasting away with the threat of the Nazis on the German frontier and the threat of the old Royalty within." The couple met Italian dictator Benito Mussolini while traveling from Naples to Trieste that September before finally embarking for the United States. Summing up his experiences in the *Gazette*, White lamented that "in practically every land east of the Rhine . . . to the Golden Gate of California, democracy is dead and gone." The dictatorships of Russia, Germany, and Italy all made war on personal liberty and individualism, differing only in whether repression was justified in the name of the upper class or the workers. Democracy survived in western Europe only because the region provided a better standard of living for its poor, which proved to White that social justice was a matter of national security.[25]

White returned from Europe "more convinced than ever that the people should rally around the Roosevelt leadership," and he was true to his promise that he would admit that his doubts about Roosevelt were unjustified. Privately, White confessed that he had been "jealous of the name Roosevelt; didn't want to see it in the White House again and was mean about it in my heart." As a result, he had been publicly generous while watchfully waiting for FDR to return to his bad habits as "the rather mediocre Governor of New York." The first year of Roosevelt's presidency had been highly successful, and White conceded that "he must have something on the ball." The New Deal's industrial recovery program had begun to struggle by 1934, but while liberals such as Lippmann and Villard had grown critical, White stood firm by declaring that Americans had to put their faith in Roosevelt as "our one fortress in this hour." The editor indulged his conservative friends by conceding that America was "in one hell of a fix" because it had to rely on either "politicians who are incompetent and easily corruptible . . . [or] greedy anti-social capitalists" who were just as incompetent and corrupt. Still, he editorialized that the best prescription for America was more New Deal: more market reform, protection for labor unions, social insurance and pensions, and progressive taxation. The editorial pleased White so greatly that he sent it to his Democratic congressman to show the president, and Roosevelt responded with a personal note of gratitude.[26]

Roosevelt's leadership still gave White reservations despite his strong support for New Deal policies, but he circulated his sentiments quietly amongst his conservative friends. Former president Hoover surprised him with a visit to Emporia in March 1934, and the two men "wrangled a little" after White rejected Hoover's conservative argument that property rights ought to be valued above all else. White attended a White House press conference at Roosevelt's invitation one month later, but he was shocked to discover that the president had no grand design for reform. Instead, FDR appeared to be experimenting, following the current, using trial and error, and drawing on his subordinates for ideas. The president's demeanor also irritated White's midwestern sensibilities, and he remarked that FDR "smiles too much for one who shakes his head so positively." White had gone "into the room an optimist . . . and for an hour or so afterwards I was a pessimist with a guilty tendency to dirty cynicism." The president was "earnest and honest in his endeavor to get us out of the mess," and he had "courage, but courage without intelligent purpose . . . becomes arrogance and if it wobbles . . . it is devastating." White was hardly alone in his frustration with Roosevelt's willingness to experiment with diverse strategies, and the experience caused him to rethink the amount of power the New Deal had accreted to the executive branch. White's fear that reactionary business interests or a demagogue could exploit a powerful executive branch to establish a dictatorship was one that he was increasingly willing to raise with liberals and conservatives alike.[27]

White had sound reasons to be concerned about the potential rise of powerful demagogues. He had seen the power of demagoguery firsthand in his fight against John Brinkley, a quack doctor in Kansas who was known for transplanting goat testicles into his patients as a remedy for a variety of illnesses. Brinkley fleeced his way into wealth by taking advantage of the desperate and the gullible, and he soon expanded along these lines by establishing radio station KFKB. Kansans were desperate for relief from the Great Depression in 1930, and Brinkley seized the moment to launch a write-in campaign for governor. He was able to use his radio station, his personal wealth,

*Herbert Hoover and White, on a subsequent visit to the latter's home on February 17,
1935. Courtesy of Kenneth Spencer Research Library, University of Kansas Libraries.*

and his vast talent for medicine-show antics to attract hordes of the
disaffected to his cause. Among other promises, Brinkley proposed
protections for family farms, free health care for the poor, and social insurance for the aged and the disabled. The problems Brinkley
highlighted were real, but he never offered a serious vision of how his
solutions would be achieved. The goat doctor came perilously close to
winning Kansas's governorship as an independent candidate in 1930
and 1932, but the New Deal helped defuse his 1934 campaign by re-
storing hope that the political system was responding to the people's
needs.[28]

White attributed Brinkley's success to his ability to "herd in a big
moron vote," and he vigorously attacked the goat doctor in all three
of his campaigns. As in his campaign against the Populists, White's
most effective attacks against Brinkley relied on Kansas pride. In
an editorial titled "Save Kansas," he asked his readers if they were
ready to be "greeted with . . . the cry of the billy goat, when they walk

the streets of other states." However, "Brinkleyism" was about more than just Brinkley. "Brinkleyism" resembled Governor Huey Long's program in Louisiana, in that it capitalized on the fact that many felt, not without reason, that the system had let them down. Long was elected to the US Senate as a Democrat from Louisiana in 1932, and White feared the "Kingfish's" rise as he honed his demagogical skills nationally. Millions of lower-middle-class Americans supported Long's gradual shift toward opposing the New Deal because they disliked Roosevelt's willingness to cooperate with large institutions, and White denounced Long as "the Hitler of the Delta" in several editorials. Brinkley and Long embodied White's fears about demagogues exploiting "the uneducated hill-billies of the backward country districts" to gain power. White warned that many had paid a heavy price for laughing at Adolf Hitler in Germany and Huey Long in Louisiana because they appeared to be clowns. The risk that Americans would "grow so tired of alphabet soup they would turn to Louisiana gumbo" was one that White took seriously.[29]

Roosevelt had lost some of his luster for White, but the Republican Party was still a poor harbor for liberals. The Republican National Committee was split into an ultraconservative faction and a more moderately conservative faction led by Hoover. The body was scheduled to meet in June 1934 to approve its midterm election platform and elect a new national chairman, and the ultraconservatives attempted to force their ideology on the party. David Hinshaw was still active in Republican politics, and he sent the ultraconservatives' proposed policy statements to White for comment in advance of the meeting. White fumed that a platform based on such ideas would cost the party "every state west of the Alleghenies," insisting that the "busted breastworks of 1929" were "gone forever." Instead, he advocated for federal protection for collective bargaining, old age pensions, unemployment and disability insurance, public employment programs, and an inflationary policy designed to free the credit markets. Ultimately, White argued that the federal government had to accept "responsibility for a decent minimum standard of living below which no man who is willing to work may be allowed to sink," or the nation would experience "a despair which will turn either to fascism or to communism, flaunting democracy as a failure." White's opposition to the platform was significant. The mere suggestion that "Mr. White and his following" would abandon the GOP if the document passed as written was sufficient to carry the issue for Hoover's RNC supporters. The final platform explicitly stated that government had to address the nation's problems, and White gave it his public endorsement.[30]

The Republican Party's reactionary bent was enough to sour White during the summer of 1934, but events conspired to compound his misery that year. The Midwest was devastated by yet another summer of extreme drought, and White chronicled the grim statistics: forty days of temperatures above 107 degrees Fahrenheit, ten days in excess of 110, and very little rainfall. The intense heat had baked the corn crop, and the portly White stewed through many a sweat-soaked day before fleeing to Colorado. The Rockies had always offered an escape, but even White's vacation turned into a curse when he was stricken with severe pain while driving in western Colorado, thirty miles from the nearest doctor, at eight o'clock at night. White was informed that he required an urgent operation, and he was immediately driven to Pueblo to pick up a hospital intern who would accompany him on the midnight train to Kansas. After a brief stop in Emporia, the Whites traveled to the Mayo Clinic for partial removal of his ulcerated prostate gland. The operation was a success, White seemed to recover quickly, and his prognosis for a full recovery was good. However, the condition might have been a harbinger of the colon cancer that ended his life a decade later.[31] The only good thing about White's illness was that it shielded him from any question of participating in the Republicans' disastrous 1934 midterm campaign. The outcome was no surprise to White, who felt that the GOP's conservative leadership had ignored his advice to "offer a program" that would give the American people economic security. Roosevelt had been "all but crowned by the people," and White editorialized that the president deserved wide latitude in his efforts to restore prosperity "so long as democratic forms persist."[32]

President Roosevelt was all the more essential to White because there appeared to be no reasonable alternative to his leadership in either party. Senator Long remained a looming danger through the massive following he built with his grandiose promises and masterful radio addresses. White was highly disturbed by rumors that Long would threaten to run for president in 1936 as a tactic to extract patronage from the Roosevelt administration, which he would use to fuel a serious campaign for the White House in 1940. To White, Senator Long was dangerous because he had mastered the art of rallying the poor white voters of the Deep South, whom White saw as a "moron" crowd. "Morons" were individuals who were not stupid in anything except politics, who were susceptible to demagogues, and who White guessed amounted to a quarter to a third of the population. The uneducated masses were with Roosevelt for the moment, but White knew that they could be captured by Long, a fascist-leaning demagogue, or a reactionary Republican who would use them to build a dictatorship in 1936 or 1940. The threat of demagoguery made it all the more important to White that the Republicans found a candidate for 1936 who understood that the nation could not go back to 1929.[33]

Ironically, White's fears about demagogues in America meshed with his concerns about Roosevelt's character to make him wary of the administration precisely as it was enacting measures he had sought for thirty years. The Roosevelt administration shifted decisively toward structural reforms in 1935. White celebrated the Wagner Act, which policed industrial relations with labor, the Social Security Act creating a social safety net, and the New Deal's various financial reform laws as a "Roosevelt revolution" that would build "a broader base for a larger consuming power in the country and so keep more fields and factories busy." The measures were real achievements that would "clip the claws of dishonest, double-dealing, tax-dodging, plug-hat respectables," and White scolded the GOP for insisting that it would repeal the New Deal. At the same time, he worried that Roosevelt's methods were establishing a pattern of emergency legislation passed by an unquestioning Congress that could be exploited by an unscrupulous successor. The danger of demagogues acquiring power

White and Albert Einstein after receiving their honorary degrees from Harvard University in June 1935. Courtesy of Emporia State University, Special Collections and Archives.

by peddling expeditious solutions during emergencies was one that had been realized in "Rome, Berlin or Moscow," and White felt that Roosevelt did not understand that his methods could be abused in the future. The New Deal was good medicine for American democracy, but White argued that it was time for the nation to return to the normal legislative process. By "normal," White meant that Congress had to stand up to the president occasionally, and the Republican Party needed to become a viable opposition party. All of this would take time, and White knew that Roosevelt occupied a nearly unassailable political position in the near term.[34]

The Republican Party's overwhelming defeat in 1934 spurred its leadership to consider White's argument that it had to develop a credible recovery program, but the outcome was the opposite of what he had desired. White had suggested that the party assemble small discussion groups of twenty grassroots delegates in each of ten or fifteen states with orders to develop ideas for the 1936 platform. The Republican establishment acted on the idea by calling the Grassroots Republican Conference to discuss platform ideas at Springfield, Illinois, in June 1935. White agreed to serve on the conference's platform committee because he expected it to be a serious, compact gathering, and because both Hoover and Kansas GOP chairman John D. Hamilton asked for his participation. Instead, the proposed convention ballooned to two thousand young conservative delegates who White knew would care only about anti-Roosevelt "indictment and hurrah-boys." The New Deal deserved constructive criticism, but White feared that "a mere indictment merely feeds the flames of men who are eventually going to vote for Huey Long."[35] White was in a quandary. He had given his word that he would participate, and he was a man who lived by his word. At the same time, that he would be prominently involved in an enterprise that was entirely at odds with his ideas was preposterous.

In desperation, White wrote to Hamilton and Hoover asking for an honorable way out of his promise to attend. To Hamilton, White pointed out that the Republican Party was divided between those who wanted to end the New Deal and those who wanted to continue it under more competent, Republican leadership. White placed himself solidly in the latter camp. Only a lasting recovery could save the United States from "violent revolution" of the Bolshevik or fascist variety, and the only way to create such a recovery was to uplift the working class so that it could consume America's industrial output. White supported liberalism, but he felt that Roosevelt was an ineffective liberal whose efforts were "just jamming the machine." The GOP had an obligation to advance a constructive, liberal agenda that would help preserve American democracy. To Hoover, White asserted that the wealthy had to accept adjustments to their ancient rights to profit, interest, and property, or they would lose everything to a demagogue establishing a "greedy plutocracy under fascism, or a dull and rapacious proletariat under communism." White protested that it would be folly for him to participate in the convention given his ideas, and perhaps he sensed the truth that he had been invited as liberal window dressing. As one of Hoover's conservative advisors noted, there would be tremendous "news value" in nailing White "down to a decently conservative platform." Hoover pressed White to make a public statement in lieu of participation, and he suggested that the statement embrace conservative ideas defending Hoover's record. The former president wanted White to denounce the New Deal and condemn "the horde of non-producers" that allegedly were leeching off the government. White gently rebuffed the idea, explaining that his objections to Roosevelt pertained to the speed rather than the substance of the New Deal.[36]

White was wise to avoid the Grassroots Conference, which produced nothing more than a mixture of partisan attacks on the administration and grudging acceptance of elements of the New Deal. The disappointing outcome left White feeling even more politically lost during the summer of 1935. To his right were the "economic Hamiltonians . . . yelling their throats sore in protest of a strongly centralized Federal Government," and to his left were the "economic Jeffersonians [who] are clamoring for more power to a bureaucratic state." The conference debacle had shown White that he could not "turn to the black conservatism of the Republican organization, and

I fear to turn definitely to the Roosevelt crowd." White utterly rejected the idea that Roosevelt had dictatorial ambitions, because the president seemed to care nothing for money, place, or power. The problem with Roosevelt was his apparent lack of "fundamental rock-bottom intellectual and moral honesty," which left White feeling that "somewhere he is built upon sand." One reason why White celebrated the Supreme Court's unanimous decision declaring the National Recovery Administration unconstitutional in May 1935 was that he hoped it would force Roosevelt to "fish or cut bait" by developing a strategy for reform instead of relying on emergency legislation.[37]

As much as Roosevelt's methods troubled White, he understood that the consequences of a Roosevelt implosion in 1936 would be far worse. America was a middle-class nation that would never accept communism, and White saw communism as dangerous only to the extent that it gave right-wing extremists a pretext for a fascist dictatorship. The same middle-class identity that immunized America against communism made it susceptible to fascism, as White had discovered during his fight against the Klan in the 1920s. He knew that "the raw material of Fascism" was already in America: "the Legion and the various Veterans Associations . . . the various red baiting leagues and societies which would flaunt the Fascist banners and let the veterans do the shooting, and finally the fear that is always in the hearts of the people." A Roosevelt implosion would encourage the Republicans to nominate a reactionary, and the resulting political upheaval would enable Long or another demagogue to win the White House.[38]

An assassin's bullet eliminated Senator Long in September 1935, but the threat of fascist demagoguery continued to loom over the nation. In his commencement speech at the Kansas State Teachers College at Pittsburg, White diagnosed the root problem as the lack of economic opportunity created by the rise of advanced industrial capitalism. Men who lacked opportunity were easily led astray by those who promised "economic security without political liberty," and the populations of Russia, Germany, Japan, and Italy had already fallen to this siren song. The United States had not succumbed, and White was careful to note that "we Americans are in no immediate danger of the world plague. But it's in the air." In the short term, Americans should not "let orators denouncing Fascism drag you into Communism. Don't let the smart, hard-bitten superpatriots lambasting Communism, lead you into Fascism." In the long term, White charged his young audience with a duty to "see to it that the American standard of living—the middle class standard . . . is maintained for all Americans who are willing to work. There is your equality of opportunity." Middle-class living standards ought to be the base from which individuals could rise, and that no one was allowed to violate through "the anti-social uses of his bad qualities." If Americans succeeded in balancing the efficiency of the modern world with democratic ideals, they would find their solution to "the material problem of the machine age. There is the lost frontier."[39] Simply put, White's prescription was nothing less than a full dose of New Deal liberalism.

Kansas governor Alf Landon had impressed White as the kind of Republican who might provide constructive criticism of the New Deal, and he was an early supporter of Landon's 1936 presidential campaign. Landon was the son of a prominent Theodore Roosevelt supporter during the Progressive Era, and the two men had become acquainted when White was a regent and Landon an undergraduate at the University of Kansas. White and Landon fought for the Progressive Party in 1912, and Landon loyally supported White's independent campaign for governor in 1924 despite the taunts of his conservative friends. Landon wrote White that year that he supported him because "your articles and editorials in my opinion did more to pave the way for the Progressive movement than anyone else, and . . . they have had more influence in my life in more ways than one." Senator Borah campaigned for the Republican nomination in 1936 as well, but White endorsed Landon partly because he owed him a debt of personal loyalty. A second reason White chose Landon was that he saw him as a fiscal conservative who was reasonably liberal on questions of social and economic justice. Third, Landon seemed to be more reliable than the fiercely independent and famously stubborn Senator Borah. White doubted that Landon could beat Roosevelt in 1936, but he believed that the candidate could advance the liberal cause by presenting a distinctly liberal position. As White put it, a man could "garner just as good a crop" through the seeds sown in a losing campaign as could be reaped through victory.[40]

White helped Landon early in the primary campaign by making a crucial ten-day talking tour to familiarize eastern Republicans with the governor's record, but he began to back away when Landon aligned himself with the hard right. In particular, White was profoundly disappointed by Landon's willingness to accept help organizing his California campaign from newspaper publisher William Randolph Hearst. White had long detested Hearst as a demagogue, and his hatred intensified when the publisher organized a vigilante campaign against striking workers in California in 1935. In White's view Hearst was guilty of supporting "crystallizing Fascism," and Landon ignored his warning that his cooperation with Hearst would alienate hordes of liberal Republicans.[41] As usual, White was to serve as both a syndicated reporter and a participant representing Landon on the platform-writing Committee on Resolutions at the 1936 Republican national convention. His doubts about Landon came to a head on the eve of the convention, and White surprised Landon by asking to be discharged from his promise to work on the platform committee because anything he wrote as a journalist would be parsed as a smoke signal from Landon's inner circle. Landon rushed to Emporia an hour before White was to depart for the convention to explain that he was counting on him, and White agreed to serve as planned. However, he made his thoughts clear when Landon asked him for his opinion on whether he would make a good president: White replied that he would either "crumble or crystallize under heat and pressure."[42]

White's concerns about serving as both a journalist and a delegate on the Committee on Resolutions were soon validated. The Supreme Court struck down a New York State minimum wage law in *Morehead v. New York ex rel. Tipaldo* on June 1, and White wrote an editorial from the convention advocating a constitutional amendment to overturn the ruling. The piece was circulated nationally, and the Resolutions Committee's conservatives demanded his dismissal because of his views. The effort failed, and White put himself to the exhausting work of trying to insert reform elements into the platform. White later reported that "for two days I didn't eat sitting down except breakfast," only to see the committee's conservative majority dismiss his efforts with "the horse-laugh in subdued and gentlemanly tones." Landon came to his defense by dramatically wiring the convention that White had his support, and the committee's conservatives were forced to give way. The committee grudgingly allowed White and Borah to write the monopoly and foreign relations planks, but White admitted that the platform was otherwise entirely conservative in outlook.[43]

The convention climaxed with Landon's acceptance speech, but the event also marked the nadir of his political association with White. Landon had asked White to comment on his draft acceptance speech, and White made several suggestions designed to temper its conservative tone. The intensely conservative speech Landon delivered showed that White's comments had been completely ignored. Although White had cultivated Landon as a man with at least some liberal tendencies, the episode convinced him that Landon was "the seed that fell among the stones." White "just didn't go to Topeka or feel that I could work with Landon intimately after" the nomination speech incident, even though Landon continued to solicit his advice. Every time Landon developed a promising idea that was even faintly liberal, White lamented, his conservative advisors ran over it "rough shod" so that "it looks like a war map of Spain" after they had finished. By September, White smirked that Landon had allowed the conservative "New York crowd" to turn him into a hybrid of "one reactionary horse and one timid progressive rabbit."[44]

Although he disagreed with Landon's politics, White still used his influence to help his friend. For instance, he persuaded liberal Republican senator Norris not to campaign on Roosevelt's behalf in Kansas on the grounds that doing so would hurt liberal Republicans in the state. For good measure, White added that it was unneighborly to campaign against Kansas's first presidential candidate in his home state. He also wrote several of his friends to ask them to consider supporting Landon, including Lippmann, influential columnist Dorothy Thompson, and novelist Upton Sinclair. The replies were not encouraging. Lippmann responded that he liked Landon, but he could not overlook John D. Hamilton's highly conservative speeches as campaign proxy. Sinclair read a Landon speech at White's suggestion, and he remarked that the candidate "sounded to me like a regular conservative making an effort to sound liberal." Thompson replied that she had begun the campaign opposed to FDR's reelection, but Landon's reactionary speeches had, ironically, persuaded her that Roosevelt was the only viable candidate.[45]

White knew that Landon would be defeated in 1936, but he found no refuge in Roosevelt's candidacy. As usual, White also attended the Democratic national convention as a reporter. He was disturbed by the structured pageantry of Roosevelt's acceptance speech, which offended him as "the most gorgeously imperial spectacle ever staged . . . on this side of Germany." The display failed to have the intended effect on White, who called it "like the chameleon that busted itself on the plaid necktie trying to do too many colors at once. It was the very size of the spectacle that turned it into brass." Still, the eruption of the Spanish Civil War in July left White ambivalent, and he confided

> that "the cause of Liberalism and progressivism will be set back by the defeat of Roosevelt by any candidate." But I also feel that the cause of liberalism and progressivism will be set back by the election of Roosevelt. Which is my way of saying that I fear that the way of fascism or at least the world revolt against democracy will reach our shores within a year and we shall have to fight the battle that is raging in Spain. It makes no difference which man is in the White House when that day comes.[46]

The fact that White had no fundamental policy disagreements with the Roosevelt administration was humorously advertised when President Roosevelt's campaign train stopped for a brief address in

The inscription refers to White's encounter with Roosevelt at the Emporia train station during the 1936 campaign. It reads: "To William Allen White—from his old friend who is for him all 48 months. Franklin D. Roosevelt." Courtesy of Emporia State University, Special Collections and Archives.

Emporia on October 13. White made his best effort to watch the president's speech inconspicuously by standing in a stationhouse doorway, but Roosevelt asked the crowd if White was present. The editor made no reply because he did not want to create an uncomfortable situation, but the crowd pointed him out and the president invited him on stage. To refuse a presidential request would be "conspicuously rude," and he had to stand there while Roosevelt joked that he was happy to have "Bill White's support for three and a half years out of every four." Landon's campaign managers were up in arms about the incident, and White calmed them by editorializing that he had not been with the president for the preceding six months. Still, there was much truth in FDR's jest. Roosevelt's appeals to the masses continued to irritate White's midwestern sensibilities during the campaign, but he made no serious attacks against the president.[47]

The 1936 election was an epic disaster for the Republican Party, and Roosevelt won by a larger margin than he had in 1932. White publicly applauded the New Deal as the culmination of forty years of efforts to shatter rugged individualism through reform, although privately he attributed the victory to Roosevelt's ability to cobble a majority coalition from southern Democrats, urban voters, individuals on relief, and organized labor. The combination struck him as dangerous because the president would have his hands full juggling the "quite unrelated and sometimes drastically opposing" interests of his coalition. As for Landon, White offered the candidate the consolation that he had fought valiantly against impossible odds. More broadly, he felt that the Republican leadership had ignored the evidence that conservatism was on the wane, and their insistence on taking a hard-right stance had allowed the GOP to be "tarred with plutocracy." Landon sealed his own fate when he chose "ultra-conservative advisors" early in the campaign. Kansas's John D. Hamilton had risen to the chairmanship of the Republican National Committee during the campaign, and White singled him out as particularly "awful. He wasn't an organizer but a fighter" who had barnstormed the country giving counterproductive speeches instead of focusing on building a campaign apparatus.[48]

The disastrous outcome of the 1936 election finally spurred the Republican Party to listen to White's advice that it devise a serious response to the Depression. Representative Hamilton Fish (R-NY) launched a drive to unseat Hamilton from the chairmanship with White's support, citing Hamilton's hyperconservative campaign rhetoric as proof that he was not the man to liberalize the GOP. The effort failed, but Chairman Hamilton finally acted on White's proposal for a series of small, grassroots meetings to write a platform that sincerely tackled the problems facing America. The effort, called the Republican Program Committee, assembled two hundred individuals in early 1938 with specific instructions to avoid "petty and vindictive faultfinding" against the Democrats . The participants were asked to be honest about the New Deal, which the RNC admitted had done many "things that should have been done long ago," some things that had failed, and some that "had dangerously undesirable objectives." The Republican Program Committee finally realized White's call for the GOP to make a sincere effort to address the Great Depression, without invective and without gazing longingly toward the glory days of 1929. Ironically, White did not participate directly because a vengeful Hamilton refused to appoint him, but his presence was still felt among the delegates. The group's study materials included one of White's speeches calling for the Republicans to embrace an active, liberal agenda, proving that the committee was very different from the highly partisan Grassroots Republican Conference that he had shunned in 1935.[49]

The 1936 election had not created any new rifts between White and Roosevelt, but the administration's postelection attempt to reform the US Supreme Court quickly convinced White that his worst fears about Roosevelt's expedient methods were justified. For decades, reformers had criticized the Supreme Court as an unelected body that subverted the people's right to legislate through Congress, and Senators Borah and Norris had proposed measures to limit judicial review during the 1920s. President Roosevelt's first term in office was marred by an unprecedented torrent of anti–New Deal Supreme

Court decisions, often rendered by a slim majority of 5 to 4 and based on arcane logic. White had editorialized in 1934 that ample precedent existed for adjusting the number of justices on the bench if the Court continued to sabotage reform. The 1936 election changed the calculus for White because the Democrats' overwhelming victory raised the specter of one-party rule. White was a political minority himself as a Republican, and he now appreciated the Supreme Court's ability to protect minorities against the tyranny of the majority.[50] The administration's Court proposal played into White's worst fears about Roosevelt's methods, spurring him into a sharp, temporary crisis of confidence in the president.

The Roosevelt administration interpreted the 1936 electoral outcome as a strong mandate to advance the New Deal, and FDR hinted at his plans in his State of the Union speech on January 6, 1937. The president paralleled White's logic that nations that treated all citizens justly remained democratic and those that did not fell to dictatorship, and he invited the Supreme Court to join with the executive and legislative branches as partners in preserving democracy. White acknowledged that the president had a legitimate grievance against the court: it had invalidated sixty-four acts of Congress over 138 years, and more than 20 percent of these occurred in the four years of the New Deal. Still, he asked for patience. Someday, a fascist Congress might pass measures designed to repress liberals, who would be glad to have a strong Supreme Court as a bulwark against reaction. Furthermore, White reminded his readers that the justices' average age of seventy-four meant that time and death would inevitably do the work of "wiping out that four to five reactionary majority."[51]

Roosevelt proposed legislation allowing him to appoint up to six additional judges to the Supreme Court on February 5, realizing White's fears that FDR wanted more fundamental changes to the judiciary. Editorially, White agreed that judicial reform was necessary and he explicitly dismissed the argument that Roosevelt wanted to be a dictator, but he maintained that the president was establishing precedents that would be dangerous. The world was full of demagogues promising a new golden age if given license to ignore the democratic process. Americans ought to be wary of the president's methods given the rise of dictatorship in the world, and White cuttingly exclaimed that Roosevelt had the people's mandate "to function as the President, not as *der fuehrer!*" He noted that the epic scale of the Depression had encouraged Congress to pass legislation without debate or due process, and this produced "an irregularity which pointed to dictatorship." White's nagging suspicions about Roosevelt's character had taken hold of him. As much as he saw Roosevelt as a well-intentioned reformer, White was angered by the thought that the president's mistrust of the people's inherent wisdom had spurred him to take a "direct backward step from democracy" that could lead to "one-man government."[52]

Although he had publicly declared his strong opposition to Roosevelt's plan, White continued working to influence the administration through Interior Secretary Ickes. Treading carefully, White wrote that he was "unhappy, but by no means heart broken" to hear that the president wanted to reform the court. If Roosevelt succeeded in pushing the Supreme Court around, White wondered, what would happen if a "Huey Long type gets into the White House"? Maintaining the court's independence was crucial, especially if the nation lurched powerfully to the right in the early 1950s. Ickes rejoined that Roosevelt had won reelection despite the Republican claim that he would pack the court, giving him a mandate. Testily, Ickes replied that "economic royalists" were behind the opposition to Roosevelt's effort to reform the Supreme Court, and he expressed frustration that conservatives were profiting from the "so-called liberals'" attacks on the president.[53]

White also reached out to Senator Norris in an attempt to influence the administration. Norris had vacillated between the position that judicial reform required a constitutional amendment and the argument that Congress had the inherent authority to accomplish reform by legislation. The senator collaborated with White in an attempt to deflect what both men regarded as the plan's most threatening aspect, which was the specter of the court's hyperpoliticization. White suggested that Norris introduce a constitutional amendment that defined interstate commerce, together with a rider calling for a speedy national referendum on the measure. Norris liked the suggestion enough to read White's letter aloud to Roosevelt, although the senator believed that an amendment by referendum was doomed to fail. Actually, White's proposal was a bid to slow the process because it would take time for the president to campaign for the people's mandate. In the meantime, as White had editorialized, time and death would solve the court problem by eliminating the conservative majority. White warned Norris that grassroots opposition to court reform was real, and his informal discussions with Roosevelt supporters around Emporia showed that this opposition was bipartisan. The editor solicited his referendum proposal to Ickes as well, who rejected it on the grounds that America did not have the decades it might take for ratification.[54]

The president had initially described his reforms as a broad bid to protect democracy, but he finally admitted in his March 9 fireside chat that his primary motive was to prevent the court from blocking his agenda. White was not persuaded, and he signaled his open opposition by remarking that "last night President Roosevelt wept on the bosoms of 40 million people." The fact that Roosevelt had not been able to appoint any new justices to the Supreme Court did not constitute a terrible judicial emergency, in White's view, and he argued that the president's patronage powers gave him effective control over Congress. The Supreme Court was the only remaining constitutional check on the executive branch, and White passionately advocated for its independence. Although he expressed faith that Roosevelt had the best of intentions, White argued that "benevolent despotism" was still despotism. The public never warmed to Roosevelt's proposal, and 51 percent of respondents opposed the measure according to a Gallup poll. The editor's call for patience seemed to be vindicated when the court drew on the Constitution's Commerce Clause to uphold the Wagner Act in *NLRB v. Jones & Laughlin Steel Corp.* and the right to set a minimum wage in *West Coast Hotel Co. v. Parrish.* The *Nation* had supported court reform, but the decisions led the journal to ask whether the court was "going liberal." It spoke volumes when the

Nation's editor, Freda Kirchwey, conceded to White that "a good liberal case can be made out against the president's plan."[55]

Court reform was mortally wounded when enough senators signaled their opposition to the bill to sustain a filibuster in April, and the coup de grâce was not long in coming. Senator Borah helped convince Justice Willis Van Devanter to announce his retirement precisely as the Judiciary Committee was rejecting the president's bill on May 18, which gave Roosevelt his first opportunity to appoint a Supreme Court justice. The need for reform was eliminated. The administration continued working for the bill's passage for several more weeks, but the effort was dead. White applauded the outcome, describing Roosevelt as a wise and patriotic man who had grown used to ruling without opposition. The episode was Roosevelt's first serious political defeat, and White counted it a net gain for the nation: the people had stood up for the Supreme Court, the court had listened to its critics and become more liberal, and Congress had asserted its independence. White hoped that Roosevelt would learn patience, although he feared for the future if the president revealed himself to be petulant in defeat.[56]

The court reform debacle had spooked White, and it took time for him to become reaccommodated to President Roosevelt's leadership. Meanwhile, he had a visceral reminder of the alternative to New Deal liberalism in the 1937 auto industry sit-down strike. Sit-down strikes were a new tactic in labor's arsenal in which striking workers gained leverage by occupying the company's factories. United Auto Workers president Walter Reuther decided to employ the method when the auto companies refused to recognize their workers' decision to unionize under the Wagner Act. Specifically, the UAW launched sit-down strikes against General Motors and Chrysler to gain their compliance with the law. White wrote a syndicated column from Detroit commenting on the strike. He entirely endorsed the workers' right to organize, picket, and bargain collectively because these rights stemmed from ancient values such as freedom of speech. However, White was opposed to depriving others of their property through the sit-down strike, which he saw as a resort to force that could lead to a dangerous cycle of conflict between labor and capital. At the same time, White felt that workers who invested part of their lives in their work deserved something like a property right to their jobs. The Wagner Act was the realization of his long-held belief that government had to protect the rights of labor and of capital to engage in collective bargaining. Although the UAW won the sit-down strike in February, White wanted labor to rely on the new law rather than resorting to such tactics.[57]

The UAW next sought to organize the Ford Motor Company, and Henry Ford soon undercut White's argument that labor should rely on the new law. White was angered when Ford insisted that his company would never obey the Wagner Act, but he was also dismayed when a UAW official retorted that Ford would negotiate with the union or it would not build cars. White's first instinct was to straddle the issue by denouncing both sides as reckless, and he advised the UAW that it was "dangerous to violate the law to get justice. It is better to get justice by changing the law." The "Battle of the Overpass" showed that it was naive to rely entirely on the law to achieve change. The battle occurred when UAW president Reuther and several colleagues distributed leaflets quoting the Wagner Act to Ford workers on a public road near the company's massive River Rouge factory on May 26. The UAW had invited the press to the event to dissuade Ford from deploying his army of union-busting thugs, but the UAW men were savagely beaten by forty Ford enforcers in front of the assembled reporters. The resulting photographs were a public relations disaster for Ford, but the company continued to ignore the Wagner Act until World War II. White was shaken, and he concluded that capital was the greater threat to the rule of law because it employed warlike weapons in an effort to drag labor "from the field of reason to the field of force." He worried that America would "pass into one of the many terrible tyrannies that are infesting the world" if the people supported business's reactionaries. White made good on his rhetoric. As soon as he had returned from Detroit, he issued a companywide memo reminding his *Gazette* employees that they had both the right and his blessing to join any union they felt would vigorously advocate for their interests.[58]

The fact that 1937 was a generally miserable year also contributed toward White's pessimism. The president's insistence on a balanced budget in 1936 had triggered the Roosevelt recession the following year, and the *Gazette*'s revenue dropped precipitously as the economy slowed. The summer was also one of the hottest on record, and both Mr. and Mrs. White suffered from several maladies. Sallie's chronic cardiovascular problems returned with full vigor that summer, and White was plagued by a restless gastrointestinal tract that made his life extremely uncomfortable. The couple planned to vacation in the American Southwest in the hope that sunshine, rest, and distractions would help, and the idea evolved into an extended stay in Mexico. The Whites thoroughly enjoyed their time in Mexico, which he described as similar to Spain or Italy in the towns and Greece or Bulgaria in the countryside. They lived "like royalty" in a Mexico City rental house that came complete with servants, but the vacation failed to yield its hoped-for therapeutic effect. Mr. and Mrs. White returned to the United States to visit New York City in the fall, but White fell victim to a hemorrhaging prostate ulcer that required emergency surgery at the Mayo Clinic. Although the prognosis was good and no cancer was detected, White's condition might have been another ominous sign of the colon cancer that killed him seven years later.[59]

Turbulence had defined 1937 for American liberalism and for White, but the following year's developments helped spur him back into Roosevelt's camp. White marked his seventieth birthday in February 1938, and he had always been highly sensitive about his age. Indeed, the prospect of becoming "old" on his fiftieth birthday in 1918 had so terrified him that he found himself "overcome by fear of impending senility" as he descended the stairs to attend his party, sat down, and cried. White gradually made his peace with Father Time, and turning seventy helped remind him that he was falling out of touch with younger reformers. In his birthday musings, he observed that "old age so often has the tendency to change progressives into reactionaries," and he credited the fact that he had never quite "passed my spiritual adolescence" for keeping his liberalism vibrant. Still, White knew that his own son, Bill, had stood to his political left since the 1920s. He regarded this as "a good thing for a youth," but he could not help grumbling to his longtime friend Milton F. Amrine that Bill was "just clear plum nuts on the New Deal. He's got to the point where Roosevelt can do no wrong." Amrine's son Michael, an apprentice at the *Gazette*, was similarly enchanted, and he went on to become a prominent liberal journalist after World War II. Political disagreements often erupted between the elder White and his young protégés during the late 1930s, but he did his best to remember that young people "cannot hold forever to our convictions. They must build a new world upon a new thesis."[60]

White knew that every generation must take leadership from its elders, as his had taken leadership from the Civil War generation during the Progressive Era. Still, he did not abandon his own beliefs merely because his generation was the one being pushed out. Instead, he spoke for his "group of Neolithic liberals" who had spent decades fighting for the reforms that had culminated in the New Deal, and who still wanted to contribute to progress. Progressive Era reformers had believed that uplifting the working class by improving their schools, housing, and environment would solve poverty. White explained that his generation had won incremental progress along these lines by influencing both politics and public opinion, but they had fallen far short of their goal because their thesis was wrong. Progressives had mistakenly believed that the patina of material equality signified a real social transformation, but the Depression had shattered this illusion. The New Deal liberals then horned White's generation of "Neolithic liberals" out of the herd, leaving them to watch in horror as the New Dealers ignored middle-class opinion in the court debacle. White agreed with the New Deal liberal view that government was a powerful force for social good, and he conceded that he and his crowd might be "outmoded, despised and rejected old dodos." However, he urged younger liberals to listen to their elders when they told them that middle-class opinion was an irresistible force that had to be considered in American politics.[61]

White published his advice in the *Gazette,* and it was reprinted nationally in the *New Republic.* His essay yielded a good response from "a lot of old fellows who want to go along with Roosevelt but who stopped at the Court deadline." Some of his correspondents hoped that court reform's failure would bring down the Democratic Party and President Roosevelt, but White rejected this view. He still wanted to reform the world and recognized that the New Deal was probably his last opportunity to see his dreams realized. True, the president was "a bound and chained patrician who must give benevolences, issue commands, and not work with those who are trying to achieve a better social order." White distrusted the Democratic Party and believed that FDR had "a God complex." However, he also knew that Roosevelt was no dictator and that the New Deal had been mostly good for America. Roosevelt "would live in history as a vigorous champion of righteous progress," because he had achieved many necessary reforms and transformed the way Americans thought about government. The business triumphalism of the 1920s and the idea that greed was a positive force in American society were both discredited. Court reform's failure had tarnished the president's aura of omnipotence and spurred both Congress and the judiciary to assert their independence. Roosevelt had succeeded in establishing the idea that it was both necessary and proper for government to act to ensure equality of opportunity for as many Americans as possible.[62]

At the same time, liberalism was under an increasingly fierce attack from the right. White foresaw that mainstream conservatives were poised for a rebound in the 1938 midterm election, months before Roosevelt's attempt to "purge" the Democratic Party of anti–New Deal conservatives had failed. In Congress, the drive for antilynching legislation ended in yet another failure in 1938, and White was convinced that "the Democratic Party is returning to its old form—the south is moving in." In Wisconsin, Governor Philip La Follette's attempt to form a progressive third party was crushed by an alliance of conservative Democrats and Republicans. The New Deal was losing steam, and conservatives were energized. Elements of the extreme right festered in dark corners around the country, including William

Dudley Pelley's Nazi-imitating Silver Shirts, Charles Coughlin's anti-Semitic Christian Front, and the openly pro-Nazi German-American *Bund*.[63]

Kansas was no exception. The state's political establishment was shocked by the rise of what White described as its "first real Nazi candidate" in 1938. Gerald B. Winrod was a Wichita-based fundamentalist Christian preacher who mounted a surprisingly strong campaign for the Republican nomination for US senator. Winrod was a "Jew baiter, peddler of Catholic intolerance, of negro-phobia," and White regarded him as more dangerous than a mere demagogue because "he is a fanatic. He has no brains and really believes what he says." White organized a desperate effort to stop Winrod, including advertisements, circulars, and a mass meeting in Emporia. The campaign succeeded when Winrod came in a distant third in the primary. Still, the incident reminded White that the only real danger to American democracy was from the right rather than the left, and it spoke volumes when White wrote the president in March 1938 asking for an autographed portrait to hang in his office beside those of Ickes, Borah, and Norris.[64]

White still had plenty of disagreements with President Roosevelt, but he had stayed true to liberalism and made his peace with the administration by the end of the 1930s. The editor proved his liberal mettle in a series of speeches he gave to several economic organizations in 1938. Middle-class business owners had shirked their duty to treat workers fairly, White argued, until the Great Depression forced the federal government to take responsibility for the working class's economic security. Middle-class business owners had foolishly resisted this effort because they wanted taxes to remain low, but they risked losing their dominant role in politics by angering millions of working-class voters. White's speech was included in the materials distributed to the Republican Program Committee with a note stating that he was a "veteran figure in Republican politics" whose opinions had to be considered. On reading the piece, White's good friend Ickes inquired, "How can you talk like this and still play around with

White at the American Society of Newspaper Editors' dinner alongside the GOP's leading presidential possibilities for the 1940 nomination. Left to right: White, Senator Robert A. Taft (OH), Thomas E. Dewey, and Senator Arthur H. Vandenberg (MI), April 21, 1939. Courtesy of Library of Congress, LC-H22-D-6396.

those dumb-bells in the Republican Party[?]" White replied that he could not see the Democratic Party as a real home for liberals as long as the South remained a key constituency. Conservative southerners could, according to White, "always ask the hill-billies, 'do you want your daughter to marry a nigger?' and stop any argument that means progress." Ickes conceded the point, while noting that the two men had spent the two decades since 1912 in a failed attempt to liberalize the GOP. In the final analysis, White saw the New Deal as a profound revolution in American political thought, and when one thought of Roosevelt, one thought: "here is a hero."[65]

White never lost his fundamental distaste for Roosevelt's personality, privately describing the president as a "double-crossing [egomaniac] with a harlot's charm and a child's emotions." It was Roosevelt's extroverted nature and his willingness to experiment that grated on White's midwestern sensibilities, who hastened to add that the president had a good brain and "a fine sense of the ultimate aims of our democracy." Roosevelt and White reconciled just as the thrust of public affairs was shifting decisively to international affairs. The world was accelerating in its long descent toward war, and, as Lippmann put it, domestic issues seemed increasingly irrelevant as Japan prosecuted its war against China in 1937 and Adolf Hitler dictated terms to the European powers at Munich the following year. The change was obvious to White as well, who perceptively remarked that the president had stepped away from liberal innovation and toward military preparedness in his January 1939 State of the Union speech. FDR laid out plans for a strong national defense and an assertive international posture, and White was glad to have a president who understood the need of the hour. The United States had to do what was necessary to protect liberal democracy in an era when militant counterrevolutionary ideologies were on the march around the world, and White soon enlisted to serve at President Roosevelt's side.[66]

CHAPTER EIGHT

FREEDOM FIGHTER

The assault on the post–World War I international order began in earnest on September 18, 1931, when Japan invaded and annexed the Chinese province of Manchuria. Japan's aggression disgusted William Allen White, who interpreted it as an attempt to stimulate the Japanese economy by employing men as workers in the armament industry and as soldiers conquering new territory. White was a strong internationalist, and he called for the League of Nations to enforce the Treaty of Versailles's collective security provisions that called for military action against Japan. Unfortunately, the Western nations were reluctant to confront Japan, and the United States pursued a less ambitious course. Secretary of State Henry Stimson issued a diplomatic note declaring that the United States would not recognize territorial gains achieved through force, a policy that came to be known as the Stimson Doctrine. The international situation worsened still further two years later when Adolf Hitler's Nazi Party ascended to power in Germany. White believed in collective security and hated Nazism and militarism, but the world's Great Powers were unwilling to stand against aggression. Under the circumstances, White concluded that strict neutrality was the only reasonable American response if a larger war broke out, and he endorsed President Franklin D. Roosevelt's rearmament proposals. Like other liberal internationalists who had supported disarmament in the 1920s, White now felt that it was prudent to rebuild America's defenses in a world spoiling for war.[1] International developments gradually persuaded him that armed neutrality was also the wrong course, and he made fighting for Woodrow Wilson's vision of a staunchly internationalist America the final campaign of his life. Twenty years after the armistice ending World War I, White had reenlisted in the fight to save the world.

Strict neutrality was White's default position on questions of international security for most of the 1930s. The *Gazette* applauded when

Congress passed the Neutrality Act banning the sale of arms and war materiel to belligerent nations in August 1935, and the law faced its first test when Italy invaded Ethiopia in October. Mr. and Mrs. White were out of the country by then, having left that month for East Asia to attend the ceremonial founding of the Philippine Commonwealth as President Manuel Quezon's guests. The Whites then spent the next four months touring Japan, Korea, and China, including Beijing, which White observed was practically overrun with Japanese troops from neighboring occupied Manchuria. The couple returned to the United States in February 1936, and White noted that the international order had completely failed. The Treaty of Versailles called for aggressors to be punished by the international community, but the aggressors had learned that no nation was willing to risk war to uphold the law. Japan violated the Versailles treaty when it invaded Manchuria in 1931, and it paid no price. Italy violated the treaty when it invaded Ethiopia in 1935, and it paid no price. Germany violated the treaty when it occupied the Rhineland on March 7, 1936, and it paid no price. No nation in the world seemed willing to stand up to the aggressors, and White was dejected to find that the doctrine that "force is mightier than reason" was spreading like a plague. Dispirited, he declared that "there is no international law. . . . We have returned to the jungle."[2]

The situation worsened when the Spanish Civil War began in July 1936. White recognized that the conflict could be the first shot in the next world war, and he reiterated his call for strict neutrality. The war in Spain quickly developed into a proxy war between Germany and Italy backing the fascist Nationalists and the Soviet Union backing the antifascist Republicans, and White began to change his mind about strict neutrality. Roosevelt reacted to the ongoing global crisis in October 1937 with his Quarantine Speech declaring that the United States would use sanctions to help contain aggression. White loudly applauded, and he took the opportunity to dramatically announce his return to collective security. In an editorial, he declared that he had spent twenty years thinking that the world could "cure war by noble ideals . . . by laying down our guns . . . by trying to reason through arbitration with nations that are denied the sources of national life." Instead, World War I had continued through conflicts in Russia, the Mediterranean, East Asia, and Ethiopia, and White saw that there would be war as long as national ambition and the unjust distribution of economic resources existed. The Spanish Civil War had made him an "isolationist with reservations," and Roosevelt's speech convinced him that Americans should rally around the president's leadership. The alternative was an isolation that would allow "the gangster nations, Germany, Italy, Japan, [to] shove us around." White felt that collective security was the best response to the totalitarian challenge, but he was not certain where it would lead. The dictatorships might push too hard and force a conflict, the democracies might wait too long to try to curb the dictatorships, or the dictatorships might collapse under the weight of their own cruelties. This uncertainty spurred White to demur when the *Nation*'s Freda Kirchwey asked him to evaluate American foreign policy from a liberal perspective.[3]

By the time Americans went to the polls in the midterm election of 1938, White and other internationally attuned liberals understood that "world politics and not domestic questions" would dominate the American political discourse. Hitler threatened to invade Czechoslovakia unless he was allowed to annex the German-speaking Sudetenland in the fall of 1938, and the Western Allies agreed to discuss the matter with him at Munich in an attempt to avert war. British prime minister Neville Chamberlain famously accepted Hitler's promise not to seek additional territory if the West agreed to his demands against the Czechs. White was outraged by Britain's decision to shirk its treaty obligation to protect Czech territorial integrity, terming Chamberlain's performance at Munich "just plain dumb." He enthusiastically endorsed President Roosevelt's request for an additional $552 million appropriation for rearmament in January, and he was unsurprised when Germany abrogated the Munich Pact by annexing the rest of Czechoslovakia on March 15, 1939. There was no appeasing an implacable enemy like Hitler, and White reminded his readers that the United States had invited the British to form a common front against Japanese aggression in China in 1931. The British had refused, and White pointed to the Czech crisis as a direct result of the international community's unwillingness to enforce the Treaty of Versailles over the preceding eight years.[4]

Lord Lothian, the British ambassador to the United States, noticed White's editorial and wrote him to discuss his assertions. The two had met when they shared a floor at the Hotel Crillon during the Versailles conference in 1919, and White was happy to renew their acquaintanceship twenty years later. In a correspondence that he first cleared with Secretary of War Henry L. Stimson, White explained to Lord Lothian that the American public had not forgotten that Britain had refused to stand up to Japan and Germany. The people were therefore skeptical of American internationalists' claims that the United States needed to help the Western Allies. Lord Lothian admitted that the Foreign Office had not behaved admirably in the Manchurian Crisis, but he explained that the British government's underlying reasoning was sound. British action against the invasion of Manchuria would have resulted in Japanese retaliation against British interests in Southeast Asia, and the United States was the only nation capable of repulsing such aggression. Simply put, the British did not believe that the Americans would back their moral outrage with military force in 1939 any more than they had in 1931. As Lord Lothian put it, the "rot" of totalitarian aggression could not be contained until the Western democracies, including the United States, stood shoulder to shoulder in their common defense.[5]

White entirely agreed with Lord Lothian's appeal for collective security, but the Neutrality Acts severely constrained the Roosevelt administration's ability to help the nations resisting aggression. America's industrial might was the best tool for helping the nations on the front lines against aggression, but the Neutrality Act of 1937 barred trade in war materials with all belligerent nations. As internationalists noted, this had the perverse effect of discouraging resistance against aggressors: any nation that stood up to aggression risked war, and war meant losing access to vital American supplies. The Roosevelt administration had proposed changing the law to allow the president to apply the Neutrality Act selectively during the spring of 1939, and White endorsed the proposal. Several prominent New York internationalists, led by the League of Nations Association's director, Clark Eichelberger, formed an independent group to lobby for the administration's proposal. Eichelberger was a midwesterner who had fought in the American Expeditionary Force during World War I, and he became an activist for internationalism after the armistice. The two men had forged a bond when they served together on the association's board of directors in the 1920s, and Eichelberger invited him to join the campaign to revise the Neutrality Act. White supported the group, but he was seventy-one, and he cited his age in declining the offer. The effort to revise the Neutrality Act failed when the Senate Foreign Relations Committee voted to postpone consideration of the measure until 1940.[6]

The Second World War began when German troops swarmed over the Polish border in the predawn hours of September 1, 1939, and President Roosevelt renewed his drive to revise the Neutrality Act by calling a special session of Congress for September 21. In the interim, isolationists such as Senator Borah, aviator Charles Lindbergh, and others who called for strict neutrality worked to turn public opinion against revision. The result was a flood of isolationist mail to Congress and the White House. Roosevelt opened the special session with a speech asking Congress for a neutrality law that would allow the sale of arms and other war materials to belligerent nations on a cash-and-carry basis. Under cash and carry, any nation could purchase goods as long as it paid cash and transported the cargo in its own vessels. The proposal would have allowed the United States to help arm the Western Allies while minimizing the danger that America might get sucked into the war. Unfortunately, the isolationists' demonstration had rattled many prorevision lawmakers. President Roosevelt knew that the isolationists had to be countered, and he wanted to persuade the public that "national security" meant aiding America's allies in addition to defending the homeland.[7] The isolationists' campaign showed the administration that a grassroots group spurring public opinion to support revision would be useful, and Eichelberger revived his organization.

The Non-Partisan Committee for Peace through Revision of the Neutrality Law was created with the full support of the Roosevelt administration, and Secretary of State Cordell Hull suggested that White serve as chair. Hull's reasoning was that White was a prominent Republican who had once supported strict neutrality but now favored revision, and White accepted the chairmanship. In his opening salvoes, White explained that a revised Neutrality Act would make the US "the world's arsenal" without the risk of war, because the cash-and-carry provision would keep American vessels out of harm's way. In contrast, strict neutrality would cause an economic collapse by denying American factories and farms access to world markets. The committee established branches in thirty states, and more than two hundred prominent Americans joined during its first two weeks. Eichelberger led the national office, while White personally lobbied congressional Republicans, made radio addresses, and helped draft policy. The group also filled the airwaves with radio talks, distributed phonograph records of its featured speakers, and mailed circulars to thousands of households. White played a particularly important role in the group's fundraising by acting as a bridge to wealthy internationalist Republicans such as Indiana corporate executive Wendell Willkie, establishing a friendship with the future presidential candidate. In a radio address on the eve of the congressional vote, White explained that Europe's democracies deserved help because they were "fighting the American battle" by resisting aggression.[8]

Congress voted in favor of the administration's proposal, and the revised Neutrality Act entered into law on November 4, 1939. White promptly dissolved the committee, and Roosevelt personally thanked him for having done "a grand job. It was effective and most helpful!" White downplayed his own role as that of "a stuffed shirt," while crediting Eichelberger for having done the real work of managing the grassroots organization. Commentator Walter Lippmann interpreted the victory as a positive statement that America was committed to opposing Nazism and communism in Europe, without entering the war itself. The United States would arm the Allies and indirectly help them hold the line, denying Germany the quick knockout blow it had hoped to score on the Western Front. Ideally, Lippmann argued, American factories would make it possible for the Allied blockade to force the Germans to sue for peace, avoiding the kind of destructive confrontation that would sow the seeds of a third world war.[9] White had long respected Lippmann's perspective on foreign policy, and his arguments increasingly found their way into White's own ideas about world affairs.

The revision campaign had won the day, and White's résumé as a respected liberal Republican with an army of influential friends made him a crucial asset for the administration. Roosevelt continued to cultivate White by assuring him that he had no intention of repeating Wilson's idealistic attempt to transform the world through the world war. America had to aid the Allies for hard, practical reasons: the August 1939 Nazi-Soviet Non-Aggression Pact had united two major totalitarian powers against the democracies, and the United States would have to choose between ruinous isolation and interminable war if western Europe fell. The president complained that "public opinion over here is patting itself on the back every morning and thanking God for the Atlantic Ocean (and the Pacific Ocean)." Americans needed to be educated about the seriousness of the totalitarian threat, and Roosevelt hinted that White ought to do the job. FDR asked for "a few helpful thoughts from the philosopher of Emporia," explaining that he did not want to see the world repeat the mistake it had made in 1918 when it had failed to craft a durable peace. White admitted being torn about "our involvement before the peace" and "letting the danger of a peace of tyranny approach too near," but he declined FDR's invitation to "spend the night at the White House and let me sit with you on the sofa after supper and talk over small matters like world problems." White claimed that he was unqualified to advise the president on foreign policy, which was a rather flimsy excuse. More likely, White knew that his credibility on neutrality stemmed from the fact that he was a loyal Republican from the isolationist Midwest, and no one could call him an administration pet.[10]

The German invasions of Norway and western Europe in the spring of 1940 dramatically intensified the isolationist-internationalist debate, and White and Eichelberger swung back into action. The two men established the Committee to Defend America by Aiding the Allies (CDAAA) on May 17, which quietly worked hand in glove with the Roosevelt administration to build public support for aiding the Allies, to fight appeasement, and to educate Americans about the fascist threat. The group had its work cut out for it, because a Gallup poll taken in late May showed that 64 percent of Americans opposed aiding the Allies if doing so increased the risk of war. The CDAAA was a well-organized, professional lobbying group that used opinion polling, volunteer telephone banks staffed by "Minute Women," a press service, and specialized divisions targeting women, labor, African Americans, and young people. White actively chaired what was known colloquially as the "White Committee," giving speeches, developing policy, raising funds, and privately consulting with Roosevelt on the group's overall strategy. Many prominent Americans spoke under its auspices, including Wendell Willkie, Freda Kirchwey, labor leader Victor Reuther, actor James Stewart, and First Lady Eleanor Roosevelt. Donations flowed in immediately, mostly from individual contributors in sums averaging twenty-five dollars.[11]

France surrendered on June 22 and the Battle of Britain began three weeks later, dispelling the widespread notion that the Allies could hold the Germans on the Continent as they had in World War I. White's son, Bill, was a war correspondent in London during the German Blitz night-bombing campaign, and his reporting strongly supported American intervention in the conflict. The specter of a Nazi victory in Europe tremendously spurred the White Committee, which soon boasted nearly three hundred local branches, $100,000 raised from 30,000 donors, and the ability to put 15,000 telegrams into Washington, DC, to support arms sales to Britain. The isolationists claimed that the United States risked war with Germany if it aided the Allies, but White rejected this argument on the grounds that the aggressor nations would inevitably turn their guns on America if they won in Europe. Echoing Lippmann, White stated that the totalitarian system was the antithesis of democracy, and "so long as the American democracy is functioning and men are living under liberty, [its existence] . . . is a menace to the totalitarian idea everywhere." A Nazi-dominated world order would produce an American economic "strangulation . . . that will envelop us in South America and force us into a drastically controlled isolationist economy." The United States would be devastated not by bombs, but by the "economic decay" of depression as Nazi-controlled foreign markets were closed to American trade. The nation's defensive front line was to be found wherever people were fighting for freedom, and White contended that the United States was too powerful to ever truly be isolated.[12]

Aiding the Allies was tremendously controversial, and White's vigorous activities on behalf of the CDAAA complicated his relationships with longtime friends who had sided with isolationism. Alf Landon expressed moral outrage at Nazi barbarism while arguing that Europe's problems were none of America's business, and he advocated rearmament rather than aiding the Allies on the grounds that Germany was likely to win the war. White kept the peace by describing himself as an amateur on foreign policy who was uncomfortable with his role as a mass propagandist, which left him feeling "like Father Coughlin." White's friendship with fiercely antiwar editor Oswald Garrison Villard was strained when the CDAAA published an ad written by New York playwright and Roosevelt speechwriter Robert Sherwood stating that "anyone who argues that [the Nazis] will wait is either an imbecile or a traitor." Roosevelt praised the ad, but Villard was offended, writing White that millions of intelligent, loyal Americans genuinely disagreed with the CDAAA's positions. White apologized, confessed that he had not read the ad before approving it, and asked a remorseful Sherwood to adopt a more respectful tone. Villard pressed the issue, pointing to the wartime oppression and disastrous outcome of World War I as proof that "if we go into this war there will be nothing left of our republic within a year." Ultimately, the two remained friends by agreeing to disagree.[13]

American arms began to flow to Britain almost as soon as the Neutrality Act of 1939 was signed, but Germany's relentless submarine campaign threatened to nullify this assistance. British prime minister Winston Churchill urgently asked Roosevelt to provide Britain with destroyers so that the British navy could defend the sea lanes in mid-May 1940, but the request had to be handled delicately due to the inevitable isolationist objections. Lippmann and Lord Lothian soon advanced the idea of trading American destroyers for access to British bases in the Western Hemisphere, while oil tycoon Armand Hammer approached White suggesting that the United States lease these bases for $500,000 per year. Although not officially part of the White Committee, Lippmann wrote a speech endorsing the exchange that was delivered under the CDAAA's auspices by General John J. Pershing, commander of the American Expeditionary Force in the First World War. Lippmann's argument was that the destroyer deal would give the United States time to rearm by helping the British hold the Nazis in Europe. If Germany did defeat Britain, then America's generosity might encourage the British fleet to continue the fight by fleeing to the United States rather than surrender to the Nazis. Pershing's speech produced tens of thousands of supportive telegrams to the White House, and an August Gallup poll showed that 60 percent of Americans favored the destroyer deal.[14]

The Roosevelt administration supported the proposal, but it was concerned that the Republican presidential nominee, Wendell Willkie, would politicize the issue in the 1940 campaign. White had supported Willkie's dark horse candidacy partly because the Republican Party was itself divided between isolationists and internationalists. Any isolationist Republican who won the nomination would be "blown out of the court" in the general election, and White argued that the GOP had no choice but to nominate a full-throated internationalist. Willkie appeared to be that internationalist when he unequivocally assured White that he would fight to keep isolationism out of the Republican platform. It also helped that White saw Willkie as a courageous and honest champion of New Deal liberalism, based on the candidate's expressed support for collective bargaining, wages and hours laws, and old age pensions. White's support for Willkie was no slur against President Roosevelt, whom the editor credited with having turned "the American people to thinking of what is roughly called distributive justice for the last ten years." Aside from the fact that White was a Republican, his primary objection to Roosevelt's reelection in 1940 was that he feared the consequences of breaking the two-term precedent.[15]

As both a Willkie supporter and an internationalist, White was uniquely positioned to help advance the destroyer deal by acting as a liaison between the campaigns. The destroyer proposal came to a head in August 1940 while White was on a working vacation at his cabin in Moraine Park. Both Lippmann and Secretary of the Interior Harold Ickes had recommended that the president invite Willkie to cosponsor the proposal, and they suggested that White serve as an intermediary because he was friends with all involved. President Roosevelt concurred, and White agreed after Roosevelt telephoned him from the White House. Willkie was staying in Colorado Springs, and White secured his promise not to make an issue of the destroyer deal. The Republican establishment was enraged, and Willkie was forced to bow to the isolationists by criticizing the deal. The destroyer exchange proceeded, and the two nations agreed to trade fifty old American destroyers for leases on British naval bases in Newfoundland and the British West Indies on September 2. White was pleased by the president's action and publicly criticized Willkie, although he still supported the Republican's candidacy. Roosevelt defeated Willkie in November, and White was proud to think that he had helped make Willkie "the recognized leader of the Republican Party who accepts the New Deal in principle and is a militant internationalist."[16]

The White Committee's activities hit full stride by the fall of 1940, and the dismayed isolationists formed the America First Committee in the hope of countering White's efforts to mold public opinion. America First's chief spokesman was Charles A. Lindbergh, who had become an international celebrity after his solo flight across the Atlantic Ocean in 1927. Lindbergh gave speeches for America First opposing aid to the Allies on the grounds that the Soviets were the

White talks with Wendell Willkie in 1943. Courtesy of Emporia State University, Special Collections and Archives.

greater threat to western Europe, and White denounced him as an appeaser who had refused to blame Germany for the war. Instead, Lindbergh and the isolationists had insisted on the same head-in-the-sand neutrality that had failed to protect Europe against Nazi aggression. As a spokesman for America First, Villard retaliated by terming White "the great warrior for England" who sought to put America into the war to save the British. Although America First grew rapidly by forging an alliance between pacifists and isolationists, Socialist Party leader and prominent America First figure Norman Thomas noted with concern that the "William Allen White Committee is gaining ground with great rapidity" by the end of 1940.[17]

Ironically, the zealous activities of the White Committee's most fervent East Coast supporters ultimately pushed White out of the organization that informally bore his name. The CDAAA's branches in New York, Baltimore, and Washington, DC, were extremely hawkish compared to its midwestern chapters, calling for the mandatory convoying of merchant vessels and other measures that were designed to put America on a war footing. For months, White had resisted such demands because he felt that the CDAAA should not get too far ahead of President Roosevelt. The New York chapter had also actively campaigned against isolationist congressman Hamilton Fish (R-NY) during the 1940 midterm election, violating the group's pledge not to intervene in elections. An exasperated White decried the New Yorkers as "my hair shirt," and he found himself constantly having to clean up after the chapter. By the fall of 1940, White warned the CDAAA's executive board that he was considering resigning the chairmanship because both he and the national organization were becoming identified with the group's radical interventionists. At the same time, White acted quickly to forestall an anti-CDAAA attack piece by his friend Roy Howard, the isolationist publisher of the Scripps-Howard newspaper chain. White reiterated that the New York chapter's activities were in violation of the national group's policies, and he wrote Howard that the whole thrust of the CDAAA's agenda was to keep America out of war. The group's policy could be summed up, White explained, by the slogan "The Yanks are Not Coming."[18]

Howard published White's letter in his newspapers, triggering the chain of events that led to White's resignation from the CDAAA. America First's Lindbergh praised the piece, and White responded with an open letter proposing that the two men collaborate on shared ideas such as increasing arms production. An America First representative applauded White's suggestion as "a complete reversal of the letter and spirit of the White Committee's official position." Naturally, the piece provoked a firestorm of criticism from the New York chapter. New York City mayor Fiorello La Guardia cuttingly denounced White for "doing a typical Laval," alluding to Pierre Laval's leadership role in the collaborationist Vichy French regime. At the same time, a *New York Times* editorial denounced White as a warmonger because of the New York chapter's aggressive activities, and Villard begged him to resign before he lost his reputation entirely. President Roosevelt tried to encourage White with a note asking him to "keep up the good work," but it was already too late. White quietly tendered his resignation as chairman on December 26, although his decision was kept private until business resumed in January after the holidays. Letters streamed in thanking him for his service, and President Roosevelt congratulated him for having educated the public about the global threat to democracy. The CDAAA continued to use his name as honorary chairman with his permission until May 1941, but he played no further role in the organization.[19]

White made many mistakes as head of the CDAAA. He was a consensus builder by nature who wanted to make everybody happy, which made him poorly suited for executive leadership. However, one must remember that White was asked to chair the CDAAA because he was a midwestern Republican internationalist who supported FDR's foreign policy. He gave the CDAAA the nonpartisan, regional, and ideological credibility it required to thrive as a national organization. Furthermore, the CDAAA's main purpose was to generate support for FDR's foreign policy. The eastern radicals who chafed against White's leadership wanted to use the CDAAA to push FDR into supporting their foreign policy. While he did make mistakes, White was able to successfully steer the CDAAA through one of the most contentious, emotional, and treacherous debates in American history. Any chairman of a group like the CDAAA would have faced a difficult task in such an environment. In fact, the reason White remained honorary chairman for so long was that the group had a difficult time finding an individual who was willing to be shot at from all sides. In the end, the CDAAA was able to move public opinion in support of aid to the Allies, proving that both it and White succeeded.[20]

The fight with the CDAAA's New York chapter was the main policy reason White resigned, but he also had a strong personal motive for disengaging from the national debate. Sallie had contracted a bad head cold in early December 1940, and the seventy-one-year-old continued to suffer from severe pain on one side of her head three weeks later. The family's doctors were unable to diagnose her condition, and Mr. and Mrs. White traveled to Tucson, Arizona, to allow her to rest. White left his wife's side only once: to attend a dinner in his honor in New York City in February 1941. At the dinner, he stated that it was necessary to subdue the dictator nations, but it was also imperative that the world establish a postwar international organization to more justly allocate the world's economic resources. White argued that world peace could only be maintained by ensuring that all nations had access to economic opportunity, and the United States had a responsibility to lead the way. Unfortunately, Sallie's condition failed to improve after three months, and the couple made plans to visit the Mayo Clinic for a neurological examination as soon as she was strong enough to make the trip. Sallie's lifelong cardiovascular problems had returned with full vigor, and she was hospitalized for observation in Tucson that March. Her doctors suspected a brain tumor or aneurysm, but she was eventually diagnosed as having suffered an undetected stroke. Sallie's health was not seriously compromised, and she recovered enough strength to do light gardening by the summer of 1942.[21]

The United States was increasingly likely to be drawn into the war by mid-1941, and White began to use America's inevitable involvement as a tool to achieve a second bite at the internationalist apple. Germany's invasion of the Soviet Union in June 1941 convinced White that the United States would soon "land in the mess on the sidewalk," and he foresaw that the Japanese would attack the United States as the last nation blocking Japanese domination of the Pacific. War would be forced on the American people, and White was proud that the CDAAA had helped President Roosevelt maintain American neutrality long enough to rearm the military, keep Britain afloat, and prevent Germany from expanding its global influence. The democratic nations would have been in an infinitely worse strategic position had the United States allowed Great Britain to fall to the Nazis in the summer of 1940. In White's view, western Europe, the United States, and China ought to join forces in a wartime international organization that would present "a solid front against the totalitarian governments." Any nation willing to pledge to give its citizens rights similar to those recognized in the American Bill of Rights would be allowed to join the proposed organization, even if it took years for the less democratic nations to make good. The democratic world order that the Allied powers pledged to create in the Atlantic Charter of August 1941 was exactly the kind of commitment White had long advocated.[22]

The war over aid to the Allies had largely been won by the summer of 1941, but White was tremendously worried that the Republican Party would repeat the mistake of 1919 by returning to isolationism after World War II. The lure of isolationism remained strong even in the summer of 1941, as Hoover and Landon demonstrated in the days following the German invasion of the Soviet Union in June. Although Hoover remained an internationalist, both he and Landon were sympathetic toward isolationist arguments, and they were outraged by Roosevelt's decision to help the Soviets resist the Nazis. The two men signed on to a joint statement denouncing collaboration with the Soviets as proof that World War II was "a war between European nations for power" and "not a world conflict between tyranny and freedom." The statement made the isolationist argument that Nazi Germany was no threat to the United States, and it claimed that American aid to the Western Allies was dragging the United States into the war. The document was released in August. That same month, the House of Representatives barely approved an administration bill to extend the length of service for six hundred thousand draftees beyond the 1940 Selective Service Act's twelve-month term by a vote of 203 in favor versus 202 against. Most of the "no" votes came from the Republicans.[23]

White was deeply troubled by such developments, and he worked with Willkie to cultivate the party's internationalist wing. Willkie had strongly and publicly supported the administration's Lend-Lease bill in March, which opened the floodgates of American aid to any nation opposing the aggressors. Willkie even traveled the country during the summer of 1941 giving two speeches a week calling for more aid to the Allies. A few days after the draft extension passed the House, White wrote Willkie that the vote showed that "we just can't let Landon and Hoover and [Senator Robert A.] Taft and [Charles] Lindbergh carry the Republican banner without a fight for it." Taft and Lindbergh were notorious isolationists, and it was significant that White placed them in the same basket as Landon and Hoover. Willkie agreed to help White assemble a small group of younger, pro–New Deal, internationalist, and up-and-coming Republicans for an informal meeting to discuss the party's future. Potential invitees included Minnesota governor Harold Stassen, managing editor of the *Kansas City Star* Roy Roberts, and Kansas governor Payne Ratner, all prominent liberal Republican midwesterners, and he proposed holding the meeting at some private location in the region. Meanwhile, Landon counterattacked with a radio address attacking the "Roosevelt-Willkie Program." The Japanese sneak attack on Pearl Harbor on December 7, 1941, disrupted these plans.[24]

The United States had finally landed in the "mess on the sidewalk," and White focused his efforts on ensuring that the GOP repudiated its flirtation with isolationism. The best way to accomplish this goal was to unite the party around a common, internationalist agenda, and both Hoover and Willkie gave White his opening. White was surprised when Hoover sent him the draft manuscript for *The Problems of Lasting Peace* in early 1942, a book he had cowritten with diplomat Hugh Gibson. The work, published in the spring, embraced a robust American role in maintaining world peace following the war, and White saw it as the beginning of a party conversation about internationalism. He sought to use the book as a "springboard" for a small gathering of Republicans that would unify the Hoover and Willkie wings on foreign policy. Willkie made his own contribution to the discussion when he returned from a 'round-the-world fact-finding trip in October, with Roosevelt's support. Willkie delivered his conclusions in a radio address calling for Americans to embrace the modern world's global nature, and he particularly thrilled White with an unvarnished attack on imperialism. Up to thirty-six million listeners heard Willkie strikingly argue that colonial subjects were "no longer willing to be Eastern slaves for Western profits." White commented that Willkie was the first major leader to demand "freedom for all mankind," which contrasted favorably against British and American promises of "freedom but with their fingers crossed for Asia and Africa" in the Atlantic Charter. Willkie was now to FDR's left, White argued, and he was undeniably the leader of the Republican Party's liberal faction. Willkie's book describing his travel experiences and thoughts about foreign policy, titled *One World,* was published in mid-1943, and it proved to be one of the best-selling books during World War II.[25]

Two of the Republican Party's major leaders had agreed that America ought to play an ongoing role in maintaining world peace, and the time seemed ripe for the party's leading figures to come together. White did all he could to bring Willkie, Hoover, and Landon together in close collaboration with RNC chairman Harrison Spangler. White proposed a private luncheon with the three men for a quiet discussion of the party's future position on foreign policy. Hoover and Willkie were willing as long as the meeting was informal, but Landon short-circuited the effort by insisting that the meeting be public and on the record. In the end, Chairman Spangler acted on White's idea that the party should sponsor a meeting to unify its internationalist and isolationist wings by organizing the Mackinac Conference, which assembled many of the Republican Party's leading lights to discuss America's postwar role in the world. White was too ill to participate in the meeting by the time it was held in September 1943, but he was generally supportive of its work.[26]

White's own hope was that the United States would embrace its responsibilities as part of a substantial postwar international organization to ensure a lasting postwar peace. Future wars would be fought over access to raw materials and markets rather than mere "political grievances," and the United States had a direct interest in shaping the postwar economic order as the world's leading industrial powerhouse. The alternatives to American leadership in the world were too dangerous to accept. One possibility was that the cycle of periodic world wars would continue until "finally the thing we call civilization will collapse." Another possibility was that other nations would exploit the power vacuum left by an isolationist United States to establish a world order friendly to their interests: "Hitler or British imperialists—either of whom will promote future wars, wars which we shall fight as we are fighting this war." America had to become "in a sense, international in our commerce, in certain political phases of our life, and in world out-look. This does not mean we shall surrender sovereignty." The United States would have to avoid the twin dangers of "militant isolationism and military American imperialism," it would have to "police and educate the victims of the aggressor nations in order to make them good customers," and it would have to "rehabilitate most of Europe to save it for capitalism which means to save it for American trade."[27] Ultimately, White's vision of the United States as an unabashedly capitalist and internationalist superpower neatly embodied the course American policy makers adopted after the Second World War.

Lippmann's 1943 work *U.S. Foreign Policy: Shield of the Republic* most closely paralleled White's ideas about the postwar settlement, and the editor worked to spread its message as widely as possible. *U.S. Foreign Policy* embraced Roosevelt's global conception of American national security, and it attacked the isolationists for having refused to either pare down American commitments or take the steps necessary for their defense. Lippmann argued for a realistic foreign policy built on a balance of powers between the Atlantic nations and the Soviet Union, and on enforcing collective security with military force. White was a member of the Book of the Month Club's selection committee, and he strongly advocated for Lippmann's book on the condition that the author add a final chapter brightening the work's gloomy conclusion about the chances for a lasting peace. The committee delegated White to call Lippmann by telephone, who agreed to state that it was possible to work out peaceful and just relations among men. In a follow-up letter, White celebrated Lippmann's book as the best expression of the "Grand Alliance" for peace that he and other internationalists wanted to create. The work was the perfect counter to the "pacifist liberals" who foolishly saw peace as the end rather than the means for human happiness.[28]

The Book of the Month Club helped *U.S. Foreign Policy* become a national best-seller, and White used the book as a tool to persuade his Republican friends to adopt internationalism. For Senator Clyde Reed (R-KS), White reduced Lippmann's proposal for a robust post-war collective security organization to "whether we shall have a debating society or an international police force. We tried the debating society and it failed." He also sent a copy to Landon with his strong recommendation, but Landon replied that he preferred "the cold blooded, realistic approach of Churchill and Stalin" in crafting an immediate postwar settlement. Landon lamented that the United States would probably follow Lippmann's internationalist path, confirming White's suspicion that his friend was an unreconstructed isolationist. Hoover also rejected Lippmann's ideas, arguing that they depended too heavily on an international balance of power backed by force rather than a voluntary international organization. Ultimately, White remained true to Lippmann's ideas, partly because he knew that a robust international organization built on American terms would be the best protection in the looming Cold War. It was obvious to White that Russia would conquer "by the logic of starvation and chaos all of Europe East of the Rhine except the Mediterranean area," and he knew that communist expansionism was "just as bad . . . as Nazi-Fascism."[29]

Ultimately, the United States did pursue the robust internationalism that White had advocated, but he did not live to see his dreams come to fruition. White was seventy-five when his health sharply declined in 1943. One attack came when the Whites were in New York City. The couple invited journalist, Republican Party operative, and White's former *Gazette* "boy" David Hinshaw to breakfast at their hotel on April 27, which was their fiftieth wedding anniversary. Hinshaw waited for them in the lobby and was horrified to see White step out of the elevator, stagger, and collapse. White was hospitalized with

White and Sallie in their cabin at Moraine Park during the summer of 1943.
Courtesy of Emporia State University, Special Collections and Archives.

double pneumonia and diabetic shock, but he recovered sufficiently to spend one final summer in Moraine Park. Much had changed in the half century since a chubby young Kansan camped in the Rockies with his fraternity brothers. The fishing in the Big Thompson River was not as good as it had once been, since Denver residents could now easily drive up to the mountains and fish the streams bare. Wartime gasoline rationing had not materially affected traffic in town, and although the Steads Ranch, the Crags Lodge, and the Stanley Hotel were closed for the war, the area's campgrounds and cabins were fully occupied. The wildlife had changed dramatically over the decades as well. Cattle and horses had roamed freely during Moraine Park's ranching days, but the ranches were closed when the area became a national park and elk now dominated. Unfortunately, the rise of the elk was the death knell for many aspen groves in Moraine Park, Glacier Creek, and Mill Creek, because the animals had developed the habit of gnawing away the trees' bark.[30] Moraine Park had changed a great deal over the decades, but the Rocky Mountains still had the power to soothe White's soul.

Politics had changed as well over the preceding half century, and White was alarmed by both parties' trajectories. The Republicans were flirting with conservative demagogues who he felt were sowing the fascist sentiment that people should "distrust your government merely because it is government." He had long worried that fascism would find a home in America after the war, and his fears multiplied after conservative Republicans won dozens of seats in the 1942 congressional election. He sharply attacked "Republican demagoguery" as protofascism in a remarkable series of editorials that were based on a visit to Washington in February 1943. The Democrats' New Deal had its flaws, but White complained that few Republicans had any interest in advancing a constructive agenda designed to solve the problems the New Deal had tried to address. Instead, too many Republicans had revealed themselves to be "cheap statesmen" like RNC chairman Spangler, who penned an article claiming that the GOP had to turn America away from "totalitarianism and state socialism," or Ohio governor John W. Bricker, whom White denounced as being "'agin' everything and 'for' nothing!" White particularly attacked the party's "leadership [for] appealing to the boys in the pool hall by calling the president a dictator and referring to the New Deal as the 'Nazi New Deal.'" The latter phrase had been used by Alf Landon on February 12, 1943, when he alleged that Roosevelt administration officials sought "to establish here what Hitler described in his early days as the National Socialistic state." Such extreme rhetoric was dangerous, White argued, because "in rallying the boys in the pool hall, those cheap morons who are easily excited by specious issues, the Republican party may be the center of a fascist movement."[31]

The Republican Party's flirtation with conservative demagoguery coincided with White's sense that Roosevelt had lost his mastery of American politics. From White's point of view, Roosevelt's New Deal coalition was an unstable hodgepodge of contradictory minority groups that included "the Old South and the negroes, the city machines and the academic mugwumps, the farmers and the laborers." Although White deeply admired the New Deal's accomplishments, he had little reason to believe that the president could exercise good leadership with such an unruly coalition. The problem with Roosevelt was that the president was a man defined by his "gambler's passion to sit at a table and play a game, the great game of world politics." As a gambler, Roosevelt had "no convictions, deep, fundamental and abiding, which he wouldn't sacrifice to win the pot on the table." White had little confidence that Roosevelt had the moral courage or intellectual conviction required to deny his supporters what they demanded, and he felt that the New Deal coalition's internal conflicts kept the president handcuffed at a time when strong leadership was required.[32] Congress was increasingly hostile and conservative, and the president seemed to have "lost the ball." White exhorted Willkie to "step out and take the moral, intellectual and political leadership of this country" by launching a national speaking tour addressing domestic and foreign policy from the liberal Republican point of view.[33]

Willkie had already begun acting on White's advice that he firmly embrace liberal Republicanism in his speeches preparing for the 1944 campaign, but White would not live to see the outcome. An extremely uncomfortable "digestive disturbance" tortured White and forced him to make his final visit to the Mayo Clinic in October 1943. The doctors conducted immediate exploratory surgery. The diagnosis was grim: White was suffering from terminal colon cancer, and he was sent home to Emporia to live out his final days. The editor continued to do what work he could, and his condition was kept a secret outside of a small circle of close friends and family. He was soon bedridden, but his interest in politics persisted: his last political request to his son was that he apologize to Willkie for his having been physically unable to help organize Kansas's delegation for the 1944 campaign. The final two weeks were terrible. Sallie described her once-cheerful husband as a shadow of "the Old Will" as his stomach rejected all but the thinnest liquids. The frustration of "dying by slow starvation" spurred uncharacteristic flashes of anger, and Sallie reported that it had been weeks since she had seen him smile. William

Allen White passed away on January 29, 1944, twelve days shy of his seventy-sixth birthday. President Roosevelt wrote Sallie expressing his sympathy over the passing of one of America's

> wisest and most beloved editors in the death of William Allen White. He made the Emporia *Gazette* a national institution. As a writer of terse, forcible and vigorous prose, he was unsurpassed. He ennobled the profession of journalism which he served with such unselfish devotion through more than two score years. To me his passing brings a real sense of personal loss for we had been the best of friends for years.[34]

EPILOGUE

Peter Pan Park is one of the biggest and busiest public spaces in Emporia today, boasting a lake, pavilions, an amphitheater, tennis courts, and other recreational facilities constructed on fifty acres of land donated by Sallie and William Allen White in their daughter Mary's memory. Under the William Allen White Foundation's auspices, American sculptor Jo Davidson crafted a memorial to White that was installed on the edge of the park's lake. The memorial was dedicated on July 11, 1950, and former president Herbert Hoover delivered the nationally broadcast keynote address. As always, Hoover could not resist the urge to try to warp White into a posthumous conservative, describing him as

> an unvarnished nineteenth-century liberal—something far different from those who would travel under that cloak today. His was a never-ceasing gospel of personal liberty. He was opposed to every governmental encroachment upon it. He opposed every domination of free men, whether by business, labor, farmers, or by group action anywhere, or at any time. For half a century his was the great voice of the Midwest which still clung to building progress through freedom of men's mind and spirits.

Hoover went on to imply that he had supported White's fight to aid the Allies before Pearl Harbor. He also stated that the United Nations was actually "an instrument to protect Red imperialism," and he endorsed the jailing of "subversives" under McCarthyism. The William Allen White whom Hoover described in his speech was a grotesque parody of the editor of the *Emporia Gazette,* who had spent his life in pursuit of a modern liberal internationalist order at home and abroad. Hoover had merely used White's good name as a camouflage for his own conservative ideas, and not for the first time.[1]

Heavy rains created so much mud that the dedication ceremony was moved from Peter Pan Park to the Emporia Civic Auditorium. White would have giggled at the irony: Hoover had delivered his caricature of White as a conservative in two venues that had been constructed with joint funding by the city of Emporia and the New Deal's Public Works Administration. Still, had he been seated on stage as the guest of honor, White would have listened politely before thanking Hoover for the kind words he had spoken. White had done so in 1908, when he sat on stage and politely listened to Senator Chester I. Long's smears. He had done the same in 1922, when he politely sat on stage next to Governor Henry J. Allen after his arrest for picketing. He had done the same in 1936, when he politely smiled as President Franklin Delano Roosevelt remarked that he was proud to have White's support for three and a half years out of every four. White would have penned frank letters to his friends analyzing Hoover's behavior after the ceremony, and he wrote two letters that provided insight about his views of the subject in 1942. In the first, he explained to Senator George W. Norris (R-NE) that Hoover was "a friendless, lonesome man who doesn't understand why he is friendless and lonesome," and who "would like to be liberal and progressive if he could. He is like the rich young man who turned away sadly for he had great wealth." To Wendell Willkie, White described Hoover as "the most contradictory and the most emotionally messed-up man I ever knew."[2]

White's faction of liberal Republicans was still in control of the national party when Hoover gave his dedication speech, but the truth was that conservatism was on the rise. White had foreseen this possibility, and he had sought to cultivate the next generation of liberal Republicans by aiding the likes of Indiana's Willkie, Minnesota's Harold Stassen, and New York's Thomas Dewey in their campaigns for national leadership. Neither Stassen nor Dewey was politically seasoned enough to win White's backing for the presidential nomination in 1940 or 1944, but both had impressed him as the kind of young men who would be the party's future leaders. White also befriended Senator Robert A. Taft (R-OH), but he confessed that he was "afraid of his conservative mind and heart."[3] Stassen's bid for national leadership petered out after World War II, but Dewey was the Republican Party's presidential standard-bearer in 1944 and 1948.

The Democrats ultimately won both contests, but liberal internationalist Dwight Eisenhower was victorious as the first Republican since Herbert Hoover to win the White House in 1952. Still, the fact that Eisenhower had won the nomination only after a stiff convention fight against Taft's conservative supporters illustrated the rise of conservatism. Eisenhower sought to rebrand his liberalism as "modern" Republicanism, punctuating liberalism's decline in the GOP. The conservative movement continued gaining strength as a diverse array of think-tank intellectuals, northern business conservatives, southern and midwestern traditionalists, middle-class Sunbelt suburbanites, and religious conservatives found ways to make common cause.[4]

White provided the best epitaph for himself in a speech titled "Between the Devil and the Deep Sea," which he delivered to the Executive Club of Chicago ten months before he passed away. He began by describing the world of his youth as one where individuals, towns, regions, and nations were relatively independent from one another. In the 1890s, it was possible for a man like White to become an independent proprietor with a small amount of capital or relatively limited training, as he had with the *Gazette*. By the 1940s, even a small-town newspaper like the *Gazette* could not operate without tremendous amounts of capital-intensive machinery, a small army of forty highly trained technicians, and a payroll of $5,000 per week, making it almost impossible for a man to be truly independent. Consequently, modern society was organized around large institutions: big business, organized labor, an active government, and international organizations. He expressed no desire to return to the simpler life of the 1890s. White appreciated the technological wonders of his day, and he understood that the opportunities he had enjoyed as a middle-class young man had not been available to the working class. Looking back, White felt that the progress reformers had made in broadening access to opportunity over the preceding half century had been worth the price of increased government involvement in Americans' economic lives.[5]

The future looked more uncertain, and White feared that large institutions would increasingly dominate the American system.

White ran the Gazette *with a handful of employees in 1896, but he required more than forty to do the same by 1938. Courtesy of Kenneth Spencer Research Library, University of Kansas Libraries.*

International capitalism had begun to grow too powerful, and White worried that massive corporations might become "unchecked by God, man or devil, unleashed save by its own instinctive demands, and soon it will transcend not only one government—all governments." On the other hand, it was dangerous to turn to government because it might become a "monster animated by pressure groups assembled into political majorities." Americans were confronted by "a ruthless and greedy totalitarianism of business" and "a similarly greedy cruel giant in the totalitarian state," which was why he had chosen the title "Between the Devil and the Deep Sea." Isolationism was not the answer to this dilemma, because the world was already international in nature. Americans had to "establish justice among men on this earth in the interest of peace, in the interests of the very forces, commerce and industry, to which the age seems to be committed." White was optimistic that the United States was equal to the task, noting that his own demographic of "middle class leaders have ridden the tide [of modernization] safely." He had faith that in the end, the American middle class would accept its moral obligation and its duty to its own self-interest by helping lead the world toward political and economic democracy. As White noted, the American people already had the necessary tools in "modern man's new weapon, the ballot."[6]

Ultimately, White looked back on his half century in American politics with pride and hope. Both the Republican and the Democratic Parties had been battlegrounds between liberals and conservatives in 1900, and both remained so in 1944. He agreed with Democratic vice president Henry A. Wallace that there was still plenty of liberalizing work to be done on each side of the partisan fence. The same was true of White's lifelong effort to advance democracy: plenty of work remained for the generations that followed, and he was optimistic that the project would succeed. He knew that progress would not be easy, but he had persisted because "doing so, I have held leadership in the Republican progressive outfit; sometimes a band of stragglers, lousy, footsore and weary, but still carrying the banner." A lifetime spent as a reformer had taught him that progress was inevitable, and "if James D. Weaver, and Bryan and Roosevelt and La Follette and Wilson and FDR had all been strangled in their infancy, the thing would have unfolded somewhat as it is." The great leaders White had known had paled in significance to the masses who had incessantly pressed for democracy, both at home and abroad. He was proud to have served as a captain in the "mighty phalanx moving steadily toward the goal that was in our hearts."[7]

NOTES

Works frequently cited have been identified by the following abbreviations:

CEP   Clark Eichelberger Papers, New York Public Library
CLP   Chester I. Long Papers, Kansas State Historical Society
EG   *Emporia Gazette*
ESU   William Allen White Collection, Emporia State University
EWG   *Emporia Weekly Gazette*
FDR   Franklin Delano Roosevelt Papers, FDR Presidential Library
HHP   Herbert Hoover Papers, Hoover Presidential Library
HIP   Harold Ickes Papers, Library of Congress
JBP   Joseph L. Bristow Papers, Kansas State Historical Society
KU   William Allen White Collection, Spencer Research Library, University of Kansas
LoC   William Allen White Papers, Library of Congress
NYT   *New York Times*
OGV   Oswald Garrison Villard Papers, Houghton Library, Harvard University
TRP   Theodore Roosevelt Papers, Library of Congress, Microfilm
UP   *Uncensored* Papers, New York Public Library
VMP   Victor Murdock Papers, Library of Congress
WLP   Walter Lippmann Papers, Sterling Library, Yale University
WWP   Wendell Willkie Papers, Lilly Library, Indiana University

INTRODUCTION: THE MAN AND HIS METHODS

1. William Allen White to Theodore Roosevelt, Feb. 13, 1904, William Allen White Papers, Manuscript Division, Library of Congress, Washington, DC.

2. What does "liberal" mean? What does "progressive" mean? The historical terms "liberal" and "progressive" are and always will be controversial because they meant different things to different people at different times. For instance, a nineteenth-century liberal might advocate laissez-faire economics, while a New Deal liberal might propose government measures to ensure economic equality of opportunity. Fortunately for this study, White was fairly consistent in his terms.

He used "liberal" and "progressive" interchangeably from 1905 to the early 1920s, and he understood these terms to mean the use of government and social institutions to create a permanent state of free and fair competition. White employed the term "liberal" almost exclusively by the mid-1920s, reserving the term "progressive" for usage in a historical sense. From the mid-1920s until his death in 1944, White's "liberalism" advocated government and social institutions that both accepted and aimed to compensate for the reality that social, political, and economic power was distributed unequally.

3. Lewis Gould, *The Republicans: A History of the Grand Old Party* (New York: Oxford University Press, 2014), 106; White to Harold Ickes, Sept. 26, 1938, LoC; Alonzo Hamby, "High Tide: Roosevelt, Truman, and the Democratic Party, 1932–1952," in *The Achievement of American Liberalism*, ed. William Chafe (New York: Columbia University Press, 2003), 22–25.

4. White, "Emporia and New York," *American Magazine*, Jan. 1907, 258–265; "Two Famous Questions," n.d., LoC; White to Carl Wheat, Nov. 30, 1916, LoC; White to Meredith Nicholson, July 6, 1917, LoC; Roosevelt to White, July 1, 1913, LoC.

5. James Shortridge, *The Middle West: Its Meaning in American Culture* (Lawrence: University Press of Kansas, 1989), 50–54.

6. "Personalizing Politics," ca. 1927, LoC; White to Walter Johnson, Nov. 2, 1942, LoC.

7. White to Borah, June 21, 1928, LoC; White to Herbert Hoover, June 18, 1928, LoC; "Exhibit C," n.d., LoC.

8. White to Hoover, June 18, 1928, LoC; Borah to White, June 19, 1928, LoC; White to Gerald Lee, Jan. 22, 1910, LoC; White to Jonathan M. Davis, Jan. 10, 1923, LoC; White to Henry A. Wallace, Jan. 3, 1939, LoC; White to Clyde Reed, May 19, 1933, LoC.

9. David Hinshaw, *A Man from Kansas: The Story of William Allen White* (New York: G. P. Putnam, 1945), 88, 179; White to George Sheldon, July 6, 1929, LoC; William Culbertson, May 7, 1911, LoC; Walter Johnson, *William Allen White's America* (New York: Henry Holt, 1947), 485–487; Biographical Sketch, n.d., William Allen White Collection, Special Collections and Archives, Emporia State University, Emporia, KS.

10. White to Henry L. Mencken, April 23, 1931, LoC.

11. Megan Barke, Rebecca Fribush, and Peter Stearns, "Nervous Break-down in 20th-Century American Culture," *Journal of Social History* 33, no. 3 (Spring 2000): 565–584; White to Henry J. Allen, Nov. 20, 1936, LoC; White to Roy Bailey, April 4, 1938, LoC.
12. White to Mary Ann White, July 4, 1914, ESU; White to Arthur Capper, Nov. 27, 1920, LoC; White to Helen Mahin, Oct. 7, 1929, LoC; Sallie White to Hayden Brothers, June 5, 1919, LoC; White to Harold Chase, Aug. 1, 1918, LoC; White to A. Hyde, Nov. 7, 1918, LoC; White to Theo-dore Roosevelt, Dec. 15, 1914, LoC.
13. Thomas Frank, *What's the Matter with Kansas?* (New York: Henry Holt, 2004), 9, 27, 60–61, 113–114.

CHAPTER 1. "HE WANTS NO OFFICE!"
1. William Gienapp, *The Origins of the Republican Party, 1852–1856* (New York: Oxford University Press, 1987), 189–191, 440; Hinshaw, *Man from Kansas*, 15.
2. Hinshaw, *Man from Kansas*, 17–19; Johnson, *White's America*, 7–18; White, Biographical Statement, Dec. 13, 1909, William Allen White Papers, Kansas Collection, Spencer Research Library, University of Kansas, Lawrence; White Statement, n.d., LoC.
3. Walter Johnson, *White's America*, 11–22; White to P. G. Young, Dec. 13, 1909, LoC; White Statement, n.d., LoC; White to Henry A. Wal-lace, Sept. 3, 1936, LoC; White to Carl Sandburg, Jan. 28, 1930, LoC; White, Commencement Speech at the Kansas State Teachers College of Pittsburg, May 28, 1936, KU.
4. Johnson, *White's America*, 9–27; William Allen White, *The Autobiogra-phy of William Allen White* (New York: Macmillan, 1946), 418; White to Young, Dec. 13, 1909, LoC; White Statement, n.d., LoC; White to Samuel Clarke, Feb. 18, 1907, LoC; White Biographical Statement, n.d., KU.
5. Hinshaw, *Man from Kansas*, 31; Jean Baker, *Affairs of Party: The Political Culture of Northern Democrats in the Mid-Nineteenth Century* (Ithaca, NY: Cornell University Press, 1983), 32–33; John DeWitt McKee, *Wil-liam Allen White: Maverick on Main Street* (Westport, CT: Greenwood, 1975), 11–12; Johnson, *White's America*, 9–27; White Statement, n.d., LoC; White Biographical Statement, n.d., KU.
6. Johnson, *White's America*, 31–43; *Emporia Gazette*, Feb. 3, 1944; White

Biographical Statement, n.d., KU; Peter H. Argersinger, "Road to a Republican Waterloo: The Farmers' Alliance and the Election of 1890 in Kansas," *Kansas History* 33, no. 4 (Winter 1967): 443–469; J. M. Satterthwaite, Dr. Allen White, as I Remember Him, n.d., KU.

7. White Biographical Statement, n.d., KU; Statement for the Fall issue of the *Jayhawker*, 1939, KU; White, *Autobiography*, 141–146, 176; Johnson, *White's America*, 42–43.

8. James H. Pickering and Nancy Thomas, *If I Ever Grew Up and Became a Man* (Estes Park, CO: Estes Park Museum Friends, 2010), 1–32; White to W. D. McPherson, May 9, 1916, LoC.

9. McKee, *Maverick*, 15; White, *Autobiography*, 89–91, 178–186, 199; Statement for the Fall issue of the *Jayhawker*, 1939, KU; Johnson, *White's America*, 40–48; White Biographical Statement, n.d., KU.

10. Peter Argersinger, *Populism and Politics: William Alfred Peffer and the People's Party* (Louisville: University Press of Kentucky, 1974), 20; O. Gene Clanton, *Kansas Populism: Ideas and Men* (Lawrence: University Press of Kansas, 1969), 12–13; Worth R. Miller, *Oklahoma Populism: A History of the People's Party in the Oklahoma Territory* (Norman: University of Oklahoma Press, 1987), 21; Argersinger, "Republican Waterloo," 443–469; White, Commencement Speech at the Kansas State Teachers College of Pittsburg, May 28, 1936, KU.

11. Clanton, *Kansas Populism*, 63–66; White Biographical Statement, n.d., KU; White, *Autobiography*, 177–187.

12. Clanton, *Kansas Populism*, 86–89; Argersinger, "Republican Waterloo," 443–469.

13. White, *Autobiography*, 195–199.

14. Ibid., 192–193, 206–223; Johnson, *White's America*, 57–60; White to W. Greason, Nov. 20, 1912, LoC; White to Mary Ann White, Mar. 1892, William Lindsay White Collection, Kansas Collection, Spencer Research Library, University of Kansas, Lawrence; White to Mary Ann White, Mar. 19, 1892, William Lindsay White Collection.

15. White, *Autobiography*, 227–239; Johnson, *White's America*, 75.

16. White, *Autobiography*, 227–230, 238–239; Johnson, *White's America*, 64–65. For more on fusion in Kansas, see John M. Peterson, "The People's Party of Kansas: Campaigning in 1898," *Kansas History* 13, no. 4 (Winter 1990): 235.

17. Johnson, *White's America*, 72–73; White, *Autobiography*, 241–246.

18. Johnson, *White's America*, 63; White, *Autobiography*, 250–257.

19. White, *Autobiography*, 257–260.
20. Ibid., 260–265; White to W. Greason, Nov. 20, 1912, LoC; White to Charles Vernon, Nov. 29, 1907, LoC; *EG*, June 3, 1895.
21. White, *Autobiography*, 263–269, 315–318; Johnson, *White's America*, 83–85.
22. Clanton, *Kansas Populism*, 191–192; White, *Autobiography*, 249–283; Johnson, *White's America*, 86–93; *Emporia Weekly Gazette*, Sept. 26, 1895; White to Henry Haskell, Aug. 11, 1936, LoC.
23. White, "What's the Matter with Kansas?" *EG*, Aug. 15, 1896.
24. Clanton, *Kansas Populism*, 191–192; Johnson, *White's America*, 94–95; Hinshaw, *Man from Kansas*, 78.
25. White, *Autobiography*, 284–292; Johnson, *White's America*, 94–104; "Lincoln Day in the East," *Salt Lake Herald*, Feb. 13, 1897.
26. White, *Autobiography*, 290–299, 577; Johnson, *White's America*, 108; McKee, *Maverick*, 49–50.
27. White, *Autobiography*, 313.
28. Ibid., 303–313; *EWG*, Oct. 7, 1897.
29. *EWG*, Feb. 3, 1898, Nov. 16, 1899, Nov. 30, 1899, Dec. 7, 1899.
30. *EWG*, Oct. 21, 1897, Oct. 28, 1897.
31. *EWG*, Mar. 10, 1898, Sept. 29, 1898, Nov. 24, 1898, Dec. 1, 1898.
32. White, *Autobiography*, 303–313; White to Charles F. Scott, Aug. 1899, LoC; White to Warren Anderson, Oct. 13, 1899, LoC.
33. White to Hanford Finney, July 3, 1899, LoC; White to Cyrus Leland, July 1899, LoC; White to W. J. Black, Aug. 15, 1899, LoC; White to W. D. Smith, Aug. 30, 1899, LoC; White to Henry Cabot Lodge, July 15, 1899, LoC; White, *Autobiography*, 322–323; *EWG*, Oct. 5, 1899.
34. White, *Autobiography*, 322; *EWG*, Sept. 28, 1899, Oct. 5, 1899.
35. *EWG*, Oct. 5, 1899.
36. White, *Autobiography*, 321; White to Francis Brogan, Apr. 11, 1901, LoC; Johnson, *White's America*, 118.

CHAPTER 2. HELL-RAISER
1. White, *Autobiography*, 319–325; White to Theodore Roosevelt, ca. Jan. 1900, LoC; White to Roosevelt, Aug. 29, 1901, LoC.
2. Johnson, *White's America*, 111; White to Roosevelt, June 28, 1899, LoC; White to Roosevelt, May 9, 1900, LoC; White to Roosevelt, June 22, 1900, LoC; Roosevelt to White, Aug. 24, 1901, LoC; Doris Kearns Goodwin, *The Bully Pulpit: Theodore Roosevelt, William Howard Taft,*

and the Golden Age of Journalism (New York: Simon & Schuster, 2013), 260; Lewis Gould, *The Presidency of Theodore Roosevelt* (Lawrence: University Press of Kansas, 2011), 6–7.

3. White to Roosevelt, July 20, 1901, LoC; White to Cyrus Leland, Aug. 15, 1901, LoC; White to Miller, Oct. 1901, LoC; White, *Autobiography,* 330.

4. White to Leland, Aug. 15, 1901, LoC; White to Roosevelt, Aug. 21, 1901, LoC; Roosevelt to White, Aug. 24, 1901, LoC; Roosevelt to White, Aug. 27, 1901, LoC; White to Roosevelt, Sept. 11, 1901, Theodore Roosevelt Papers, Manuscript Division, Library of Congress, Washington, DC.

5. Roosevelt to White, Sept. 7, 1901, LoC; White to Roosevelt, Sept. 14, 1901, LoC; White, *Autobiography,* 338–339.

6. White, *Autobiography,* 430; R. Alton Lee, "Joseph Ralph Burton and the 'Ill Fated' Senate Seat of Kansas," *Kansas History* 32, no. 4 (Winter 2009): 246–265; Robert S. La Forte, *Leaders of Reform: Progressive Republicans in Kansas, 1900–1916* (Lawrence: University Press of Kansas, 1974), 18–19.

7. Cyrus Leland to Joseph L. Bristow, Sept. 27, 1897, Joseph Bristow Papers, Kansas State Archives, Topeka, KS; Johnson, *White's America,* 124.

8. Bristow to J. D. Bowersock, Sept. 20, 1901, JBP; Leland to Bristow, Sept. 20, 1901, JBP; White to Roosevelt, Oct. 14, 1901, TRP; White to Roosevelt, Oct. 25, 1901, TRP.

9. Roosevelt to White, Oct. 25, 1901, TRP; Roosevelt to White, Nov. 2, 1901, TRP; White to Roosevelt, Oct. 30, 1901, TRP.

10. White to Roosevelt, Nov. 6, 1901, TRP; White to Roosevelt, Nov. 10, 1901, TRP; Leland to White, Nov. 16, 1901, LoC; Roosevelt to White, Nov. 6, 1901, LoC.

11. Leland to Bristow, Nov. 26, 1901, JBP; Bristow to Leland, Dec. 5, 1901, JBP; Bristow to Leland, Dec. 6, 1901, JBP; Leland to Bristow, Dec. 3, 1901, JBP; Leland to Bristow, Dec. 11, 1901, JBP.

12. Bristow to Leland, Dec. 12, 1901, JBP; Bristow to Leland, Dec. 14, 1901, JBP; White to Roosevelt, Dec. 13, 1901, TRP; White to Roosevelt, Dec. 13, 1901, TRP.

13. Bristow to Allen, Dec. 27, 1901, JBP; Leland to Bristow, Dec. 30, 1901, JBP; White to Roosevelt, Dec. 14, 1901, TRP; White to George Cortelyou, Dec. 18, 1901, TRP.

14. White, *Autobiography,* 335; William Allen White, "Platt," *McClure's,* Dec. 1901, 145–153; Goodwin, *Bully Pulpit,* 282.

15. White to Cortelyou, Dec. 17, 1901, LoC; White to Roosevelt, Dec. 17, 1901, LoC; Roosevelt to White, Dec. 3, 1901, LoC; Johnson, *White's America*, 134–135; White, *Autobiography*, 347–349.

16. White, *Autobiography*, 347–349; White to Roosevelt, Feb. 10, 1902, TRP; White to Angelo Scott, Sept. 26, 1916, LoC.

17. White to Roosevelt, Dec. 22, 1904, LoC; *EG*, Jan. 23, 1902, Feb. 13, 1902; Roosevelt to White, June 4, 1902, LoC; Lee, "Joseph Ralph Burton," 246–265; Gould, *Roosevelt Presidency*, 51.

18. White to Roosevelt, Apr. 9, 1902, TRP; White to Roosevelt, Apr. 23, 1902, TRP; White to Roosevelt, Apr. 26, 1902, TRP; White to Roosevelt, June 5, 1902, TRP.

19. Lee, "Joseph Ralph Burton," 246–265; White to Roosevelt, June 5, 1902, TRP; White to Cortelyou, June 19, 1902, TRP; Roosevelt to White, June 4, 1902, LoC.

20. Bristow to Leland, June 11, 1902, JBP; Lee, "Joseph Ralph Burton," 246–265; Roosevelt to White, June 23, 1902, LoC.

21. White, *Autobiography*, 350–366.

22. Chester Long to Bristow, July 21, 1902, JRB; White, *Autobiography*, 352–353; La Forte, *Leaders of Reform*, 27.

23. White, *Autobiography*, 353; Lee, "Joseph Ralph Burton," 246–265; White to Long, Apr. 14, 1903, LoC; La Forte, *Leaders of Reform*, 42.

24. Lee, "Joseph Ralph Burton," 246–265; Johnson, *White's America*, 139–140; La Forte, *Leaders of Reform*, 39; White to Roosevelt, July 11, 1903, LoC.

25. Michael Wolraich, *Unreasonable Men: Theodore Roosevelt and the Republican Rebels Who Created Progressive Politics* (New York: Palgrave Macmillan, 2014), 1–8; White to Charles Gleed, May 3, 1904, LoC; La Forte, *Leaders of Reform*, 73.

26. La Forte, *Leaders of Reform*, 31–42; White to C. C. Coleman, Oct. 12, 1904, LoC.

27. White to Ed Hoch, Oct. 7, 1904, LoC.

28. Roosevelt to White, Dec. 2, 1904, LoC; William Allen White, "The Reorganization of the Republican Party," *Saturday Evening Post*, Dec. 3, 1904.

29. R. Alton Lee, *Farmers vs. Wage Earners: Organized Labor in Kansas, 1860–1960* (Lincoln: University Press of Nebraska, 2005), 96; La Forte, *Leaders of Reform*, 44–58, 69–71; Gould, *Roosevelt Presidency*, 146–147.

30. White to Frank Hunt, Jan. 20, 1905, LoC; White to I. B. Perrine, Mar. 2, 1905, LoC; White, *Autobiography*, 365–368; J. Anthony Lukas, *Big Trouble* (New York: Simon & Schuster, 1997), 715.

31. David J. Hoeveler, *John Bascom and the Origins of the Wisconsin Idea* (Madison: University of Wisconsin Press, 2016), 191–192; White to Hoch, Mar. 7, 1905, LoC; White to Scott Hopkins, June 7, 1907, LoC; White to the Editor of the "Kansan," Dec. 14, 1908, LoC; Johnson, *White's America*, 151; Clifford S. Griffin, *The University of Kansas: A History* (Lawrence: University Press of Kansas, 1974), 255.

32. La Forte, *Leaders of Reform*, 68–74; Gould, *Roosevelt Presidency*, 150–159.

33. Gould, *Republicans*, 119; White to George T. Nicholson, Apr. 5, 1906, LoC.

34. La Forte, *Leaders of Reform*, 72–77; White, *Autobiography*, 367; White to Roosevelt, Aug. 16, 1906, LoC.

35. White to Hoch, May 6, 1906, LoC; White to Hoch, May 24, 1906, LoC.

36. La Forte, *Leaders of Reform*, 75–79; White to Robert La Follette, July 6, 1906, LoC; White to Ralph Stout, Aug. 9, 1906, LoC; J. B. Dykes to Chester Long, Feb. 1, 1908, Chester I. Long Papers, Kansas State Archives, Kansas Historical Society, Topeka, KS.

37. La Forte, *Leaders of Reform*, 77–78; White to Roosevelt, Aug. 16, 1906, LoC; White to W. R. Stubbs, Oct. 16, 1906, LoC.

38. White to Stubbs, Oct. 16, 1906, LoC.

39. La Forte, *Leaders of Reform*, 80–83; White to Roosevelt, Oct. 18, 1906, LoC; White to Henry Allen, Jan. 15, 1907, LoC.

40. La Forte, *Leaders of Reform*, 84–88; Long to Morton Albaugh, Feb. 6, 1907, Chester Long Papers, Kansas State Archives, Topeka, KS; Long to W. Y. Morgan, Feb. 8, 1907, CLP; Long to F. Dumont Smith, Feb. 8, 1907, CLP.

41. Gould, *Roosevelt Presidency*, 8; White to Roosevelt, Mar. 11, 1907, LoC; Roosevelt to White, Mar. 20, 1907, LoC.

42. White to Senator Marcus Hanna, Nov. 29, 1902, LoC; White to Hanna, Dec. 8, 1902, LoC.

43. White to Roosevelt, May 1, 1907, LoC; White to Borah, May 1, 1907, LoC; Borah to White, n.d., LoC; Roosevelt to White, May 8, 1907, LoC; Lukas, *Big Trouble*, 714–715.

44. White to Roosevelt, July 25, 1907, LoC; Roosevelt to White, July 30, 1907, LoC.

45. Roosevelt to White, Aug. 30, 1907, LoC; Roosevelt to White, Mar. 24, 1908, LoC; White, *Autobiography,* 374–375; Lukas, *Big Trouble,* 716–717, 731–748.
46. White to Henry Allen, Apr. 29, 1907, LoC; White to W. R. Stubbs, May 31, 1907, LoC; White to Robert Stone, June 14, 1907, LoC.
47. La Forte, *Leaders of Reform,* 86–95; White, *Autobiography,* 395; Morton Albaugh to Long, Feb. 7, 1908, CLP; White to Victor Murdock, Mar. 1908, LoC; White to J. N. Dolley, June 29, 1908, LoC.
48. Chandler to Long, Apr. 3, 1908, CLP; R. K. Faxon to Long, Apr. 11, 1908, CLP; White to T. Johnston, Apr. 16, 1908, LoC; White to Oswald Garrison Villard, Apr. 15, 1908, LoC; White to Bristow, May 9, 1908, LoC; White to D. C. McCollum, May 27, 1908, LoC; White to T. B. Murdock, June 9, 1908, LoC.
49. White to Bristow, May 4, 1908, LoC; Bristow to White, May 7, 1908, LoC; Bristow to White, May 8, 1908, LoC.
50. Ralph Faxon to Long, May 12, 1908, CLP; Mort Albaugh to Long, May 13, 1908, CLP; F. Grimes to Long, May 13, 1908, CLP.
51. White, *Autobiography,* 395; Faxon to Long, May 21, 1908, CLP; Albaugh to Long, May 23, 1908, CLP; Albaugh to Long, May 26, 1908, CLP; Long to Albaugh, May 22, 1908, CLP.
52. Long to Albaugh, May 31, 1908, CLP; Albaugh to Long, June 1, 1908, CLP; White to Willey, July 29, 1908, LoC; White to Paul Lovell, Aug. 6, 1908, LoC.
53. Henry Allen to Morgan, July 11, 1908, CLP; Albaugh to Long, July 11, 1908, CLP; White to Bristow, June 23, 1908, LoC; White to Bristow, June 27, 1908, LoC; White to Victor Murdock, June 29, 1908, LoC; White to Bristow, July 13, 1908, LoC.
54. White, *Autobiography,* 397; La Forte, *Leaders of Reform,* 106–107; Long to Grimes, May 14, 1908, CLP; Long to Roosevelt, July 19, 1908, CLP; White to Ralph Tennal, June 30, 1908, LoC; White to La Follette, July 1, 1908, LoC.
55. White, *Autobiography,* 401; La Forte, *Leaders of Reform,* 106–108; White to Frank Ward, Jan. 5, 1909, LoC; White to Paul Lovell, Aug. 6, 1908, LoC; White to Allen, Aug. 11, 1908, LoC; White to Roosevelt, Aug. 8, 1908, LoC; White to Alex Miller, Aug. 13, 1908, LoC.
56. White to Stubbs, Nov. 6, 1908, LoC; White to Clad Hamilton, Nov. 24, 1908, LoC; White to La Follette, Nov. 30, 1908, LoC; White to

Oskinson, Dec. 15, 1908, LoC; White to Ray S. Baker, Mar. 25, 1909, LoC; La Forte, *Leaders of Reform*, 123–127.

57. Johnson, *White's America*, 140–141; White to G. W. Folk, Aug. 12, 1908, LoC; White to William Bobbs, Oct. 24, 1908, LoC; White to Borah, Aug. 11, 1908, LoC; White to Ben Lindsey, Aug. 31, 1908, LoC; White to Charles E. Hughes, Nov. 21, 1908, LoC.

58. Gilbert Fite, *Peter Norbeck: Prairie Statesman* (Columbia: University of Missouri, 1948), 49; White, *Autobiography*, 401; Johnson, *White's America*, 165; White to George Hooker, Dec. 18, 1908, LoC; White to La Follette, Nov. 14, 1908, LoC; White to John S. Phillips, Sept. 9, 1908, LoC; White to Ben Lindsey, Feb. 1, 1909, LoC.

59. White to Roosevelt, Oct. 16, 1908, LoC; White to Roosevelt, Oct. 8, 1906, LoC; Roosevelt to White, Aug. 11, 1906, LoC; William H. Taft to White, Feb. 26, 1908, LoC; Roosevelt to White, Oct. 17, 1907, LoC; Goodwin, *Bully Pulpit*, 538.

60. White to Taft, Mar. 16, 1909, LoC; White to Irvine Dungan, Nov. 25, 1908, LoC; Taft to White, Mar. 20, 1909, LoC; Taft to White, Mar. 12, 1909, LoC.

61. White, *Autobiography*, 363–364; White to Roosevelt, July 25, 1907, LoC.

62. Daniel T. Rodgers, *Atlantic Crossings: Social Politics in a Progressive Age* (Cambridge, MA: Harvard University Press, 1998), 57; White, *Autobiography*, 401–411; Johnson, *White's America*, 168–169; White to John Phillips, Oct. 26, 1908, LoC; White to Harry Baker, Mar. 25, 1909, LoC; White to Helen Mahin, Oct. 7, 1929, LoC.

CHAPTER 3. A WAR OF CONQUEST

1. White, *Autobiography*, 381, 423; White to W. Sage, May 10, 1910, LoC; George Brett to White, Oct. 8, 1909, LoC; Theodore Roosevelt to White, Dec. 10, 1909, LoC; White to Helen Mahin, Oct. 7, 1929, LoC; White to Edna Ferber, Oct. 31, 1936, LoC; *La Follette's*, Oct. 23, 1909, 4.

2. White to F. S. Jackson, Dec. 14, 1909, LoC; White to Jackson, Dec. 18, 1909, LoC; Stuart Rochester, *American Liberal Disillusionment in the Wake of World War I* (University Park: Pennsylvania State University Press, 1977), 30–31.

3. Lewis Gould, *The William Howard Taft Presidency* (Lawrence: University Press of Kansas, 2009), 46–47, 61–62; Roger E. Wyman, "Insurgency in Minnesota: The Defeat of James A. Tawney in 1910,"

Minnesota History 40, no. 7 (Fall 1967): 313–329; White to Dr. Hamilton Mable, Sept. 1909, LoC; White to William R. Nelson, Sept. 23, 1909, LoC; White to Alice Post, Oct. 9, 1909, LoC; La Forte, *Leaders of Reform*, 154–163.

4. Gould, *Taft Presidency*, 99; Richard Lowitt, *George W. Norris: The Making of a Progressive, 1861–1912* (Syracuse, NY: Syracuse University Press, 1963), 176–179; White to Maurice Crowther, June 7, 1910, LoC; White to Henry Haskell, June 6, 1910, LoC; White to Henry Beasley, Feb. 18, 1910, LoC; White to William H. Taft, Feb. 3, 1910, LoC; White to H. C. O'Laughlin, Jan. 19, 1910, LoC; White to H. W. Mabie, Oct. 23, 1909, LoC; Victor Murdock to White, Dec. 19, 1909, LoC; Taft to White, May 20, 1910, LoC; White to Henry Pringle, Sept. 7, 1939, LoC.

5. White to Winston Churchill, Aug. 11, 1910, LoC; White to Samuel Gompers, Aug. 8, 1910, LoC; White to Sheffield Ingalls, July 22, 1910, LoC.

6. White to E. Riley, Apr. 22, 1910, LoC; White to Ralph Stout, Aug. 20, 1910, LoC; White to J. Carnahan, Aug. 22, 1910, LoC; White to Smith, Sept. 7, 1910, LoC; La Follette to White, Sept. 15, 1910, LoC; William E. Borah to White, Sept. 26, 1910, LoC; Walter Lippmann to White, Oct. 4, 1910, LoC.

7. Gould, *Taft Presidency*, 109–110; White to Dante Barton, June 20, 1910, LoC; White to Barton, n.d., LoC.

8. Roosevelt to White, Aug. 9, 1910, LoC; Robert La Forte, "Theodore Roosevelt's Osawatomie Speech," *Kansas History* 32, no. 2 (Summer 1966): 187–200; White, *Autobiography*, 438.

9. White to Gifford Pinchot, Sept. 21, 1910, LoC.

10. White to Fred Davis, Dec. 5, 1910, LoC; White to Murdock, Feb. 4, 1911, LoC; White to Roosevelt, Nov. 12, 1910, LoC; Roosevelt to White, Nov. 11, 1910, LoC; Bristow to White, Jan. 16, 1911, LoC.

11. Roosevelt to White, Dec. 12, 1910, LoC; White to Albert Beveridge, Nov. 22, 1910, LoC; White to Mark Sullivan, Nov. 23, 1910, LoC; White to Roosevelt, Nov. 28, 1910, LoC; White to Oswald Garrison Villard, Dec. 5, 1910, LoC; White to Gifford Pinchot, Nov. 29, 1910, LoC; White to George Record, Dec. 7, 1910, LoC; White to Roosevelt, Jan. 17, 1911, LoC; William Allen White, "The Insurgence of Insurgency: What the Radical Wing of the Republican Party Stands for, and What It Has Accomplished," *American Magazine*, Dec. 1910, 170.

12. White to La Follette, Jan. 3, 1911, LoC; La Follette to White, Dec. 28, 1910, LoC; Roosevelt to White, Jan. 24, 1911, LoC.

13. White to Murdock, Feb. 4, 1911, LoC; White to J. Burnette, Feb. 13, 1911, LoC; White to Brewster, Feb. 18, 1911, LoC; White to Nelson, May 10, 1911, LoC; White to Murdock, Aug. 20, 1911, LoC.

14. White to Harwell and Cannon, May 16, 1911, LoC; White to Fred Trigg, May 29, 1911, LoC; White to Murdock, Aug. 20, 1911, LoC; White to Roosevelt, Oct. 16, 1911, LoC.

15. White to Roosevelt, Oct. 16, 1911, LoC; White to Roosevelt, Nov. 16, 1911, LoC; Roosevelt to White, Oct. 24, 1911, LoC.

16. White to Henry Vincent, Sept. 3, 1910, LoC; White to Henry Allen, Jan. 17, 1912, LoC; White to Bristow, Dec. 28, 1911, LoC; White to A. Brown, Dec. 17, 1909, LoC. On the contrast between Roosevelt's and La Follette's views on the fundamental problems facing American democracy, see Sidney Milkis, *Theodore Roosevelt, the Progressive Party, and the Transformation of American Democracy* (Lawrence: University Press of Kansas, 2009).

17. White, *Autobiography*, 448–449; Nancy Unger, *Fighting Bob La Follette: The Righteous Reformer* (Chapel Hill: University of North Carolina Press, 2000), 200–207; White to Rodney Elward, Nov. 9, 1912, LoC; White to Fola La Follette, Feb. 8, 1938, LoC; Bristow to White, Jan. 11, 1912, LoC; Bristow to White, Jan. 19, 1912, LoC; Bristow to White, Dec. 20, 1911, ESU; Goodwin, *Bully Pulpit*, 674–675.

18. White to Bristow, Jan. 8, 1912, LoC; White to Murdock, Jan. 11, 1912, LoC; White to Mort Albaugh, Jan. 13, 1912, LoC; White to Albaugh, Jan. 18, 1912, LoC; White to Charles F. Scott, Feb. 10, 1912, LoC; White to Murdock, Apr. 29, 1912, LoC; White to Roland Rees, Apr. 29, 1912, LoC.

19. White, *Autobiography*, 457, 466; White to John Phillips, May 15, 1912, LoC; White to Charles Davidson, May 15, 1912, LoC; Bristow to White, Apr. 17, 1912, LoC.

20. White, *Autobiography*, 464–468; White to Allen, May 23, 1912, LoC; White to Charles Van Hise, May 24, 1912, LoC; White to Charles Sheldon, Sept. 16, 1912, LoC.

21. Gould, *Taft Presidency*, 178–181; White, *Autobiography*, 469–473, 494.

22. White to B. Blaker, July 13, 1912, LoC; White to W. Cunningham, July 23, 1912, LoC; White to Roosevelt, July 24, 1912, LoC; White to G. Franklin, Aug. 12, 1912, LoC; White to E. Jackson, Aug. 31, 1912, LoC; Johnson, *White's America*, 203.

23. White, *Autobiography*, 461, 484–494; White to Medill McCormick, Aug. 26, 1912, LoC; White to John Phillips, Aug. 28, 1912, LoC; White to Paul U. Kellogg, Aug. 30, 1912, LoC; White to George Brett, Oct. 5, 1912, LoC; La Forte, *Leaders of Reform*, 196–203; White to George Adams, Jan. 24, 1916, LoC.

24. White Letter to Delegates, Sept. 18, 1912, LoC; White to O. K. Miller, Sept. 27, 1912, LoC; White to O. W. Dawson, Oct. 8, 1912, LoC; Samuel Blythe, "The Mix in the Middle West," *Saturday Evening Post*, Sept. 21, 1912, 6.

25. Kendrick Clements, *The Presidency of Woodrow Wilson* (Lawrence: University Press of Kansas, 1992), 5–11; White to Charles F. Scott, Sept. 26, 1912, LoC; White to Frank Wade, July 10, 1912, LoC; White to John Phillips, July 20, 1912, LoC; White to A. Torrance, Oct. 17, 1912, LoC; White to Elmer Peterson, Sept. 20, 1912, LoC.

26. White to William Vernon, May 10, 1912, LoC; White, *Autobiography*, 479; White to F. Miller, Nov. 9, 1912, LoC; White to Robert Stone, Nov. 16, 1912, LoC; White to Chester Aldrich, Dec. 2, 1912, LoC; Roosevelt to White, Nov. 15, 1912, LoC; Bristow to White, Dec. 1, 1912, LoC; Bristow to White, Dec. 3, 1912, LoC; Dolley to White, Sept. 26, 1912, LoC; Milkis, *Theodore Roosevelt*, 2.

27. Clements, *Wilson*, 28; White, *Autobiography*, 490; White to Roosevelt, Nov. 25, 1912, LoC; Roosevelt to Pinchot, Nov. 13, 1912, LoC.

28. White, *Autobiography*, 497; White to Allen, Nov. 1912, LoC; White to Roosevelt, Nov. 14, 1912, LoC; White to Charles F. Scott, Jan. 10, 1914, LoC; White to John Phillips, June 6, 1913, LoC; White to George Perkins, June 5, 1913, LoC.

29. White to Roosevelt, Sept. 24, 1913, LoC.

30. White to Allen, Sept. 23, 1913, LoC; White to Allen, Sept. 27, 1913, LoC; White to J. Moore, Jan. 19, 1914, LoC; Bristow to White, June 19, 1913, LoC.

31. Clements, *Wilson*, 38–44; White to Arthur Capper, Sept. 30, 1913, LoC; White to Bristow, Oct. 26, 1913, LoC; Capper to White, Oct. 11, 1913, LoC.

32. White to Bristow, Nov. 1, 1913, LoC; Bristow to White, Oct. 25, 1913, LoC; Bristow to White, Nov. 12, 1913, LoC; David Hinshaw to White, Dec. 17, 1913, LoC; Allen to White, Jan. 6, 1914, LoC.

33. White to Arthur Capper, Nov. 28, 1913, LoC; White to Roosevelt, Mar.

7, 1914, LoC; White to F. D. Coburn, Feb. 6, 1914, LoC; White to O. W. Dawson, Apr. 24, 1914, LoC; White Circular Letter, May 4, 1914, LoC; U. S. Sartin to White, Apr. 14, 1914, LoC.

34. White to Murdock, Dec. 4, 1913, LoC; White to Roosevelt, Mar. 7, 1914, LoC; White to N. James, Jan. 8, 1914; Murdock to White, Dec. 16, 1913, LoC.

35. White to Allen, Jan. 6, 1914, LoC; White to Stubbs, Jan. 6, 1914, LoC; White to John Landon, Feb. 20, 1914, LoC; White to H. Motter, Mar. 8, 1914, LoC; White to Murdock, Mar. 7, 1914, LoC.

36. White to L. Valentine, Jan. 20, 1914, LoC.

37. White to McCormick, Dec. 29, 1913, LoC; White to Gifford Pinchot, Apr. 20, 1914, LoC; Perkins to White, May 27, 1914, LoC; Perkins to White, Apr. 10, 1914, LoC; Gifford Pinchot to White, Apr. 15, 1914, LoC.

38. White to Murdock, June 12, 1914, LoC; Roosevelt to White, July 6, 1914, LoC; U. S. Sartin to White, July 28, 1914, LoC; Allen to White, Oct. 12, 1914, LoC; Allen to White, Aug. 31, 1914, LoC; A. Bower Sageser, *Joseph L. Bristow: Kansas Progressive* (Lawrence: University Press of Kansas, 1968), 151.

39. White to O. K. Davis, Sept. 12, 1914, LoC; Secretary to Bristow et al., n.d., LoC; White to Mrs. Charles Scott, Jan. 27, 1915, LoC; White to W. T. Lute, Feb. 22, 1916, LoC; White to George Brett, Mar. 4, 1916, LoC.

40. White to Theodore Roosevelt, Dec. 15, 1914, LoC.

41. White to Arthur Capper, Nov. 5, 1914, LoC; White to G. Bertch, n.d., LoC; White to J. Jones, Nov. 10, 1914, LoC.

42. White to Jim Garfield, Nov. 18, 1914, LoC; Roosevelt to White, Nov. 7, 1914, LoC.

43. George Perkins to White, Nov. 21, 1914, LoC; David Hinshaw to White, Nov. 7, 1914, LoC; Raymond Robins to White, Jan. 12, 1915, LoC; White to Allen, Nov. 9, 1914, LoC; White to Perkins, Nov. 18, 1914, LoC; White to Hiram Johnson, Nov. 29, 1914, LoC.

44. White to Robins, Jan. 16, 1915, LoC; White to Lilla Monroe, Nov. 7, 1914, LoC; White to Morton Albaugh, Dec. 23, 1914, LoC.

45. White to Perkins, May 13, 1915, LoC; White to Hinshaw, Feb. 8, 1915, LoC; White to Frank Lloyd Wright, Feb. 17, 1915, LoC; Enos Mills to White, Nov. 19, 1913, LoC; Mills to White, Jan. 10, 1915, LoC.

46. White to Roosevelt, Apr. 6, 1916, LoC; White to Perkins, Jan. 25, 1916,

LoC; White to Fredrick Cowper, Feb. 3, 1916, LoC; White to George Lamb, Mar. 8, 1916, LoC.

47. Gould, *Republicans*, 148–149; White, *Autobiography*, 522–527; White to George Adams, Jan. 24, 1916, LoC; White to Harold Ickes, May 17, 1937, LoC.

48. White to Gifford Pinchot, June 23, 1916, LoC; Pinchot to White, June 30, 1916, LoC; Paul U. Kellogg to White, July 13, 1916, LoC; White to Roosevelt, June 17, 1916, LoC; White to Victor Murdock, June 19, 1916, Victor Murdock Papers, Manuscripts Division, Library of Congress, Washington, DC.

49. White, *Autobiography*, 528–531; White to Ralph Tennal, June 17, 1916, LoC; White to Henry Forman, Sept. 11, 1916, LoC; White to Norman Hapgood, Oct. 15, 1916, LoC.

50. Clements, *Wilson*, 81; White to Ray S. Baker, Jan. 27, 1917, LoC; White to Scott Nearing, Nov. 3, 1916, LoC; Allen to White, Dec. 14, 1916, LoC; Harold Ickes to White, Nov. 11, 1916, LoC; Ickes to White, Feb. 5, 1917, LoC.

51. See Karen A. J. Miller, *Populist Nationalism: Republican Insurgency and American Foreign Policy Making, 1918–1925* (Westport, CT: Greenwood, 1999).

CHAPTER 4. SAVING THE WORLD

1. "Our Other War," *EG*, Apr. 29, 1914; "The Cruel War," *EG*, Aug. 6, 1914.

2. White, *Autobiography*, 515, 533; White to Edward Lyman, Nov. 30, 1914, LoC; White to Clinton Woodruff, Jan. 19, 1915, LoC; White to Murdock, Sept. 15, 1915, LoC; Roosevelt to White, Aug. 3, 1915, LoC.

3. Clements, *Wilson*, 128; Ross A. Kennedy, *The Will to Believe: Woodrow Wilson, World War I, and America's Strategy for Peace and Security* (Kent, OH: Kent State University Press, 2009), 54; "The World Is Mad," *EG*, May 10, 1915; Charles Forcey, *The Crossroads of Liberalism: Croly, Weyl, Lippmann, and the Progressive Era, 1900–1925* (New York: Oxford University Press, 1961), 235–236; White to Theodore Roosevelt, Aug. 27, 1915, LoC.

4. "The Roosevelt Method," *EG*, Jan. 8, 1916; "The Monroe Doctrine," *EG*, Jan. 11, 1916; Taft to White, Dec. 1, 1915, LoC.

5. White to Howard Fielder, Apr. 17, 1916, LoC; "Germany's Note," *EG*,

May 6, 1916; White to Frank Polk, Mar. 13, 1916, LoC; White to Wray, Mar. 13, 1916, LoC.

6. White to Roosevelt, Apr. 22, 1916, LoC; Memorial Day Address of Theodore Roosevelt at Kansas City, May 30, 1916, LoC; Roosevelt to White, May 22, 1916, LoC.

7. Rochester, *American Liberal Disillusionment*, 38–39; Lloyd Ambrosius, *Woodrow Wilson and the American Diplomatic Tradition: The Treaty Fight in Perspective* (Cambridge: Cambridge University Press, 1987), 30–31; N. Gordon Levin, *Woodrow Wilson and World Politics: America's Response to War and Revolution* (London: Oxford University Press, 1968), 42–43; "War," *EG*, Mar. 21, 1917; "Fight and Fight Hard," *EG*, Mar. 27, 1917.

8. Alan Dawley, *Changing the World: American Progressives in War and Revolution* (Princeton, NJ: Princeton University Press, 2003), 120–140; "He Kept Us Out of War," *EG*, Apr. 3, 1917; "A Holy Day," *EG*, Apr. 6, 1917; Statement Issued by Hiram Johnson, Gifford Pinchot, Harold Ickes, William Allen White, and Others, Apr. 23, 1917, Harold Ickes Papers, Manuscript Division, Library of Congress, Washington, DC.

9. Joseph McCartin, *Labor's Great War: The Struggle for Industrial Democracy and the Origins of Modern American Labor Relations, 1912–1921* (Chapel Hill: University of North Carolina Press, 1991), 40–58, 84–95; "The Changing World," *EG*, June 30, 1917; "The Glorious," *EG*, July 4, 1917; "Let's Look at the Cause," *EG*, Jan. 4, 1918; White to W. S. Woods, n.d., LoC; Clements, *Wilson*, 86–89; Rochester, *American Liberal Disillusionment*, 40–41.

10. Shelton Stromquist, *Reinventing "The People"* (Urbana: University of Illinois Press, 2006), 4; "The Bolsheviki," *EG*, Jan. 25, 1918; White to Nicholas Murray Butler, Feb. 19, 1918, LoC; "Let It Be Permanent," *EG*, Sept. 6, 1918; "The Changing World," *EG*, June 30, 1917.

11. White to Rodney Elward, June 8, 1917, LoC; "Congress and the President," *EG*, June 1, 1917; "A Splendid Precedent," *EG*, May 31, 1917; "Freedom under the Law," *EG*, July 30, 1917; William Allen White, *Masks in a Pageant* (New York: Macmillan, 1928), 368–369; "A Lesson from the Old South," *EG*, Dec. 3, 1917.

12. White to George Brett, June 29, 1917, LoC.

13. White to George Brett, July 23, 1917, LoC; Henry Allen to White, July 30, 1917, LoC; White to Mary Ann White, Aug. 8, 1917, KU; Johnson, *White's America*, 277–282.

14. White to Thomas Page, Dec. 15, 1917, LoC; White to Charles Gleed, Apr. 24, 1918, LoC; White to Henry Allen, Apr. 24, 1918, LoC; Walter Lippmann to White, May 7, 1918, LoC; Henry Cabot Lodge to White, Apr. 24, 1918, LoC.

15. White to Jay House, Sept. 25, 1918, LoC; White to Chauncey Williams, Mar. 13, 1918, LoC; White to Helen, Nov. 6, 1918, LoC; White to Frank Adams, Sept. 11, 1918, LoC.

16. Clements, *Wilson Presidency*, 155–164; "Democracy and the Censor," *EG*, Jan. 8, 1918; "Our Censored News," *EG*, May 2, 1918; White to Villard, Sept. 30, 1918, LoC; Bruce Barton to White, Nov. 20, 1917, LoC.

17. "Win the War by Honesty," *EG*, Jan. 17, 1918; White to Vernon Kellogg, Jan. 15, 1918, LoC; White to Vernon Kellogg, n.d., LoC.

18. White to Henry Allen, Dec. 10, 1917, LoC; White to J. Brooks, Feb. 5, 1918, LoC; White to Allen, Mar. 5, 1918, LoC; White to Homer Hoch, Oct. 3, 1918, LoC.

19. James Robertson, "Progressives Elect Will H. Hays Republican National Chairman, 1918," *Indiana Magazine of History* 64, no. 3 (September 1968): 173–190; White to Ickes, Feb. 28, 1918, LoC; White to Will Hays, Mar. 4, 1918, LoC; White to Roosevelt, Mar. 25, 1918, LoC; Roosevelt to White, Apr. 2, 1918, LoC; Ickes to White, Feb. 25, 1918, LoC.

20. White to Roosevelt, Mar. 29, 1918, LoC.

21. White to Roosevelt, Apr. 24, 1918, LoC; White to Hays, May 15, 1918, LoC.

22. Richard W. Resh, "A Vision in Emporia: William Allen White's Search for Community," *Midcontinent American Studies* 10, no. 2 (Fall 1969): 20–22; White to Brett, May 27, 1918, LoC; White to Martin, Oct. 18, 1918, LoC; White to Charles Russel, Oct. 22, 1918, LoC; White to Helen Mahin, Oct. 7, 1929, LoC.

23. White to Medill McCormick, Sept. 16, 1918, LoC; White to Hays, Sept. 17, 1918, LoC.

24. Seward Livermore, *Politics Is Adjourned: Woodrow Wilson and the War Congress, 1916–1918* (Middletown, CT: Wesleyan University Press, 1966), 69, 80, 136, 221–223; "Wilson Winning the War," *EG*, Sept. 24, 1918; "Mexicanizing America," *EG*, Oct. 28, 1918; White to Will Carruth, Nov. 4, 1918, LoC; White to Villard, Sept. 30, 1918, LoC.

25. Livermore, *Politics Is Adjourned*, 225–226; "The Republican Party," *EG*, Nov. 6, 1918; White to Helen, Nov. 6, 1918, LoC; White to William Ingersoll, Nov. 13, 1918, LoC.

26. White to George Lorimer, May 7, 1918, LoC; White to Theodore Roosevelt, Nov. 18, 1918, LoC; "Exit the Kings," *EG*, Nov. 11, 1918; "Bolsheviki," *EG*, Nov. 13, 1918; "The Power of Democracy," *EG*, Nov. 19, 1918; "Counting Our Gains," *EG*, Dec. 3, 1918.

27. White, *Autobiography*, 551; White to Borah, Nov. 19, 1918, LoC; "Why Wilson Went," *EG*, Dec. 21, 1918; White to Henry Allen, July 29, 1919, LoC.

28. Clements, *Wilson*, 172–173; Villard to Henry R. Mussey, Jan. 20, 1919, Oswald Garrison Villard Papers, Houghton Library, Harvard University, Cambridge, MA; Lippmann Memorandum on Press Correspondents, n.d., Walter Lippmann Papers, Manuscripts and Archives, Sterling Library, Yale University, New Haven, CT; Ronald Steel, *Walter Lippmann and the American Century* (Boston: Little, Brown, 1980), 145–153; Johnson, *White's America*, 296.

29. David McFadden, *Alternative Paths: Soviets and Americans, 1917–1920* (New York: Oxford University Press, 1993), 200–208; White, *Autobiography*, 562–563; White to Upton Sinclair, July 29, 1919, LoC; White to Sinclair, Oct. 26, 1939, LoC; Norman Saul, "William Allen White and the Russian Revolution," *Kansas History* 38, no. 4 (Winter 2015): 268–282; White to Victor Murdock, Jan. 14, 1918, VMP.

30. Clements, *Wilson*, 174–175; White, *Autobiography*, 556; "Realists or Idealists?" *EG*, Feb. 1, 1919; "Three Leagues of Nations," *EG*, Feb. 15, 1919; Johnson, *White's America*, 304–309.

31. "Russia and World Peace," *EG*, Mar. 29, 1919; "Reputation a Bugbear," *EG*, Apr. 10, 1919; "The Second Coming of Wilson," *EG*, Apr. 19, 1919; "Unrest of Little Peoples," *EG*, June 2, 1919.

32. Clements, *Wilson*, 190–197; White, *Autobiography*, 577; Ambrosius, *Woodrow Wilson*, 176–177; Levin, *Woodrow Wilson*, 253–260; White to Arthur Capper, Aug. 21, 1919, LoC; Johnson, *White's America*, 318–319.

33. "Republicans and the League," *EG*, Sept. 13, 1919; White to S. G. Thackrey, Sept. 13, 1919, LoC; "A Weakness of the League," *EG*, Oct. 7, 1919; White to Leonard Wood, Aug. 20, 1919, LoC.

34. "Sphinx That Is Wilson," *EG*, Dec. 3, 1919; "The Treaty and Senate," *EG*, Dec. 8, 1919; "A Sad Situation," *EG*, Feb. 3, 1920; White to Isaiah Bowman, Sept. 12, 1919, LoC.

35. "The Dead Treaty," *EG*, Mar. 20, 1920.

36. Thomas Knock, *To End All Wars: Woodrow Wilson and the Quest for a*

New World Order (New York: Oxford University Press, 1992), 268–269; "The Dead Treaty," *EG*, Mar. 20, 1920; White to Walter R. Berdgman, Apr. 21, 1920, LoC; White to James Causey, Oct. 27, 1919, LoC.

CHAPTER 5. A HARD-BOILED WORLD

1. David Kennedy, *Over Here: The First World War and American Society* (New York: Oxford University Press, 1980), 247–250; Robert Murray, *Red Scare: A Study in National Hysteria, 1919–1920* (Minneapolis: University of Minnesota Press, 1955), 57–67, 80–84, 132, 143; White to Lyman B. Moses, June 22, 1920, LoC.

2. Murray, *Red Scare*, 228–230, 242–244; "Seeing Red," *EG*, Jan. 8, 1920; White, *Autobiography*, 622; White to Ernest Harvier, Jan. 10, 1920, LoC; White to Arthur Capper, Nov. 25, 1922, LoC.

3. White to John Davis, Jan. 10, 1923, LoC.

4. White to Leonard Wood, Aug. 7, 1919, LoC; White to Henry Allen, Apr. 27, 1918, LoC; White to Wood, May 24, 1918, LoC; White to Frederick Moore, Dec. 1, 1919, LoC; White to Wood, Dec. 26, 1919, LoC; White to Herbert Hadley, Jan. 14, 1920, LoC.

5. White to Oswald Garrison Villard, May 22, 1920, LoC; Will Hays to White, Dec. 17, 1919, LoC; Ickes to White, Feb. 4, 1920, LoC; White to Hays, Dec. 30, 1919, LoC; White to Victor Murdock, Feb. 4, 1920, LoC; White to Harold Ickes, Mar. 25, 1920, LoC; White to Victor Murdock, Feb. 4, 1920, VMP.

6. Borah to White, Apr. 3, 1922, LoC; White, *Autobiography*, 582–588; White to Edward Duffield, July 14, 1920, LoC; Harold Ickes to White, June 24, 1920, LoC; "Be a Sport," *EG*, June 24, 1920; Ickes to White, June 30, 1920, HIP; White to Rodney Elward, June 15, 1920, LoC; Johnson, *White's America*, 324–325.

7. White to Sen. Warren G. Harding, July 10, 1920, LoC; White to Ickes, July 12, 1920, LoC; "The League Still Lives," *EG*, Sept. 6, 1920; White to Gifford Pinchot, July 10, 1920, LoC; White to Victor Murdock, July 19, 1920, LoC.

8. Gould, *Republicans*, 163; White, *Autobiography*, 591; White to FDR, Aug. 1, 1921, LoC; White to FDR, Aug. 17, 1921, LoC; "A Hard Boiled World," *EG*, Nov. 11, 1920; White, *Masks*, 410–411; White to Victor Murdock, Dec. 20, 1920, LoC.

9. White to Henry Haskell, July 27, 1921, LoC; White to Will Hays, June

1, 1921, LoC; White to Herbert Hoover, Aug. 16, 1921, LoC; White to Victor Murdock, Sept. 23, 1921, LoC; White, *Autobiography*, 592–595.

10. White to Murdock, Aug. 14, 1923, LoC; White to Henry Allen, July 19, 1926, LoC; White to Vernon Kellogg, June 14, 1926, LoC; White to George Lorimer, May 29, 1926, LoC; White to Walt Mason, July 15, 1926, LoC; White to William Mayo, Apr. 2, 1926, LoC.

11. Robert Farrell, *The Presidency of Calvin Coolidge* (Lawrence: University Press of Kansas, 1998), 42; White to Ickes, Mar. 22, 1922, HIP; William Allen White, "The Best Minds, Incorporated: Who's Who in the Harding Administration and What to Expect from It," *Collier's Weekly*, Mar. 4, 1922, LoC.

12. On Hoover's groundbreaking career at Commerce, see Ellis W. Hawley, "Herbert Hoover, the Commerce Secretariat, and the Vision of an 'Associative State,' 1921–1928," *Journal of American History* 61, no. 1 (June 1974): 116–140; "What Do Moderates Want?" *EG*, Nov. 2, 1922; "The Rise of Borah," *EG*, Nov. 29, 1922; "A Brave Man," *EG*, Apr. 21, 1923; White to Helen Mahin, June 23, 1922, LoC; "Hope Springs Eternal," *New York Tribune*, 1922, LoC; White to Vernon Kellogg, Nov. 23, 1922, LoC.

13. White to Theodore Roosevelt, Jr., July 15, 1926, LoC.

14. White, *Masks*, 391; White, *Autobiography*, 619; Warren G. Harding to White, Aug. 11, 1921, LoC.

15. William Allen White, *A Puritan in Babylon: The Story of Calvin Coolidge* (New York: Macmillan, 1938), 444; Farrell, *Coolidge*, 39; "Coolidge's Conservatism," *EG*, Sept. 26, 1925; White to Norris, Jan. 19, 1926, LoC; White to Ickes, Mar. 18, 1926, LoC; White to Vernon Kellogg, Sept. 20, 1923, LoC; Calvin Coolidge to White, Aug. 15, 1924, LoC; White to M. F. Amrine, Dec. 6, 1924, LoC; White to Walter Lippmann, Dec. 1, 1924, LoC.

16. Stromquist, *Reinventing "The People,"* vii; White to Charles Scott, Oct. 27, 1919, LoC; "The Coal Strike," *EG*, Nov. 5, 1919; "Why the Conference Failed," *EG*, Nov. 7, 1919; "Slowly Veering Round," *EG*, Nov. 25, 1919; Melvyn Dubofsky and Warren Van Tine, *John L. Lewis: A Biography* (New York: Quadrangle, 1977), 50–55; "Labor Is Waiting," *EG*, Oct. 9, 1919; "Strikes and Things," *EG*, Sept. 17, 1919; McCartin, *Labor's Great War*, 184–190.

17. Christopher Tomlins, *The State and the Unions: Labor Relations, Law,*

    and the Organized Labor Movement in America, 1880–1960 (Cambridge: Cambridge University Press, 1985), 90–94; Dubofsky, *John L. Lewis,* 32–33, 52–63; White to Hutchinson, Jan. 15, 1920, LoC; White to Leonard Wood, Nov. 12, 1919, LoC; White to Clyde Reed, Dec. 3, 1919, LoC.

18. Farrell, *Coolidge,* 79; Lee, *Farmers vs. Wage Earners,* 152–156; "Courts of Industrial Injustice," *Nation,* Apr. 3, 1920, 416; White to Hutchinson, Jan. 15, 1920, LoC; *The Kansas Court of Industrial Relations: A Modern Weapon* (Topeka: Kansas State Printer, 1921), 8; Henry J. Allen, *The Party of the Third Part* (New York: Harper, 1921), 71–91; Message of Governor Henry J. Allen to the Kansas Legislature, Jan. 5, 1920, Henry J. Allen Papers, Manuscript Division, Library of Congress, Washington, DC; White to W. H. Dodderidge, Jan. 25, 1920, LoC; "Some Friendly Advice," *EG,* Jan. 30, 1920; White to Henry Allen, Feb. 4, 1920, LoC.

19. James G. Pope, "Labor's Constitution of Freedom," *Yale Law Journal* 106, no. 4 (Jan. 1997): 964–965; Eldon Eisenach, *The Lost Promise of Progressivism* (Lawrence: University Press of Kansas, 1994), 195; W. F. Wilkerson, *The Court of Industrial Relations: Selected Opinions and Orders, Including Rules, Practices, and Procedure* (Topeka: Kansas State Printing Plant, 1922), 11–15; Domenico Gagilardo, *The Kansas Industrial Court: An Experiment in Compulsory Arbitration* (Lawrence: University Press of Kansas, 1941), 72–75, 236; "A Working Law," *EG,* July 30, 1920; "The Open Shop," *EG,* Dec. 28, 1920; "Some Sense in This," *EG,* June 3, 1921.

20. Herbert Rabinowitz, "The Kansas Industrial Court Act," *California Law Review* 12, no. 1 (Nov. 1923): 1–16; "Howat's Meeting," *EG,* Aug. 15, 1921; "Kansas Industrial Court Held Legal," *EG,* June 12, 1921; "The Old Cat Is Dying," *EG,* Oct. 29, 1921; William Allen White, "Industrial Justice—Not Peace," *Nation's Business,* May 1922, 14–16; White to Walter Lippmann, May 19, 1922, WLP.

21. David Montgomery, *The Fall of the House of Labor: The Workplace, the State, and American Labor Activism, 1865–1925* (New York: Cambridge University Press, 1987), 400–405; "Toward Understanding the Railroad Strike," *Nation,* Nov. 2, 1921, 491; Colin Davis, *Power at Odds: The 1922 National Railroad Shopmen's Strike* (Urbana: University of Illinois Pres, 1997), 54–61, 74; "The Railway Strike," *EG,* Oct. 28, 1921.

22. "They Have a Kick Coming," *EG,* June 19, 1922; White, *Autobiography,*

611; Allen to White, June 29, 1922, HAP; White to Allen, June 30, 1922, LoC.

23. "Emporia and the Strike," *EG*, July 3, 1922; Davis, *Power at Odds*, 74, 83–86; White to Allen, July 7, 1922, LoC; "Next Week's Trouble," *EG*, July 8, 1922.

24. Allen to White, July 10, 1922, LoC; Davis, *Power at Odds*, 85; White to Allen, July 11, 1922, LoC; Allen to White, July 12, 1922, LoC; George Lathrop to Allen, July 8, 1922, HAP; Allen to White, July 12, 1922, LoC.

25. White to the *Nation*, July 24, 1922, OGV; *EG*, July 22, 1922; White to Borah, Aug. 3, 1922, LoC; Charles Spencer to Allen, July 28, 1922, HAP; Allen to Barnard Macy, Feb. 3, 1923, HAP; J. McDermott to Allen, July 8, 1922, HAP; Sam Ferguson to Allen, July 21, 1922, HAP.

26. Borah to White, Aug. 1, 1922, LoC; Frank Cobb to White, Aug. 1, 1922, LoC; White, *Autobiography*, 613–614; White to Albert Beveridge, Aug. 22, 1922, LoC; Felix Frankfurter to White, July 1922, LoC; Roger Baldwin to White, Sept. 18, 1922, LoC; Allen to Homer Caldwell, Aug. 5, 1922, HAP; Allen to J. E. Jones, July 24, 1922, HAP; Allen to M. M. Studebaker, July 22, 1922, HAP; Allen to L. E. Moses, Feb. 3, 1923, HAP; White to Baldwin, Sept. 13, 1922, LoC.

27. Davis, *Power at Odds*, 87–88, 104–108, 135–145; Charles B. Driscoll, "Kansas Cleans Up Governor Allen," *Nation*, Dec. 6, 1922, 600–601; Allen to Albert T. Cooper, Sept. 9, 1922, HAP; Draft Manuscript, 1922, LoC.

28. "The Union Victory," *EG*, Aug. 16, 1922; "The Isolation of Labor," *EG*, Sept. 7, 1922; Lippmann to Newton Baker, Feb. 14, 1921, WLP; White to Henry Haskell, Aug. 7, 1922, LoC; Manuscript, July/Aug. 1922, LoC; Johnson, *White's America*, 486–487.

29. Allen to White, Nov. 18, 1922, LoC; Allen to White, Nov. 27, 1922, LoC; White to Allen, Nov. 28, 1922, LoC; "Wrongs of 'Bill' White," *New York Times*, Dec. 20, 1922; W. L. Huggins to White, Dec. 11, 1922, LoC; White to Rodney Elward, Aug. 7, 1922, LoC.

30. Davis, *Power at Odds*, 148; "The Industrial Court," *EG*, June 12, 1923; "Conservative Labor," *EG*, Sept. 15, 1923; Rabinowitz, "Kansas Industrial Court," 1–16; "Await the Resurrection," *EG*, Apr. 14, 1925.

31. George McJimsey, *The Presidency of Franklin Delano Roosevelt* (Lawrence: University Press of Kansas, 2000), 84; "Labor Vincit," *EG*, June 28, 1935.

32. Robert Ferrell, *Peace in Their Time: The Origins of the Kellogg-Briand Pact* (New Haven, CT: Yale University Press, 1952), 263–265; Joan Hoff Wilson, *American Business and Foreign Policy, 1920–1933* (Lexington: University Press of Kentucky, 1971), xvi; Miller, *Populist Nationalism*, 97–102; White to W. S. Dickey, Apr. 29, 1920, LoC.

33. Marian C. McKenna, *Borah* (Ann Arbor: University of Michigan Press, 1961), 178; Karen A. J. Miller, *Populist Nationalism*, 104–105; Robert Maddox, *William E. Borah and American Foreign Policy* (Baton Rouge: Louisiana State University Press, 1969), 86–94; "Continuous Foreign Policy," *EG*, May 19, 1921; Wilson, *American Business*, 32–33, 38–39.

34. "Hughes, the Diplomat," *EG*, Nov. 23, 1921; Miller, *Populist Nationalism*, 122–126; Maddox, *William E. Borah*, 105–106; White, *Autobiography*, 599–602; "Big Doings," *EG*, July 2, 1921; Borah to White, July 5, 1921, LoC.

35. White to Borah, Mar. 31, 1922, LoC; Maddox, *William E. Borah*, 114–115; "'Two,'" *EG*, Mar. 25, 1922; Miller, *Populist Nationalism*, 153–157; "The Better Epoch," *EG*, Feb. 10, 1922.

36. Miller, *Populist Nationalism*, 162; "A Brave Man," *EG*, Apr. 21, 1923.

37. Ferrell, *Coolidge*, 20; White to Coolidge, Jan. 27, 1925, LoC; "Borah," *EG*, Nov. 5, 1924; "Coolidge," *EG*, Feb. 3, 1925; "Our Eloquent President," *EG*, Jan. 28, 1925.

38. White, "Mediterranean Cruise," 1924, ESU.

39. Ibid.; White to Sherwood Eddy, Sept. 26, 1926, LoC; White to Allen, June 4, 1925, LoC; J. Davis to White, Mar. 24, 1925, LoC.

40. Johnson, *White's America*, 123–124; "Dollar Diplomacy," *EG*, Jan. 18, 1927.

41. Robert Johnson, *The Peace Progressives and American Foreign Relations* (Cambridge, MA: Harvard University Press, 1995), 128–137; Allan Millett, *Semper Fidelis: The History of the United States Marine Corps* (New York: Free Press, 1991), 250; Johnson, *White's America*, 132; "Blood or Bonds," *EG*, Feb. 13, 1928; Burton K. Wheeler, "Keep Marines Away," *EG*, Feb. 17, 1928; "Orphans of the Storm," *EG*, Apr. 25, 1928.

42. Ferrell, *Coolidge*, 125–126; Ethan Ellis, *Frank B. Kellogg and American Foreign Relations, 1925–1929* (New Brunswick, NJ: Rutgers University Press, 1961), 25, 44–48; Johnson, *White's America*, 122; Borah to White, May 14, 1927, LoC; White to Borah, May 17, 1927, LoC.

43. Ellis, *Frank B. Kellogg*, 48–49; Steel, *Walter Lippmann*, 93, 236–241;

Lippmann to Borah, Dec. 15, 1927, William Borah Papers, Manuscript Division, Library of Congress, Washington, DC; Johnson, *White's America*, 126; Dwight Morrow to White, July 11, 1927, LoC; White to Morrow, July 15, 1927, LoC; Maddox, *William E. Borah*, 176; Lippmann to Dwight Morrow, Dec. 2, 1927, WLP; Lars Schoultz, *Beneath the United States: A History of U.S. Policy toward Latin America* (Cambridge, MA: Harvard University Press, 1998), 275–283.

44. Steel, *Walter Lippmann*, 240–241; "The White Knight," *EG*, Dec. 20, 1927; Ellis, *Frank B. Kellogg*, 50–51.

CHAPTER 6. MAIN STREET CULTURE WARRIOR

1. Jon Lauck, *From Warm Center to Ragged Edge: The Erosion of Midwestern Literary and Historical Regionalism, 1920–1965* (Iowa City: University of Iowa Press, 2017), 29–33; White to M. F. Amrine, Jan. 22, 1926, LoC; White to Herbert Croley, Dec. 9, 1920, LoC; White to Sinclair Lewis, Nov. 23, 1920, LoC.

2. Shortridge, *Middle West*, 54–60; White, "The Blood of the Conquerors," *Collier's*, Mar. 10, 1923, 5–6; Craig Miner, *Kansas: The History of the Sunflower State, 1854–2000* (Lawrence: University Press of Kansas, 2002), 190–220, 246–269.

3. John E. Miller, *Small-Town Dreams: Stories of Midwestern Boys Who Shaped America* (Lawrence: University Press of Kansas, 2014), 7, 125–126; Edward Argan, *"Too Good a Town": William Allen White, Community, and the Emerging Rhetoric of Middle America* (Fayetteville: University of Arkansas Press, 1998), 88–91; White, "Blood of the Conquerors," 5–6; White, *Autobiography*, 439, 542, 625–627; Sally Foreman Griffith, *Home Town News: William Allen White and the Emporia Gazette* (New York: Oxford University Press, 1989), 14; "Why Kansas Is Kansas," *EG*, Dec. 29, 1925; "Lyon County," *EG*, Feb. 15, 1926.

4. William Allen White, "What's the Matter with America?" *Collier's*, July 1, 1922, LoC; Gary Gerstle, *American Crucible: Race and Nation in the Twentieth Century* (Princeton, NJ: Princeton University Press, 2001), 4.

5. Rory McVeigh, *The Rise of the Ku Klux Klan: Right-Wing Movements and National Politics* (Minneapolis: University of Minnesota Press, 2009), 4–31, 55–75; Michael Kazin, *The Populist Persuasion: An American History* (Ithaca, NY: Cornell University Press, 1998), 1–6, 60.

6. Jack Wayne Traylor, "William Allen White's 1924 Gubernatorial Campaign," *Kansas Historical Quarterly* 42, no. 2 (Summer 1976): 180–191;

White to H. B. Swope, Sept. 17, 1921, LoC; McVeigh, *Rise of the Klan,* 4, 25–27; Miner, *Kansas,* 252–257; Nancy MacLean, *Behind the Mask of Chivalry: The Making of the Second Ku Klux Klan* (New York: Oxford University Press, 1994), xii–xiii, 10–32, 54–73, 99, 158.

7. White to Walt Mason, June 21, 1923, LoC; White to Gifford Pinchot, Sept. 11, 1923, LoC; White, "Mediterranean Cruise," 1924, ESU.

8. Traylor, "White's 1924 Gubernatorial Campaign," 180–191; White to Charles Scott, Sept. 2, 1924, LoC; White to Victor Murdock, Aug. 14, 1924, LoC; White to Borah, Nov. 24, 1924, LoC; White, *Autobiography,* 439, 542, 625–627.

9. "White Announces," *EG,* Sept. 20, 1924; "Klanism vs Americanism," *EG,* Sept. 26, 1924; "The Governorship," *EG,* Sept. 16, 1924; Robert Slayton, *Empire Statesman* (New York: Free Press, 2001), 211; McKee, *William Allen White,* 170–171; White to Borah, Nov. 24, 1924, LoC.

10. Walter Lippmann to Sallie White, Oct. 8, 1924, WLP; Anne O'Hare McCormick, "Editor White Tilts at the Kansas Klan," *NYT,* Oct. 5, 1924; "White States Issue," *EG,* Sept. 26, 1924; "Shake Off Klan Control Is Plea of Independents," *EG,* Oct. 29, 1924; "At the Crossroads," *EG,* Nov. 1, 1924; "Nothing Radical in the Platform," *EG,* Oct. 13, 1924; White to Scott, Sept. 2, 1924, LoC; White to Borah, Nov. 24, 1924, LoC; "The Prodigal's Return," *EG,* Nov. 3, 1924; White to Col. House, Nov. 25, 1924, LoC; White to Lippmann, Nov. 19, 1924, LoC.

11. "White Continues Fight on Paulen," *EG,* Sept. 24, 1924; "Calls White an Andy Gump," *EG,* Oct. 25, 1924; Charles W. Sloan, "Kansas Battles the Invisible Empire: The Legal Ouster of the KKK from Kansas, 1922–1927," *Kansas Historical Quarterly* 40, no. 3 (Fall 1974): 393–409; "Klansmen Enter Negro Church," *EG,* Oct. 30, 1924; "Unknown Vandals Cut Down White Banner in Iola," *EG,* Sept. 26, 1924; Charles Isely to White, Nov. 11, 1924, LoC; Kansas Federation of Non-Partisan Voters Pamphlet, LoC; Harold McGugin to M. F. Amrine, Oct. 26, 1924, LoC; Speech, Sept. 23, 1924, LoC; "Davis Strikes Back," *EG,* Oct. 6, 1924; "Huggins Pulls for Paulen," *EG,* Oct. 28, 1924.

12. Isely to White, Nov. 6, 1924, LoC; Campaign Financial Statement, Nov. 3, 1924, LoC; "Kansas Swatted the Klan," *EG,* Nov. 7, 1924; White to Paul A. Jones, Nov. 13, 1924, LoC; Charles Isley to White, Nov. 11, 1924, LoC; Alf Landon to White, Nov. 19, 1924, LoC; White to Landon, Nov. 24, 1924, LoC.

13. "Wiped Out," *EG,* Aug. 5, 1926; Traylor, "White's 1924 Gubernatorial

Campaign," 180–191; White to Lippmann, Nov. 9, 1924, WLP; White to Villard, Nov. 19, 1924, LoC; White, "Annihilate the Klan!" *Nation,* Jan. 7, 1925, 7; "Our American Right," *EG,* Apr. 18, 1924.

14. "The Council Grove Case," *EG,* Feb. 10, 1926; "Sees Klan's Hand in DAR Blacklist," *NYT,* Apr. 6, 1928; "Emporia Scoreboard Offends Ministers," *NYT,* Oct. 10, 1926; "The Blue Menace," *Nation,* Apr. 18, 1928, 422; White to Rolla Clymer, June 12, 1925, LoC; White to Henry Haskell, July 8, 1927, LoC.

15. Farrell, *Coolidge,* 88–93; "Thoughts on Prohibition," *EG,* Mar. 12, 1926; "The New Rebellion," *EG,* July 9, 1926; White to H. L. Mencken, Apr. 29, 1922, LoC; White to Nicholas Butler, July 5, 1928, LoC; White to Gibson Gardner, July 24, 1924, LoC.

16. Fite, *Peter Norbeck,* 108; White to Borah, June 21, 1928, LoC; White to Herbert Hoover, June 18, 1928, LoC; Borah to White, June 19, 1928, LoC.

17. William Allen White, "The Education of Herbert Hoover," *Collier's,* June 9, 1928, 8–9; "The Sunrise Trumpet," *EG,* June 18, 1928; "Snorts at Convention," *EG,* June 16, 1928; Allan Lichtman, *Prejudice and the Old Politics: The Presidential Election of 1928* (Chapel Hill: University of North Carolina Press, 1979), 5–8; White to Capper, July 11, 1927, LoC; Martin Fausold, *The Presidency of Herbert C. Hoover* (Lawrence: University Press of Kansas, 1985), 22.

18. William Allen White, "Al Smith, City Feller," *Collier's,* Aug. 21, 1926; White, *Masks,* 467; "Editorial Correspondence," *EG,* June 26, 1928; Walter Lippmann, "The Sick Donkey," *Harper's,* Sept. 1927, LP; Slayton, *Empire Statesman,* 30, 84–85, 129–133, 169–174, 240.

19. "Editorial Correspondence," *EG,* June 30, 1926; "Smith Amends the Platform," *EG,* July 2, 1928; "Not Obey—Observe," *EG,* July 6, 1928; "Al Smith's Record," *EG,* July 7, 1928; Slayton, *Empire Statesman,* 196–199, 256–275.

20. Frederick J. Hoffman, "Philistine and Puritan in the 1920s: An Example of the Misuse of the American Past," *American Quarterly* 1, no. 3 (Autumn 1949): 247–263; "White Calls Smith Menace to Nation," *NYT,* July 13, 1928; "Gov. Smith vs. William Allen White," *New York World,* July 18, 1928; "Puritan 'Bill' White," *NYT,* July 14, 1928; "Al Smith Denies Charges," *EG,* July 14, 1928; "Tammanizing America," *EG,* July 21, 1928; White to Paul Jones, July 20, 1928, LoC; Felix Frankfurter to White, Aug. 1, 1928, LoC; William L. White to Frankfurter, Aug. 11, 1928, LoC; Borah to White, July 18, 1928, LoC.

21. Lippmann to Frankfurter, Aug. 2, 1928, WLP; White to Mahin, Dec. 18, 1928, LoC; "The Hoover Whispering Campaign," *Nation*, Sept. 28, 1928, p. 263; "Smith Strikes Back at White's Charges," *NYT*, July 15, 1928; "White Withdraws Part of Charges," *EG*, July 31, 1928; "White Withdraws Smith Vice Charges," *NYT*, Aug. 1, 1928; "White Now Stands by Smith Charges," *NYT*, Aug. 15, 1928; White, *Autobiography*, 634; White to Herbert Hoover, July 12, 1928, Herbert Hoover Papers, Herbert Hoover Presidential Library, West Branch, IA; Johnson, *White's America*, 410–411.

22. The passage "Catholic so-called religion" has been incorrectly attributed to White. See Fausold, *Hoover*, 29; "Hoover Whispering Campaign," *Nation*, 263; John T. McGreevy, "Thinking on One's Own: Catholicism in the American Intellectual Imagination, 1928–1960," *Journal of American History* 84, no. 1 (June 1997): 97–131; Slayton, *Empire Statesman*, 284–287, 300–309; Lichtman, *Prejudice*, 59–76, 245; "William Allen White Says," Pamphlet, HHP.

23. "White Links Smith to Tammany 'Evils,'" *NYT*, Oct. 20, 1928; White Speech at Independence, KS, Oct. 19, 1928, LoC; "'Retracted Nothing,' White Says at Home," *NYT*, Oct. 2, 1928; White to Allen, Oct. 18, 1928, LoC; "A Personal Word," *EG*, Oct. 2, 1928; Hoover to White, July 24, 1928, HHP.

24. White at Independence, KS, Oct. 19, 1928, LoC; "A Very Personal Matter," *EG*, Nov. 5, 1928; Lichtman, *Prejudice*, 59–61; Slayton, *Empire Statesman*, 258–259, 312.

25. Fausold, *Hoover*, 25; Richard Lowitt, *George W. Norris: The Persistence of a Progressive, 1913–1933* (Urbana: University of Illinois Press, 1971), 414–424; Lippmann, Radio Statement, Nov. 6, 1928, WLP; "Hoover Wins," *Nation*, Nov. 14, 1928, 510; Villard to Ramsay MacDonald, Dec. 6, 1928, OGV; Oswald Garrison Villard, *Fighting Years: Memoirs of a Liberal Editor* (New York: Harcourt, Brace, 1939), 469; Slayton, *Empire Statesman*, 268, 321–324; Lichtman, *Prejudice*, 25.

26. By "Buick-radio age," Lippmann meant "modern." White to Henry Haskell, Nov. 20, 1928, LoC; Lippmann to Herbert Croly, Nov. 21, 1928, WLP; "Hoover and Progress," *EG*, Nov. 6, 1928; White to Ickes, Nov. 23, 1928, HIP; Lippmann Speech, Kansas City, Nov. 15, 1928, WLP; MacLean, *Behind the Mask*, 92–97; Lichtman, *Prejudice*, 63–64; Slayton, *Empire Statesman*, 284–286; Steel, *Walter Lippmann*, 249.

27. Lippmann to White, Nov. 7, 1928, WLP.

28. "A Foundation of Sand," *EG*, Apr. 19, 1929; "Stop, Look, Listen," *EG*, May 8, 1929; White to Lippmann, Jan. 9, 1931, LoC; "The Need of a Leader," *EG*, Dec. 13, 1930.

29. Ronald Feinman, *Twilight of Progressivism: The Western Republican Senators and the New Deal* (Baltimore: Johns Hopkins University Press, 1981), 91.

CHAPTER 7. RELUCTANT NEW DEALER

1. Walter Lippmann Diary, Oct. 29, 1929, WLP; David M. Kennedy, *Freedom from Fear: The American People in Depression and War, 1929–1945* (New York: Oxford University Press, 1999), 38, 51; John Kenneth Galbraith, *The Great Crash: 1929* (New York: Houghton Mifflin, 1997), 24–29; "Stock Values," *EG*, Oct. 30, 1929; "Post Mortem," *EG*, Nov. 20, 1929.

2. White's use of the Russian word "ukase" is significant: it means an arbitrary edict from the tsar. Arthur Capper to White, Oct. 19, 1929, LoC; White to Herbert Hoover, May 6, 1929, LoC; White to Lippmann, May 9, 1929, LoC; Borah to White, Dec. 19, 1929, LoC; White to David Hinshaw, Aug. 24, 1929, LoC.

3. Borah to White, Dec. 19, 1929, LoC; White to Harold Ickes, Nov. 1, 1929, LoC; White to Hoover, Oct. 4, 1929, LoC; White to Hoover, Sept. 12, 1929, LoC; Fausold, *Hoover*, 46.

4. White to Hinshaw, Dec. 3, 1929, LoC; White to George Lorimer, Mar. 19, 1931, LoC; White to Arthur Capper, Aug. 30, 1931, LoC.

5. Feinman, *Twilight of Progressivism*, 18–21; White to Allen, May 15, 1930, LoC; White to Borah, Nov. 11, 1929, LoC; White to Allen, Sept. 18, 1930, LoC; White to Henry Haskell, Aug. 2, 1930, LoC; Fausold, *Hoover*, 131.

6. White to William Culbertson, Dec. 31, 1930, LoC; White to Hinshaw, Dec. 26, 1930, LoC; White to David Lawrence, Jan. 6, 1931, LoC.

7. White to Bruce Bliven, Jan. 17, 1931, LoC; Arthur Schlesinger, Jr., *The Age of Roosevelt: The Crisis of the Old Order, 1919–1933* (Boston: Houghton Mifflin, 1956), 170, 392–393; Feinman, *Twilight*, 20–21; Borah to A. C. Voorhees, Feb. 12, 1931, Borah Papers; White to Hoover, May 17, 1930, LoC; White to Oswald Garrison Villard, Aug. 21, 1931, LoC; White to Hinshaw, Feb. 13, 1931, LoC.

8. Fausold, *Hoover*, 110–111; White to Gifford Pinchot, ca. 1931, LoC; White to Herbert Hoover, Oct. 18, 1920, HHP.

9. Fausold, *Hoover*, 54, 86; White to M. F. Amrine, Aug. 17, 1932, LoC; White to Paul Kellogg, Mar. 3, 1931, LoC; White to Amrine, Feb. 4, 1931, LoC.

10. Gould, *Republicans*, 184–186; "The Need of a Leader," *EG*, Dec. 13, 1930; Schlesinger, *Crisis*, 278; White to Franklin D. Roosevelt, Dec. 17, 1930, LoC; "Grape-vine," *EG*, Dec. 31, 1930; White to Lippmann, Jan. 9, 1931, LoC; Lippmann to White, Jan. 13, 1931, LoC; White to Roosevelt, Mar. 21, 1931, LoC.

11. Feinman, *Twilight*, 26–29; "Hoover's Speeches," *EG*, June 16, 1931; "Queer Days," Mar. 12, 1931, *EG*; White to Judson King, Mar. 13, 1931, LoC; White to David Hinshaw, Mar. 17, 1931, LoC.

12. "Justice or Trouble," *EG*, Aug. 3, 1931; Schlesinger, *Crisis*, 222–223, 256; "The Menace," *EG*, Sept. 14, 1931; Feinman, *Twilight*, 29; White to H. L. Mencken, Apr. 23, 1931, LoC; White to Charles Curtis, Apr. 21, 1931, LoC; White to Sherwood Eddy, June 16, 1931, LoC.

13. White to Edward Costigan, Aug. 23, 1931, LoC; Hinshaw to White, Aug. 15, 1931, LoC; White to Hinshaw, Aug. 10, 1931, LoC; White to Roy Roberts, July 2, 1931, LoC; White to Capper, Aug. 30, 1931, LoC; Hinshaw to White, Apr. 25, 1931, LoC; Fausold, *Hoover*, 150.

14. White to Haskell, Oct. 1, 1931, LoC; White to Hinshaw, Nov. 6, 1931, LoC; White to William Mayo, Oct. 26, 1931, LoC; White to William Green, Sept. 1, 1931, LoC.

15. Feinman, *Twilight*, 29–30; "The Way Out," *EG*, Dec. 8, 1931; Schlesinger, *Crisis*, 233–238; "'We Change with Them,'" *EG*, Dec. 10, 1931; "Our Peculiar Constitution," *EG*, Dec. 23, 1931; White to Lippmann, Jan. 27, 1932, WLP; White to Judson King, Dec. 1, 1931, LoC; Fausold, *Hoover*, 152–155.

16. White to Lippmann, Apr. 19, 1932, LoC; White to Lippmann, Apr. 26, 1932, LoC; "A Progressive Program," *EG*, May 21, 1932. White to Allen, May 29, 1932, LoC; White to Capper, May 17, 1932, LoC; White to Capper, Apr. 2, 1932, LoC.

17. Donald Ritchie, *Electing FDR: The New Deal Campaign of 1932* (Lawrence: University Press of Kansas, 2007), 48–55; "Our Liberal Court," *EG*, May 17, 1932; "We Beg to Differ," *EG*, May 27, 1932; White to Capper, May 23, 1932, LoC; Feinman, *Twilight*, 30–31.

18. "Convention Notes," *EG*, June 28, 1932; Schlesinger, *Crisis*, 296–311; "The Final Word," *EG*, July 4, 1932.

19. McJimsey, *FDR*, 18; "The Republican Ticket," *EG*, July 5, 1932;

Schlesinger, *Crisis*, 420–421; White to Ickes, July 14, 1932, LoC; White to Clyde Reed, June 2, 1932, LoC; White to Walt Mason, Aug. 6, 1932, LoC.

20. McJimsey, *FDR*, 24–25; Schlesinger, *Crisis*, 430–431; Feinman, *Twilight*, 38; "The Speech You Missed," *EG*, Oct. 4, 1932; White, "Hails the Genius of Hoover," Republican National Committee pamphlet, LoC; Hinshaw to White, July 24, 1932, LoC; White to Henry Allen, Oct. 7, 1932, LoC; White to Allen, Sept. 20, 1932, LoC.

21. "The Old Bull Moose," *EG*, Oct. 21, 1932; "President Roosevelt," *EG*, Nov. 9, 1932; White to Hinshaw, Dec. 30, 1932, LoC; White to Clyde Reed, Nov. 7, 1932, LoC; White to Haskell, Nov. 11, 1932, LoC.

22. Schlesinger, *Crisis*, 442–465; "Hell's A-Poppin," *EG*, Jan. 3, 1933; "'Do Sumpin',''' *EG*, Jan. 4, 1933; "Amazing," *EG*, Feb. 3, 1933; White to Capper, Jan. 3, 1933, LoC; Capper to White, Jan. 6, 1933, LoC; White to Roy Roberts, Dec. 29, 1932, LoC.

23. McJimsey, *FDR*, 36; Arthur Schlesinger, Jr., *The Age of Roosevelt: The Coming of the New Deal* (Boston: Houghton Mifflin, 1959), 1–21, 45, 101–102, 180, 264, 282, 320–325; "President Roosevelt," *EG*, Mar. 4, 1933.

24. White to Ickes, Mar. 6, 1933, HIP; White to Ickes, May 23, 1933, LoC; Roosevelt to Ickes, May 31, 1933, Franklin D. Roosevelt Papers, Franklin D. Roosevelt Presidential Library, Hyde Park, NY; White to Walt Mason, Apr. 25, 1933, LoC; Adam Cohen, *Nothing to Fear: FDR's Inner Circle and the Hundred Days That Created Modern America* (New York: Penguin, 2009), 284–287.

25. White, *Autobiography*, 636; White to Ickes, Nov. 14, 1933, LoC; "Life among the Tyrants," *EG*, Oct. 25, 1933; White to Edna Ferber, Oct. 23, 1933, LoC; Norman Saul, "The 'Russian' Adventures of Henry and Me: William Allen White and Henry Justin Allen in Stalin's Russia," *Kansas History* 39, no. 1 (Spring 2016): 32–47.

26. White to Ickes, Nov. 14, 1933, LoC; "Life among the Tyrants," *EG*, Oct. 25, 1933; Villard, "The Plight of Liberalism," *Modern Thinker*, 34–37, n.d., OGV; "The President's Job," *EG*, Jan. 10, 1934; "Congress and Roosevelt," EG, Jan. 3, 1934; Dudley Doolitle to Marvin McIntyre, Jan. 4, 1934, FDR; White to Theodore Roosevelt, Jr., Dec. 5, 1933, LoC; FDR to White, Jan. 22, 1934, LoC; White to Roberts, May 8, 1934, LoC.

27. Alan Brinkley, "The New Deal Experiments," in Chafe, 1–3; Schlesinger, *New Deal*, 486–487; White to Herbert Hoover, May 3, 1934, LoC; White to Capper, Apr. 2, 1934, LoC; White to Lippmann, Mar. 30, 1936, LoC.

28. R. Alton Lee, *The Bizarre Careers of John R. Brinkley* (Louisville: University Press of Kentucky, 2002), 118–152.

29. "Save Kansas," *EG*, quoted in Lee, *John R. Brinkley*, 118–152; Alan Brinkley, *Voices of Protest: Huey Long, Father Coughlin and the Great Depression* (New York: Vintage, 1982), ix–xiii, 3; Schlesinger, *New Deal*, 392–394, 471; Arthur M. Schlesinger, Jr., *The Age of Roosevelt: The Politics of Upheaval* (Boston: Houghton Mifflin, 1960), 1–25, 53–69; "The Demagog," *EG*, Nov. 22, 1934; "Heil Huey," *EG*, Aug. 29, 1934; White to Reed, July 24, 1934, LoC.

30. Gary Dean Best, *Herbert Hoover: The Postpresidential Years, 1933–1964* (Stanford, CA: Hoover Institution Press, 1983), 1:21–24; Hinshaw to Hoover, June 19, 1934, LoC; White to Hinshaw, June 9, 1934, LoC; White to Hinshaw, May 25, 1934, LoC.

31. White to Henry A. Wallace, Sept. 21, 1934, LoC; White to Allen, Sept. 7, 1934, LoC; White to Allen, Sept. 13, 1934, LoC.

32. "The New Deal," *EG*, Nov. 7, 1934; White to Frank Knox, Oct. 9, 1934, LoC.

33. Brinkley, *Voices of Protest*, 71–74, 241; "Washington in the Fog," *EG*, Feb. 4, 1935; White to Ickes, Feb. 7, 1935, LoC; "The New Dred Scott," *EG*, May 30, 1935.

34. White to Hoover, Feb. 19, 1936, LoC; "Getting Away with It," *EG*, Mar. 24, 1936; White to Lippmann, Mar. 30, 1936, LoC; White to Lippmann, Apr. 7, 1936, WLP; "Roosevelt Wins," *EG*, Aug. 26, 1935.

35. White to Capper, May 17, 1935, LoC; White to Rolla Clymer, May 6, 1935, LoC; White to Hoover, May 8, 1935, HHP.

36. White to John Hamilton, May 11, 1935, LoC; White to Hoover, May 4, 1935, LoC; Hoover to White, May 10, 1935, LoC; White to Hoover, June 28, 1935, LoC; Hoover to White, May 10, 1935, LoC; Arthur Hyde to Hoover, Apr. 29, 1935, HHP.

37. Best, *Herbert Hoover*, 39; McJimsey, *FDR*, 72–76; Feinman, *Twilight*, 118–119; "The New Dred Scott," *EG*, May 30, 1935; "Exit NRA R. I. P.," *EG*, May 28, 1935; White to Allen, May 9, 1935, LoC; White to Gifford Pinchot, June 11, 1935, LoC; White to Pinchot, Aug. 9, 1935, LoC.

38. White to Hoover, June 28, 1935, LoC; Brinkley, *Voices of Protest*, 192–194, 249–262; White to Dorothy Canfield Fisher, Mar. 18, 1936, LoC.

39. William Allen White, Commencement Speech at the Kansas State Teachers College at Pittsburg, May 28, 1936, KU.

40. White to Raymond Clapper, Sept. 12, 1936, LoC; White to Judson

King, Apr. 10, 1936, LoC; White to Ickes, Mar. 22, 1933, LoC; Landon to White, June 8, 1927, LoC.

41. White to Landon, Apr. 21, 1936, LoC; White to Borah, Sept. 23, 1935, LoC; White to Hoover, Apr. 6, 1936, LoC; Johnson, *White's America*, 452–453.

42. White to Borah, Apr. 8, 1936, LoC; White to Clapper, Aug. 13, 1936, LoC; White to Hoover, July 1, 1936, LoC; Johnson, *White's America*, 455.

43. Schlesinger, *Politics of Upheaval*, 540–546, 579; Feinman, *Twilight*, 100; White to Nicholas M. Butler, Sept. 9, 1936, LoC; White to Reed, July 8, 1936, LoC.

44. White to Haskell, Aug. 13, 1936, LoC; White to Landon, July 31, 1936, LoC; White to Clapper, Sept. 2, 1936, LoC; White to Clark Eichelberger, May 28, 1943, LoC.

45. Dorothy Thompson to White, Sept. 29, 1936, LoC; Upton Sinclair to White, Aug. 4, 1936, LoC; Lippmann to White, Aug. 11, 1936, LoC; White to George Norris, Sept. 30, 1936, LoC.

46. White to Josephus Daniels, Aug. 8, 1936, LoC; Benjamin Alpers, *Dictators, Democracy, and American Public Culture: Envisioning the Totalitarian Enemy, 1920s–1950s* (Chapel Hill: University of North Carolina Press, 2003), 78–79; White to Haskell, July 2, 1936, LoC.

47. White to Newton D. Baker, Nov. 4, 1936, LoC; "Some Afterthoughts," *EG*, Nov. 7, 1936; White to Roberts, Oct. 14, 1936, LoC.

48. Alonzo Hamby, "High Tide: Roosevelt, Truman, and the Democratic Party, 1932–1952," in Chafe, *American Liberalism*, 22–25; White, *Autobiography*, 639–640; Feinman, *Twilight*, 102–103; Schlesinger, *Politics of Upheaval*, 595, 615, 632–642; "Some Afterthoughts," *EG*, Nov. 7, 1936; White to Joseph Bristow, Dec. 8, 1936, LoC; White to Landon, Nov. 5, 1936, LoC.

49. Hamilton Fish to White, Dec. 8, 1936, LoC; Fish to White, Dec. 21, 1936, LoC; Dr. Glenn Frank, The Problem of the Republican Program Committee, Feb. 28, 1938, HHP; Facts about the Republican Program Committee, Brochure, HHP; William Hard to Members of the Committee, June 2, 1938, HHP; Johnson, *White's America*, 467.

50. "In the Offing," *EG*, Mar. 16, 1934; Schlesinger, *Politics of Upheaval*, 447–467; Feinman, *Twilight*, 212–213; Barry Cushman, *Rethinking the New Deal Court: The Structure of a Constitutional Revolution* (New York: Oxford University Press, 1998), 12; David M. Kennedy, *Freedom*

from Fear, 329–330; White to Norris, Nov. 14, 1936, LoC; Jeff Shesol, *Supreme Power: Franklin Roosevelt vs. the Supreme Court* (New York: W. W. Norton, 2010), 2–5.

51. Feinman, *Twilight,* 210–218; Shesol, *Supreme Power,* 3–4; Marian McKenna, *Franklin Roosevelt and the Great Constitutional War: The Court-Packing Crisis of 1937* (New York: Fordham University Press, 2002), 260–267; "The Supreme Court Issue," *EG,* Jan. 26, 1937; William Leuchtenburg, *The Supreme Court Reborn: The Constitutional Revolution in the Age of Roosevelt* (New York: Oxford University Press, 1995), 96–97, 156–162.

52. Feinman, *Twilight,* 218–219; "Adroit," *EG,* Feb. 6, 1937; "The Democratic Process," *EG,* Feb. 18, 1937.

53. White to Ickes, Feb. 8, 1937, LoC; Ickes to White, Feb. 25, 1937, LoC.

54. Lowitt, *George W. Norris,* 186–191; White to Norris, Feb. 22, 1937, LoC; Norris to White, Feb. 27, 1937, LoC; White to Norris, Mar. 1, 1937, George W. Norris Papers, Manuscript Division, Library of Congress, Washington, DC; Ickes to White, Mar. 23, 1937, LoC.

55. Shesol, *Supreme Power,* 329; H. W. Brands, *Traitor to His Class: The Privileged Life and Radical Presidency of Franklin Delano Roosevelt* (New York: Doubleday, 2008), 473–475; "The Fireside Talk," *EG,* Mar. 10, 1937; David M. Kennedy, *Freedom from Fear,* 334; "Court Follows Flag," *EG,* Apr. 13, 1937; "Is the Supreme Court Going Liberal?" *Nation,* Apr. 3, 1937, 367–368; White to Freda Kirchwey, June 9, 1937, LoC; Kirchwey to White, June 16, 1937, LoC.

56. Feinman, *Twilight,* 128–135, 221; James T. Patterson, *Congressional Conservatism and the New Deal: The Growth of the Conservative Coalition in Congress, 1933–1939* (Lexington: University Press of Kentucky, 1967), 118; Cushman, *Rethinking,* 15–25; McKenna, *Supreme Court,* 454; White to Rudolph Spreckles, Sept. 9, 1937, LoC; "A Democracy," *EG,* July 21, 1937; "Net Gain," *EG,* July 26, 1937; White to Hoover, May 4, 1937, LoC.

57. Nelson Lichtenstein, *The Most Dangerous Man in Detroit: Walter Reuther and the Fate of American Labor* (New York: HarperCollins, 1995), 56–86; David M. Kennedy, *Freedom from Fear,* 309–317; "The Sit Down Strike," *EG,* Feb. 3, 1937; "The Labor Row," *EG,* Mar. 31, 1937; White to Felix Frankfurter, Apr. 2, 1937, LoC.

58. Feinman, *Twilight,* 136–137; Lichtenstein, *Most Dangerous,* 80–86; "Tolerance," *EG,* June 12, 1937; Patterson, *Congressional Conservatism,*

137; "Moving on Ford," *EG*, Apr. 9, 1937; White to *Gazette* Staff, June 22, 1937, LoC.

59. White to Haskell, Apr. 16, 1937, LoC; White to Haskell, Oct. 25, 1937, LoC; White to Hinshaw, Nov. 18, 1937; White to Villard, Dec. 8, 1937, LoC.

60. White to Frankfurter, Oct. 20, 1920, LoC; White to Amrine, Nov. 29. 1936, LoC; White to Capper, Aug. 14, 1937, LoC; White to Norris, Feb. 12, 1938, LoC; White, "Thoughts at 65," Feb. 10, 1933, KU.

61. Otis Graham, *An Encore for Reform: The Old Progressives and the New Deal* (New York: Oxford University Press, 1967), 98–104; "A Yip from the Doghouse," *EG*, Dec. 20, 1937, also published under the same title in *New Republic*, Dec. 15, 1937, 160–161.

62. White to Villard, Dec. 8, 1937, OGV; "Five Years of It," *EG*, Mar. 3, 1938; White to FDR, Mar. 1, 1938, FDR; White to Walt Mason, Sept. 9, 1937, LoC; Johnson, *White's America*, 470–473.

63. Patterson, *Congressional Conservatism*, 333–335; Smith, *To Save a Nation: American Countersubversives, the New Deal, and the Coming of World War II* (New York: Basic Books, 1973), 3–9; John Miller, *Governor Philip F. La Follette, the Wisconsin Progressives, and the New Deal* (Columbia: University of Missouri Press, 1982), 158–160; White to Murdock, Jan. 7, 1938, LoC; White to Villard, July 28, 1937, LoC.

64. White to FDR, Mar. 1, 1938, FDR; White to Bruce Bliven, July 28, 1938, LoC; FDR to White, June 8, 1938, LoC; White to FDR, June 10, 1938, LoC; White to Capper, Feb. 1, 1938, LoC; White to Rolla Clymer, July 25, 1938, LoC.

65. White, "The Challenge to the Middle Class," ca. 1938, LoC; Kennedy, *Freedom from Fear*, 346–349; Ickes to White, Sept. 23, 1938, LoC; White to Ickes, Sept. 26, 1938, LoC; Patterson, *Congressional Conservatism*, 145; White to Villard, Jan. 28, 1939, LoC; Ickes to White, Sept. 29, 1938, LoC; Facts about the Republican Program Committee, Brochure, HHP; William Hard to Members of the Committee, June 2, 1938, HHP.

66. "The President's Message," *EG*, Jan. 5, 1939; White to George F. Milton, Aug. 16, 1939, LoC.

CHAPTER 8. FREEDOM FIGHTER

1. Robert Divine, *The Illusion of Neutrality* (Chicago: University of Chicago Press, 1962), 25, 30–31; Steel, *Walter Lippmann*, 328–329; "A Japanese Cure," *EG*, Jan. 25, 1932; Robert Dallek, *Franklin D. Roosevelt*

and American Foreign Policy, 1932–1945 (New York: Oxford University Press, 1979), 75; "Big Navy," *EG*, Jan. 31, 1934; Michael S. Sherry, *In the Shadow of War: The United States since the 1930s* (New Haven, CT: Yale University Press, 1995), 20–21.

2. Divine, *Illusion of Neutrality*, 100–115, 122–134; "Japan," *EG*, Feb. 28, 1936; Kennedy, *Freedom from Fear*, 384; "International Outlawry," *EG*, May 16, 1936; White to Edna Ferber, Apr. 7, 1936, LoC; Secretary to Bruce Bliven, Oct. 24, 1935, LoC; White to Herbert Hoover, Dec. 16, 1935, HHP.

3. "Armistice," *EG*, Nov. 11, 1937; "Inching Along," *EG*, Oct. 6, 1936; "Support the President," *EG*, Jan. 3, 1938; "The New Day," *EG*, Jan. 30, 1938; Freda Kirchwey to White, Mar. 4, 1938, LoC; White to Kirchwey, Mar. 17, 1938, LoC.

4. Kennedy, *Freedom from Fear*, 418–419; "Jump in the Dark," *EG*, Oct. 26, 1938; Divine, *Illusion of Neutrality*, 234–238; "The President's Message," *EG*, Jan. 5, 1939; "The Chamberlain Alibi," *EG*, Mar. 18, 1939; "Britain's Humiliation," *EG*, June 1, 1939.

5. White to Lord Lothian, Mar. 16, 1939, LoC; Lothian to White, Apr. 6, 1939, LoC; White to Stimson, June 8, 1939, LoC; White to Lothian, June 8, 1939, LoC; White to Stimson, Nov. 27, 1939, LoC.

6. Divine, *Illusion of Neutrality*, 251, 279; "Neutrality," *EG*, June 14, 1939; Eichelberger to White, Mar. 24, 1939, LoC; White to Eichelberger, Mar. 29, 1939, LoC.

7. Smith, *To Save a Nation*, 152–157; Divine, *Illusion of Neutrality*, 287–306; Sherry, *Shadow of War*, 32–34.

8. Divine, *Illusion of Neutrality*, 302–306; Eichelberger to White, Oct. 4, 1939, LoC; Sherry, *Shadow of War*, 32–34; Eichelberger to Stimson, Oct. 29, 1939, Clark Eichelberger Papers, Manuscripts and Archives, New York Public Library, New York, NY; White, "The Hour Is Striking," Speech, CBS, Oct. 15, 1939, CEP; White to Claude Pepper, Nov. 13, 1939, LoC; White to Raymond Clapper, Nov. 25, 1940, LoC.

9. Divine, *Illusion of Neutrality*, 330–331; FDR to White, Nov. 8, 1939, FDR; White to Eichelberger, Nov. 14, 1939, LoC; Walter Lippmann, "American Policy and the Allied Strategy," *New York Herald-Tribune*, Nov. 7, 1939; "Friendship's Garland," *EG*, Jan. 22, 1940; White to Thomas Lamont, Nov. 25, 1939, LoC.

10. FDR to White, Dec. 14, 1939, LoC; White to Alfred Landon, Jan. 4, 1940, LoC; White to FDR, Dec. 22, 1939, LoC.

11. CDAAA Statement of Program, July 3, 1940, LoC; White to Landon, July 5, 1940, LoC; Proposed Speakers for Mass Meetings, ND, CEP; Wayne S. Cole, *Roosevelt and the Isolationists, 1932–1945* (Lincoln: University of Nebraska Press, 1983), 365; Kennedy, *Freedom from Fear*, 438; Margaret Olson to White, Dec. 9, 1940, LoC; Eichelberger to Kenneth Colegrove, Nov. 18, 1940, CEP; Memo for the President, June 15, 1940, FDR; Edwin Watson to White, June 28, 1940, FDR; Justus Doenecke, *Storm on the Horizon: The Challenge to American Intervention, 1939–1941* (Oxford: Rowman & Littlefield, 2000), 106; White to Felix Frankfurter, May 31, 1940, LoC.

12. White to Landon, July 5, 1940, LoC; White to Ralph Coghlan, Oct. 11, 1940, LoC; White to Charles Crandon, July 26, 1940, LoC; Address by William Allen White at the Dinner Given by Dr. Alexander Doudon, New York City, June 22, 1940, CEP; Karen M. Smith, "Father, Son, and Country on the Eve of War: William Allen White, William Lindsay White, and American Isolationism, 1940–1941," *Kansas History* 28, no. 1 (Spring 2005): 30–43.

13. White to Landon, July 5, 1940, LoC; White to Villard, June 14, 1940, LoC; Villard to White, June 12, 1940, LoC; White to Robert Sherwood, June 14, 1940, OGV; Villard to White, June 19, 1940, LoC; Villard to White, July 8, 1940, LoC; Address of Alf Landon before the Johnson County Republicans, May 17, 1940, Wendell Willkie Papers, Lilly Library, Indiana University, Bloomington, IN.

14. Steel, *Walter Lippmann*, 384; Dallek, *FDR*, 244; Kennedy, *Freedom from Fear*, 444–445; Armand Hammer to White, June 13, 1940, LoC; Walter Lippmann, "The Problem of the Destroyers," *New York Herald-Tribune*, Aug. 6, 1940; White to Knox, May 31, 1940, LoC; General Pershing Speech, 1940, WLP; "Suppose Britain Loses," CDAAA Pamphlet, ca. July 1940, *Uncensored* Papers, Manuscripts and Archives, New York Public Library, New York, NY; Doenecke, *Storm on the Horizon*, 125.

15. Donald Johnson, *The Republican Party and Wendell Willkie* (Urbana: University of Illinois Press, 1960), 140; White to Judson King, Aug. 30, 1940, LoC; White to Knox, May 24, 1940, LoC; White to Raymond Clapper, Nov. 25, 1940, LoC.

16. Steve Neal, *Dark Horse: A Biography of Wendell Willkie* (Garden City, NJ: Doubleday, 1984), 140; Ross Gregory, "Seeking the Presidency: Willkie as Politician," in *Wendell Willkie: Hoosier Internationalist*, ed.

James Madison (Bloomington: Indiana University Press, 1992), 61; Johnson, *Republican Party*, 127; Steel, *Walter Lippmann*, 385; Ickes Diary, Aug. 4, 1940, HIP; Kennedy, *Freedom from Fear*, 460–461; Ickes Diary, Sept. 8, 1940, HIP; White to Reuben Peterson, Sept. 7, 1940, LoC; "White Defends Roosevelt in British Deal," *New York Herald-Tribune*, Sept. 7, 1940, CEP; White to Henry Allen, Sept. 3, 1940, LoC; White to Clapper, Nov. 25, 1940, LoC; White to Eichelberger, Aug. 11, 1940, LoC; White to Freda Kirchwey, Nov. 8, 1940, LoC.

17. "Lindbergh, the Appeaser," *EG*, Oct. 17, 1940; Villard, "Should We Unite Behind the President?" *Uncensored*, Nov. 9, 1940, OGV; Ronald Radosh, *Prophets on the Right: Profiles of Conservative Critics of American Globalism* (New York: Simon & Schuster, 1975), 83; Smith, *To Save a Nation*, 176; Norman Thomas to Frederick Libby, Nov. 28, 1940, UP.

18. Dallek, *FDR*, 258; White to Villard, Apr. 12, 1941, OGV; White to Eichelberger, Dec. 3, 1940, LoC; White to Roy Howard, Dec. 20, 1940, LoC; White to Eichelberger, Oct. 22, 1940, LoC; White to Willkie, Jan. 11, 1941, WWP.

19. White to Villard, Apr. 12, 1941, OGV; White to Felix Frankfurter, Dec. 12, 1940, LoC; Herbert Swope to White, Dec. 24, 1940, LoC; White to Eichelberger, Dec. 26, 1940, LoC; Villard to White, Dec. 30, 1940, LoC; America First Press Release, Dec. 26, 1940, UP; Open Letter from White to Lindbergh, Dec. 26, 1940, LoC; FDR to White, Dec. 31, 1940, LoC; White to Villard, Jan. 27, 1941, LoC; White to Eichelberger, Apr. 23, 1941, LoC; David Kennedy attributes White's resignation to the Lend-Lease controversy, but White's correspondence does not support this conclusion. See Kennedy, *Freedom from Fear*, 471.

20. For a critical view of White's CDAAA leadership, see William Tuttle, "Aid-to-the-Allies Short-of-War versus American Intervention, 1940: A Reappraisal of William Allen White's Leadership," *Journal of American History* 56, no. 4 (Mar. 1970): 848–858.

21. White to Victor Murdock, Dec. 21, 1940, LoC; White to Frank Clough, Mar. 25, 1941, LoC; White to Eichelberger, Mar. 17, 1941, LoC; White to Edna Ferber, July 21, 1942, LoC; White, Welding New Weapons of Democracy, Award Dinner of The Churchman to William Allen White, Feb. 25, 1941, KU.

22. Kennedy, *Freedom from Fear*, 482; White to Landon, July 19, 1941, LoC; White to Eichelberger, July 29, 1941, LoC; White to Hoover, Sept. 29,

1941, LoC; David Schmitz, *The Triumph of Internationalism: Franklin D. Roosevelt and a World in Crisis, 1933–1941* (Washington, DC: Potomac, 2007), 81; White to Sherwood, Oct. 10, 1940, LoC. See also Elizabeth Borgwardt, *A New Deal for the World: America's Vision for Human Rights* (Cambridge, MA: Harvard University Press, 2005).

23. Best, *Hoover*, 1:191; McJimsey, *FDR*, 206; Johnson, *Republican Party*, 188–189; White to Herbert Hoover, Apr. 15, 1942, LoC; Hoover to Landon, June 30, 1941, HHP; Hoover to Landon, July 1, 1941, HHP.

24. Johnson, *Republican Party*, 191; White to Willkie, Aug. 16, 1941, LoC; White to Willkie, Sept. 4, 1941, LoC; Willkie to White, Aug. 29, 1941, LoC.

25. Howard Jones, "One World: An American Perspective," in Madison, *Wendell Willkie*, 115; Hoover to White, Mar. 28, 1942, LoC; White to Hoover, July 7, 1942, LoC; White to Willkie, Dec. 5, 1942, WWP; Wendell Willkie, "Our Reservoir of World Respect and Hope," in *Vital Speeches of the Day*, vol. 9, 34–39; White, Syndicated Column Typescript, Oct. 28, 1942, WWP; Best, *Hoover*, 1:219–240.

26. White to Hinshaw, Apr. 2, 1943, LoC; Best, *Hoover*, 1:219–240.

27. Victoria de Grazia, *Irresistible Empire: America's Advance through Twentieth-Century Europe* (Cambridge, MA: Harvard University Press, 2006), 3; White to Capper, Feb. 4, 1942, LoC; White to Capper, July 11, 1942, LoC; White to Ed Rees, Sept. 29, 1943, LoC; White to Herbert Hoover, Dec. 5, 1942, ESU.

28. Walter Lippmann, *U.S. Foreign Policy: Shield of the Republic* (Boston: Little, Brown, 1943), xii–xiii, 37–58, 71–77, 107, 134–136, 152–153; Steel, *Walter Lippmann*, 406–410; White to Lippmann, Apr. 16, 1943, LoC; White to Haskell, June 9, 1943, LoC.

29. White to Landon, June 24, 1943, LoC; Landon to White, June 28, 1943, LoC; White to Clyde Reed, Mar. 29, 1943, LoC; Hoover to White, May 27, 1943, HHP; White to Hoover, Mar. 29, 1943, ESU; White to Landon, Feb. 10, 1943, ESU.

30. Hinshaw, *Man from Kansas*, 292; White to Hinshaw, May 11, 1943, LoC; White to Ida Tarbell, May 22, 1943, LoC; White to Ronald Finney, July 23, 1943, LoC.

31. David M. Jordan, *FDR, Dewey, and the Election of 1944* (Bloomington: University of Indiana Press, 2011), 15; Bricker quoted in Johnson, *Republican Party*, 230–231; White to Capper, Mar. 16, 1942, LoC; White,

"Out and Around," Feb. 25–27, 1943, WWP; "Landon Assails 'Nazi New Dealers,'" *NYT*, Feb. 13, 1943.

32. White to Alf Landon, Jan. 27, 1943, ESU; White to Henry Allen, June 24, 1943, LoC.

33. White to Willkie, June 26, 1943, LoC; White to Willkie, July 20, 1943, LoC; Susan Dunn, *1940: FDR, Willkie, Lindbergh, Hitler—The Election amid the Storm* (New Haven, CT: Yale University Press, 2013), 314–316.

34. Sallie White to Villard, Jan. 18, 1944, OGV; Franklin D. Roosevelt to Sallie White, Jan. 29, 1944, FDR; Dorothy Canfield Fisher to Sallie White, Nov. 2, 1943, LoC; Secretary to Henry Allen, Oct. 16, 1943, LoC; William L. White to Willkie, Jan. 29, 1944, WWP; Sallie White to Victor Murdock, Jan. 15, 1944, VMP; Sallie White to Victor Murdock, Dec. 8, 1943, VMP.

EPILOGUE

1. Herbert Hoover, "World Peace and the United Nations," Emporia, July 11, 1950, HHP.

2. Ibid.; Frank Clough, *William Allen White of Emporia* (New York: McGraw-Hill, 1941; reprint, Westport, CT: Greenwood, 1970), 113; White to Willkie, Dec. 15, 1942, WWP; White to George W. Norris, June 27, 1942, LoC.

3. White to Alf Landon, May 8, 1940, LoC.

4. Kim Phillips-Fein, "Conservatism: A State of the Field," *Journal of American History* 98, no. 3 (Dec. 2011): 723–743.

5. William Allen White, "Between the Devil and the Deep Sea," 1943, KU.

6. Ibid.

7. White to Harry Slattery, May 29, 1942, LoC; White to Henry A. Wallace, Aug. 10, 1943, LoC; Thomas Devine, *Henry Wallace's 1948 Presidential Campaign and the Future of Postwar Liberalism* (Chapel Hill: University of North Carolina Press, 2013), 15–16.

BIBLIOGRAPHY

PRIMARY SOURCES

Manuscripts

Henry J. Allen Papers. Manuscript Division. Library of Congress, Washington, DC.

William E. Borah Papers. Manuscript Division. Library of Congress, Washington, DC.

Joseph L. Bristow Papers. Kansas State Archives, Topeka, KS.

Clark Eichelberger Papers. Manuscripts and Archives. New York Public Library, New York, NY.

Herbert Hoover Papers. Herbert Hoover Presidential Library, West Branch, IA.

Harold Ickes Papers. Manuscript Division. Library of Congress, Washington, DC.

Walter Lippmann Papers. Manuscripts and Archives. Yale University, New Haven, CT.

Chester I. Long Papers. Kansas State Archives, Topeka, KS.

Victor Murdock Papers. Manuscript Division. Library of Congress, Washington, DC.

George W. Norris Papers. Manuscript Division. Library of Congress, Washington, DC.

Franklin D. Roosevelt Papers. Franklin D. Roosevelt Presidential Library, Hyde Park, NY.

Theodore Roosevelt Papers. Manuscript Division. Library of Congress, Washington, DC.

Uncensored Papers. Manuscripts and Archives. New York Public Library, New York, NY.

Oswald Garrison Villard Papers. Houghton Library. Harvard University, Cambridge, MA.

William Allen White Papers. Special Collections and Archives. Emporia State University, Emporia, KS.

William Allen White Papers. Kansas Collection. Kenneth Spencer Research Library, University of Kansas, Lawrence, KS.

William Allen White Papers. Manuscript Division. Library of Congress, Washington, DC.

William Lindsay White Papers. Kansas Collection. Kenneth Spencer Research Library, University of Kansas, Lawrence, KS.

Wendell Willkie Papers. Lilly Library, Indiana University, Bloomington, IN.

Books

Allen, Henry J. *The Party of the Third Part*. New York: Harper, 1921.

Clough, Frank. *William Allen White of Emporia*. New York: McGraw-Hill, 1941. Reprint, Westport, CT: Greenwood, 1970.

The Kansas Court of Industrial Relations: A Modern Weapon. Topeka: Kansas State Printer, 1921.

Lippmann, Walter. *U.S. Foreign Policy: Shield of the Republic*. Boston: Little, Brown, 1943.

White, William Allen. *The Autobiography of William Allen White*. New York: Macmillan, 1946.

———. *The Martial Adventures of Henry and Me*. New York: Macmillan, 1918.

———. *Masks in a Pageant*. New York: Macmillan, 1928.

———. *A Puritan in Babylon: The Story of Calvin Coolidge*. New York: Macmillan, 1938.

Wilkerson, W. F. *The Court of Industrial Relations: Selected Opinions and Orders, Including Rules, Practices, and Procedure*. Topeka: Kansas State Printing Plant, 1922.

Periodicals

American Magazine

Collier's magazine

Emporia Gazette

Emporia Weekly Gazette

Harper's Magazine

La Follette's magazine

McClure's magazine

Nation

Nation's Business

New York Times

Saturday Evening Post

SECONDARY SOURCES
Books

Alpers, Benjamin. *Dictators, Democracy, and American Public Culture: Envisioning the Totalitarian Enemy, 1920s–1950s.* Chapel Hill: University of North Carolina Press, 2003.

Ambrosius, Lloyd. *Woodrow Wilson and the American Diplomatic Tradition: The Treaty Fight in Perspective.* Cambridge: Cambridge University Press, 1987.

Argan, Edward. *"Too Good a Town": William Allen White, Community, and the Emerging Rhetoric of Middle America.* Fayetteville: University of Arkansas Press, 1998.

Argersinger, Peter. *Populism and Politics: William Alfred Peffer and the People's Party.* Louisville: University Press of Kentucky, 1974.

Baker, Jean. *Affairs of Party: The Political Culture of Northern Democrats in the Mid-Nineteenth Century.* Ithaca, NY: Cornell University Press, 1983.

Best, Gary Dean. *Herbert Hoover: The Postpresidential Years, 1933–1964.* Vol. 1. Stanford, CA: Hoover Institution Press, 1983.

Borgwardt, Elizabeth. *A New Deal for the World: America's Vision for Human Rights.* Cambridge, MA: Harvard University Press, 2005.

Brands, H. W. *Traitor to His Class: The Privileged Life and Radical Presidency of Franklin Delano Roosevelt.* New York: Doubleday, 2008.

Brinkley, Alan. "The New Deal Experiments." In Chafe, *Achievement of American Liberalism,* 1–19.

———. *Voices of Protest: Huey Long, Father Coughlin and the Great Depression.* New York: Vintage, 1982.

Chafe, William, ed. *The Achievement of American Liberalism.* New York: Columbia University Press, 2003.

Clanton, O. Gene. *Kansas Populism: Ideas and Men.* Lawrence: University Press of Kansas, 1969.

Clements, Kendrick. *The Presidency of Woodrow Wilson.* Lawrence: University Press of Kansas, 1992.

Cohen, Adam. *Nothing to Fear: FDR's Inner Circle and the Hundred Days That Created Modern America.* New York: Penguin, 2009.

Cole, Wayne S. *Roosevelt and the Isolationists, 1932–1945.* Lincoln: University of Nebraska Press, 1983.

Cushman, Barry. *Rethinking the New Deal Court: The Structure of a Constitutional Revolution.* New York: Oxford University Press, 1998.

Dallek, Robert. *Franklin D. Roosevelt and American Foreign Policy, 1932–1945*. New York: Oxford University Press, 1979.

Davis, Colin. *Power at Odds: The 1922 National Railroad Shopmen's Strike*. Urbana: University of Illinois Press, 1997.

Dawley, Alan. *Changing the World: American Progressives in War and Revolution*. Princeton, NJ: Princeton University Press, 2003.

de Grazia, Victoria. *Irresistible Empire: America's Advance through Twentieth-Century Europe*. Cambridge, MA: Harvard University Press, 2006.

Devine, Thomas. *Henry Wallace's 1948 Presidential Campaign and the Future of Postwar Liberalism*. Chapel Hill: University of North Carolina Press, 2013.

Divine, Robert. *The Illusion of Neutrality*. Chicago: University of Chicago Press, 1962.

Doenecke, Justus. *Storm on the Horizon: The Challenge to American Intervention, 1939–1941*. Oxford: Rowman & Littlefield, 2000.

Dubofsky, Melvyn, and Warren Van Tine. *John L. Lewis: A Biography*. New York: Quadrangle, 1977.

Dunn, Susan. *1940: FDR, Willkie, Lindbergh, Hitler—The Election amid the Storm*. New Haven, CT: Yale University Press, 2013.

Eisenach, Eldon. *The Lost Promise of Progressivism*. Lawrence: University Press of Kansas, 1994.

Ellis, L. Ethan. *Frank B. Kellogg and American Foreign Relations, 1925–1929*. New Brunswick, NJ: Rutgers University Press, 1961.

Farrell, Robert. *The Presidency of Calvin Coolidge*. Lawrence: University Press of Kansas, 1998.

Fausold, Martin. *The Presidency of Herbert C. Hoover*. Lawrence: University Press of Kansas, 1985.

Feinman, Ronald. *Twilight of Progressivism: The Western Republican Senators and the New Deal*. Baltimore: Johns Hopkins University Press, 1981.

Ferrell, Robert. *Peace in Their Time: The Origins of the Kellogg-Briand Pact*. New Haven, CT: Yale University Press, 1952.

Fite, Gilbert. *Peter Norbeck: Prairie Statesman*. Columbia: University of Missouri, 1948.

Forcey, Charles. *The Crossroads of Liberalism: Croly, Weyl, Lippmann, and the Progressive Era, 1900–1925*. New York: Oxford University Press, 1961.

Frank, Thomas. *What's the Matter with Kansas?* New York: Henry Holt, 2004.

Gagilardo, Domenico. *The Kansas Industrial Court: An Experiment in Compulsory Arbitration.* Lawrence: University Press of Kansas, 1941.

Galbraith, John Kenneth. *The Great Crash: 1929.* New York: Houghton Mifflin, 1999.

Gerstle, Gary. *American Crucible: Race and Nation in the Twentieth Century.* Princeton, NJ: Princeton University Press, 2001.

Gienapp, William. *The Origins of the Republican Party, 1852–1856.* New York: Oxford University Press, 1987.

Goodwin, Doris Kearns. *The Bully Pulpit: Theodore Roosevelt, William Howard Taft, and the Golden Age of Journalism.* New York: Simon & Schuster, 2013.

Gould, Lewis. *The Presidency of Theodore Roosevelt.* Lawrence: University Press of Kansas, 2011.

———. *The Republicans: A History of the Grand Old Party.* New York: Oxford University Press, 2014.

———. *The William Howard Taft Presidency.* Lawrence: University Press of Kansas, 2009.

Graham, Otis. *An Encore for Reform: The Old Progressives and the New Deal.* New York: Oxford University Press, 1967.

Gregory, Ross. "Seeking the Presidency: Willkie as Politician." In Madison, *Wendell Willkie,* 47–70.

Griffin, Clifford S. *The University of Kansas: A History.* Lawrence: University Press of Kansas, 1974.

Griffith, Sally F. *Home Town News: William Allen White and the Emporia Gazette.* New York: Oxford University Press, 1989.

Hamby, Alonzo. "High Tide: Roosevelt, Truman, and the Democratic Party, 1932–1952." In Chafe, *Achievement of American Liberalism,* 21–61.

Hinshaw, David. *A Man from Kansas: The Story of William Allen White.* New York: G. P. Putnam, 1945.

Hoeveler, David J. *John Bascom and the Origins of the Wisconsin Idea.* Madison: University of Wisconsin Press, 2016.

Johnson, Donald. *The Republican Party and Wendell Willkie.* Urbana: University of Illinois Press, 1960.

Johnson, Robert. *The Peace Progressives and American Foreign Relations.* Cambridge, MA: Harvard University Press, 1995.

Johnson, Walter. *William Allen White's America.* New York: Henry Holt, 1947.

Jones, Howard. "One World: An American Perspective." In Madison, *Wendell Willkie*, 103–124.

Jordan, David M. *FDR, Dewey, and the Election of 1944*. Bloomington: University of Indiana Press, 2011.

Kazin, Michael. *The Populist Persuasion: An American History*. Ithaca, NY: Cornell University Press, 1998.

Kennedy, David M. *Freedom from Fear: The American People in Depression and War, 1929–1945*. New York: Oxford University Press, 1999.

———. *Over Here: The First World War and American Society*. New York: Oxford University Press, 1980.

Kennedy, Ross. *The Will to Believe: Woodrow Wilson, World War I, and America's Strategy for Peace and Security*. Kent, OH: Kent State University Press, 2009.

Knock, Thomas J. *To End All Wars: Woodrow Wilson and the Quest for a New World Order*. New York: Oxford University Press, 1992.

La Forte, Robert S. *Leaders of Reform: Progressive Republicans in Kansas, 1900–1916*. Lawrence: University Press of Kansas, 1974.

Lauck, Jon. *From Warm Center to Ragged Edge: The Erosion of Midwestern Literary and Historical Regionalism, 1920–1965*. Iowa City: University of Iowa Press, 2017.

Lee, R. Alton. *The Bizarre Careers of John R. Brinkley*. Louisville: University Press of Kentucky, 2003.

———. *Farmers vs. Wage Earners: Organized Labor in Kansas, 1860–1960*. Lincoln: University of Nebraska Press, 2005.

Leuchtenburg, William. *The Supreme Court Reborn: The Constitutional Revolution in the Age of Roosevelt*. New York: Oxford University Press, 1995.

Levin, N. Gordon. *Woodrow Wilson and World Politics: America's Response to War and Revolution*. London: Oxford University Press, 1968.

Lichtenstein, Nelson. *The Most Dangerous Man in Detroit: Walter Reuther and the Fate of American Labor*. New York: HarperCollins, 1995.

Lichtman, Allan. *Prejudice and the Old Politics: The Presidential Election of 1928*. Chapel Hill: University of North Carolina Press, 1979.

Livermore, Seward W. *Politics Is Adjourned: Woodrow Wilson and the War Congress, 1916–1918*. Middletown, CT: Wesleyan University Press, 1966.

Lowitt, Richard. *George W. Norris: The Making of a Progressive, 1861–1912*. Syracuse, NY: Syracuse University Press, 1963.

———. *George W. Norris: The Persistence of a Progressive, 1913–1933*. Urbana: University of Illinois Press, 1971.

─────. *George W. Norris: The Triumph of a Progressive, 1933–1944*. Urbana: University of Illinois Press, 1978.

Lukas, J. Anthony. *Big Trouble*. New York: Simon & Schuster, 1997.

MacLean, Nancy. *Behind the Mask of Chivalry: The Making of the Second Ku Klux Klan*. New York: Oxford University Press, 1994.

Maddox, Robert. *William E. Borah and American Foreign Policy*. Baton Rouge: Louisiana State University Press, 1969.

Madison, James, ed. *Wendell Willkie: Hoosier Internationalist*. Bloomington: Indiana University Press, 1992.

McCartin, Joseph. *Labor's Great War: The Struggle for Industrial Democracy and the Origins of Modern American Labor Relations, 1912–1921*. Chapel Hill: University of North Carolina Press, 1991.

McFadden, David. *Alternative Paths: Soviets and Americans, 1917–1920*. New York: Oxford University Press, 1993.

McJimsey, George. *The Presidency of Franklin Delano Roosevelt*. Lawrence: University Press of Kansas, 2000.

McKee, John DeWitt. *William Allen White: Maverick on Main Street*. Westport, CT: Greenwood, 1975.

McKenna, Marian C. *Borah*. Ann Arbor: University of Michigan Press, 1961.

─────. *Franklin Roosevelt and the Great Constitutional War: The Court-Packing Crisis of 1937*. New York: Fordham University Press, 2002.

McVeigh, Rory. *The Rise of the Ku Klux Klan: Right-Wing Movements and National Politics*. Minneapolis: University of Minnesota Press, 2009.

Milkis, Sidney. *Theodore Roosevelt, the Progressive Party, and the Transformation of American Democracy*. Lawrence: University Press of Kansas, 2009.

Miller, John E. *Governor Philip F. La Follette, the Wisconsin Progressives, and the New Deal*. Columbia: University of Missouri Press, 1982.

─────. *Small-Town Dreams: Stories of Midwestern Boys Who Shaped America*. Lawrence: University Press of Kansas, 2014.

Miller, Karen A. J. *Populist Nationalism: Republican Insurgency and American Foreign Policy Making, 1918–1925*. Westport, CT: Greenwood, 1999.

Miller, Worth R. *Oklahoma Populism: A History of the People's Party in the Oklahoma Territory*. Norman: University of Oklahoma Press, 1987.

Millett, Allan R. *Semper Fidelis: The History of the United States Marine Corps*. New York: Free Press, 1991.

Miner, Craig. *Kansas: The History of the Sunflower State, 1854–2000*. Lawrence: University Press of Kansas, 2002.

Montgomery, David. *The Fall of the House of Labor: The Workplace, the State, and American Labor Activism, 1865–1925*. New York: Cambridge University Press, 1987.

Murray, Robert K. *Red Scare: A Study in National Hysteria, 1919–1920*. Minneapolis: University of Minnesota Press, 1955.

Neal, Steve. *Dark Horse: A Biography of Wendell Willkie*. Garden City, NJ: Doubleday, 1984.

Patterson, James T. *Congressional Conservatism and the New Deal: The Growth of the Conservative Coalition in Congress, 1933–1939*. Lexington: University Press of Kentucky, 1967.

Pickering, John M., and Nancy Thomas. *If I Ever Grew Up and Became a Man*. Estes Park, CO: Estes Park Museum Friends, 2010.

Radosh, Ronald. *Prophets on the Right: Profiles of Conservative Critics of American Globalism*. New York: Simon & Schuster, 1975.

Ritchie, Donald. *Electing FDR: The New Deal Campaign of 1932*. Lawrence: University Press of Kansas, 2007.

Rochester, Stuart. *American Liberal Disillusionment in the Wake of World War I*. University Park: Pennsylvania State University Press, 1977.

Rodgers, Daniel T. *Atlantic Crossings: Social Politics in a Progressive Age*. Cambridge, MA: Harvard University Press, 1998.

Sageser, A. Bower. *Joseph L. Bristow: Kansas Progressive*. Lawrence: University Press of Kansas, 1968.

Schlesinger, Arthur, Jr. *The Age of Roosevelt: The Coming of the New Deal*. Boston: Houghton Mifflin, 1959.

———. *The Age of Roosevelt: The Crisis of the Old Order*. Boston: Houghton Mifflin, 1956.

———. *The Age of Roosevelt: The Politics of Upheaval*. Boston: Houghton Mifflin, 1960.

Schmitz, David F. *The Triumph of Internationalism: Franklin D. Roosevelt and a World in Crisis, 1933–1941*. Washington, DC: Potomac, 2007.

Schoultz, Lars. *Beneath the United States: A History of U.S. Policy toward Latin America*. Cambridge, MA: Harvard University Press, 1998.

Sherry, Michael S. *In the Shadow of War: The United States since the 1930s*. New Haven, CT: Yale University Press, 1995.

Shesol, Jeff. *Supreme Power: Franklin Roosevelt vs. the Supreme Court*. New York: W. W. Norton, 2010.

Shortridge, James. *The Middle West: Its Meaning in American Culture*. Lawrence: University Press of Kansas, 1989.

Slayton, Robert. *Empire Statesman*. New York: Free Press, 2001.

Smith, Geoffrey S. *To Save a Nation: American Countersubversives, the New Deal, and the Coming of World War II*. New York: Basic Books, 1973.

Steel, Ronald. *Walter Lippmann and the American Century*. Boston: Little, Brown, 1980.

Stromquist, Shelton. *Reinventing "The People."* Urbana: University of Illinois Press, 2006.

Tomlins, Christopher L. *The State and the Unions: Labor Relations, Law, and the Organized Labor Movement in America, 1880–1960*. Cambridge: Cambridge University Press, 1985.

Unger, Nancy. *Fighting Bob La Follette: The Righteous Reformer*. Chapel Hill: University of North Carolina Press, 2000.

Villard, Oswald Garrison. *Fighting Years: Memoirs of a Liberal Editor*. New York: Harcourt, Brace, 1939.

Wilson, Joan Hoff. *American Business and Foreign Policy, 1920–1933*. Lexington: University Press of Kentucky, 1971.

Wolraich, Michael. *Unreasonable Men: Theodore Roosevelt and the Republican Rebels Who Created Progressive Politics*. New York: Palgrave Macmillan, 2014.

Articles

Argersinger, Peter H. "Road to a Republican Waterloo: The Farmers' Alliance and the Election of 1890 in Kansas." *Kansas History* 33, no. 4 (Winter 1967): 443–469.

Barke, Megan, Rebecca Fribush, and Peter Stearns. "Nervous Breakdown in 20th-Century American Culture." *Journal of Social History* 33, no. 3 (Spring 2000): 565–584.

Hawley, Ellis. "Herbert Hoover, the Commerce Secretariat, and the Vision of an 'Associative State,' 1921–1928." *Journal of American History* 61, no. 1 (June 1976): 116–140.

Hoffman, Frederick T. "Philistine and Puritan in the 1920s: An Example of the Misuse of the American Past." *American Quarterly* 1, no. 3 (Autumn 1949): 247–263.

La Forte, Robert. "Theodore Roosevelt's Osawatomie Speech." *Kansas History* 32, no. 2 (Summer 1966): 187–200.

Lee, R. Alton. "Joseph Ralph Burton and the 'Ill Fated' Senate Seat of Kansas." *Kansas History* 32, no. 4 (Winter 2009): 246–265.

McGreevy, John T. "Thinking on One's Own: Catholicism in the American

Intellectual Imagination, 1928–1960." *Journal of American History* 84, no. 1 (June 1997): 97–131.

Peterson, John M. "The People's Party of Kansas: Campaigning in 1898." *Kansas History* 13, no. 4 (Winter 1990): 235–258.

Phillips-Fein, Kim. "Conservatism: A State of the Field." *Journal of American History* 98, no. 3 (December 2011): 723–743.

Pope, James G. "Labor's Constitution of Freedom." *Yale Law Journal* 106, no. 4 (January 1997): 941–1031.

Rabinowitz, Herbert. "The Kansas Industrial Court Act." *California Law Review* 12, no. 1 (November 1923): 1–16.

Resh, Richard. "A Vision in Emporia: William Allen White's Search for Community." *Midcontinent American Studies* 10, no. 2 (Fall 1969): 19–35.

Robertson, James O. "Progressives Elect Will H. Hays Republican National Chairman, 1918." *Indiana Magazine of History* 64, no. 3 (September 1968): 173–190.

Saul, Norman. "The 'Russian' Adventures of Henry and Me: William Allen White and Henry Justin Allen in Stalin's Russia." *Kansas History* 39, no. 1 (Spring 2016): 32–47.

———. "William Allen White and the Russian Revolution." *Kansas History* 38, no. 4 (Winter 2015): 268–282.

Sloan, Charles W. "Kansas Battles the Invisible Empire: The Legal Ouster of the KKK from Kansas, 1922–1927." *Kansas Historical Quarterly* 40, no. 3 (Fall 1974): 393–409.

Smith, Karen M. "Father, Son, and Country on the Eve of War: William Allen White, William Lindsay White, and American Isolationism, 1940–1941." *Kansas History* 28, no. 1 (Spring 2005): 30–43.

Traylor, Jack W. "William Allen White's 1924 Gubernatorial Campaign." *Kansas Historical Quarterly* 42, no. 2 (Summer 1976): 180–191.

Tuttle, William. "Aid-to-the-Allies Short-of-War versus American Intervention, 1940: A Reappraisal of William Allen White's Leadership." *Journal of American History* 56, no. 4 (March 1970): 840–858.

Wyman, Roger E. "Insurgency in Minnesota: The Defeat of James A. Tawney in 1910." *Minnesota History* 40, no. 7 (Fall 1967): 317–329.

INDEX